# Guide to Information Sources in the Forensic Sciences

**Recent Titles in Reference Sources in Science and Technology**
*Judith A. Matthews, Series Editor*

American Military History: A Guide to Reference and Information Sources
*Daniel K. Blewett*

Education: A Guide to Reference and Information Sources
*Nancy Patricia O'Brien*

Northern Africa: A Guide to Reference and Information Sources
*Paula Youngman Skreslet*

Zoological Sciences: A Guide to Reference and Information Sources
*Diane Schmidt*

Guide to Information Sources in Mathematics and Statistics
*Martha A. Tucker and Nancy D. Anderson*

Computer Science and Computing: A Guide to the Literature
*Michael Knee*

Guide to Reference and Information Sources in Plant Biology, Third Edition
*Diane Schmidt, Melody M. Allison, Kathleen A. Clark, Pamela F. Jacobs, and Maria A. Porta*

# Guide to Information Sources in the Forensic Sciences

Cynthia Holt

Foreword by Moses S. Schanfield

**Reference Sources in Science and Technology**
*Judith A. Matthews, Series Editor*

## LIBRARIES
UNLIMITED
A Member of the Greenwood Publishing Group

Westport, Connecticut • London

**Library of Congress Cataloging-in-Publication Data**

Holt, Cynthia.
  Guide to information sources in the forensic sciences / by Cynthia Holt ;
foreword by Moses S. Schanfield.
     p.  cm.—(Reference sources in science and technology)
  Includes bibliographical references and index.
  ISBN 1-59158-221-0 (alk. paper)
  1. Forensic sciences—Bibliography.  2. Forensic sciences—Reference books—
Bibliography.  3. Forensic sciences—Information services—Directories.
4. Forensic sciences—Databases—Directories.  I. Title.  II. Series: Reference
sources in science and technology series.

Z7503.4.C728H65 2006
[HV8073]
016.36325—dc22      2005030801

British Library Cataloguing in Publication Data is available.

Library of Congress Catalog Card Number: 2005030801
ISBN: 1-59158-221-0

First Published in 2006

Libraries Unlimited, 88 Post Road West, Westport, CT 06881
A Member of the Greenwood Publishing Group, Inc.
www.lu.com

Printed in the United States of America

The paper used in this book complies with the
Permanent Paper Standard issued by the National
Information Standards Organization (Z39.48–1984).

10 9 8 7 6 5 4 3 2 1

This book is dedicated to my family, who were so supportive of me—especially to my sister Catherine, who "encouraged" me through the process in her own special way.

# CONTENTS

# FOREWORD

The information age has radically changed how scientists do business, and the forensic scientists are no exception. The advancement of forensic science was relatively slow until the latter quarter of the twentieth century. Because forensic science is an applied science it has had to rely on the basic sciences (e.g., biology, chemistry, physics) to make great strides. From Sir Francis Galton's description of fingerprints and their first applications in the late nineteenth and early twentieth centuries, to the beginnings of forensic microscopy to compare bullets, fibers, and hairs, to the first use of ABO blood groups and the creation of micro-crystalline tests for drugs and other innovations, the field has become progressively more complex. Also, with the invention of the transistor and other technological advances, instrumentation at all levels—including the gas chromatograph, electrophoresis, DNA technology, and lasers—has made leaps forward.

Forensic science, or criminalistics as some individuals refer to it, has changed from a field in which one person could do a little of everything to a field of specialists. Minimally, the field has consisted of drug chemists, firearms examiners, biologists, trace evidence analysts, identification specialists (e.g., fingerprints), and crime scene investigators. In recent years, however, forensic science has expanded to include computer forensics, document examination, and a myriad of other applied specialties. The age of the generalist has passed.

Though the microscope has remained largely unchanged in several hundred years, the ability to store images electronically has radically changed how forensic scientists do business. We now live in a digital era. Photography using silver-based images has been replaced with high-resolution digital images used in recording crime scenes, documenting evidence, or in laboratory tests. Tests are digitized and compared to other laboratory results, whether they be fingerprints, bullets, cartridge cases, or DNA profiles within the United States or around the world.

How do these changes affect the teachers, researchers, and practitioners of forensic science? Just as the world of basic science has expanded explosively, particularly in the last ten years, so has the amount of information specific and relevant to the forensic sciences. How do we keep track of it? Not very well. We have Web sites that collate information, we can do Web searches, and we can use our libraries. Thanks to the O. J. Simpson case and the ever-increasing number of television shows emphasizing forensic science—e.g., *Law and Order, CSI, NCIS, Crossing Jordan* and other related shows—the public is sensitized and curious about the world of forensic science. Students interested in forensic science degrees far outstrip the number of educational opportunities and the number of positions available. There is no shortage of educational programs being created to fill this vacuum. Pressures from consumers of services and individuals interested in educational opportunities, as well as the increasing scrutiny of the courts on forensic evidence, have placed an increasing burden on the forensic community to manage and access the information available.

I would like to thank Miss Holt for making the effort to pull together the various sources from the highly diverse areas of forensic science to aid librarians that support academic and research forensic scientists. I think this work will also be useful to lawyers looking up material in esoteric areas for legal cases, as well as to students, crime laboratories, and other individuals interested in the forensic sciences.

Moses S. Schanfield
Professor and Chair
Department of Forensic Sciences
The George Washington University

# PREFACE

As an academic librarian serving a graduate-level forensic sciences department, I have seen firsthand how confusing the multitude of information sources can be for researchers, so I set out to try to bring order to the chaos of these resources. This book is not the type one reads from cover to cover. It is intended instead to serve as a reference guide to the major information resources in the forensic sciences. It will be helpful both for new researchers in the forensic sciences fields and for working forensic scientists in need of additional information resources outside their normal spheres of study. It will also serve as an introduction and guide for librarians seeking information about, and looking to build a collection in, the forensic sciences.

This monograph is intended to provide a strong overview of the literature and tools in this field, but it is by no means exhaustive. Tools are primarily in English, with a few non-English titles included because of their significance in the forensic sciences.

The literature of forensics is expanding at a rapid rate, mostly due to an increasing number of subdisciplines and the subject's popularity with the public. The introductory chapter aims to clarify the distinctions between the major forensic sciences specialties. It also provides an overview of the hierarchy of various classification systems for the forensics literature.

All subjects need a solid basis in the historical. The forensic sciences are no exception. Interestingly, historical bibliographies seem to have been popular until the 1980s but seem to have since fallen out of fashion in forensics. In many ways this makes sense, as much of the development of the field occurred in the nineteenth and early twentieth centuries—but there seems to be an opportunity for a historically inclined forensic scientist to fill the gap from the 1980s to the present. Certainly the biographical literature on forensic scientists is greatly lacking.

The bulk of this book is the bibliography of resources recommended to support research in the forensic sciences and its various subspecialties. I have grouped these materials by type of material (e.g., journals, abstracts and indexes, books), as indicated in the table of contents.

I would like to acknowledge the Gelman Library at The George Washington University, which provided the support and time I needed to complete this research. In addition, I would like to thank Liz Harter and Dr. Moses Schanfield for their assistance in the final review of the manuscript. Their suggestions and comments were invaluable to me in ensuring an accurate and useful guide. I would also like to thank my friend and colleague, Bill Poluha, for his constant encouragement and belief in me.

# INTRODUCTION

The forensic sciences refer to the application of principles and methods of specialized scientific and/or technical knowledge to criminal and civil legal questions. The term forensic medicine is often used interchangeably with the term forensic science, but it is actually a subspecialty of the forensic sciences dealing with the relationships and applications of medical facts to legal questions. Forensic medicine is also referred to as legal medicine and medical jurisprudence. Forensic scientists include, but are not limited to, pathologists, psychiatrists, odontologists, toxicologists, molecular biologists, entomologists, and criminalists. What distinguishes a forensic scientist from other scientists working in the various disciplines that make up forensics is that they must also be able to present their results convincingly under oath in a court of law. Practitioners are finding themselves increasingly in demand in the courtroom as expert witnesses.

The public often uses the terms forensic pathologist, medical examiner, and coroner synonymously but they are distinct vocations. A coroner is an elected or appointed official responsible for determining and certifying the cause and manner of death. The requirements for the office of coroner vary widely across the United States. Many are laypersons, whereas in other areas the coroner is required to be a physician, and in a few areas a coroner is required be a forensic pathologist. A medical examiner is an appointed government official who is also a medical physician—and often, but not necessarily, a forensic pathologist—responsible for investigating sudden and unexpected deaths or deaths from injuries. A forensic pathologist is a physician with specialized medical and forensic science training and knowledge. Forensic pathologists are commonly involved in the investigation of death scenes, performance of forensic autopsies, review of medical records, interpretation of toxicology and other laboratory studies, certification of sudden and unnatural deaths, and testifying in court in criminal and civil law proceedings. Forensic autopsies have a different focus from that of hospital autopsies, which are conducted in cases of natural death.

Due to the interdisciplinary nature of this field, researchers may need to access literature in a wide variety of disciplines other than strictly "forensic science." Written for researchers in the forensic sciences and for those who guide them, such as librarians who serve a scientific or technical clientele, this book highlights the most important research tools in the forensic sciences, including those of the interrelated disciplines of anthropology, chemistry, engineering, entomology, dentistry, and psychology, among others.

# Specialties in the Forensic Sciences

Contrary to how they are portrayed on television shows such as *CSI: Crime Scene Investigation*, most forensic scientists specialize in one aspect of forensics, that is, they only deal with firearms, they only analyze DNA evidence, or they only process a crime scene. Usually the person who collects the evidence at the scene does not also run the lab tests on that evidence, although that person's level of specialization can depend on the size of the lab at which he or she works.

Ballistics is the "study of a projectile in motion" (Brenner 2004), whereas firearms identification is primarily concerned with determining if "a bullet, cartridge case or other ammunition component was fired by a particular firearm" (Brenner 2004). These terms are often confused. Tool marks are marks left on an item by a tool; in the case of firearms, they are marks left by a part of the firearm on a cartridge case.

Crime scene investigation involves the use of scientific methods, physical evidence, deductive reasoning, and their interrelationships to gain knowledge of the series of events that surround the commission of a crime.

Criminalistics applies to the identification, preservation, and interpretation of all types of physical evidence in a case. Criminalistics includes forensic chemistry, forensic biology, and trace evidence analysis. Depending on the size of a department or laboratory, criminalists might handle a general workload in smaller facilities, whereas in larger departments they might be more specialized.

Forensic accounting involves providing an accounting analysis (financial information) that is suitable in a court of law. It encompasses both litigation support and investigative accounting. Litigation support encompasses the provision of accounting assistance in matters involving existing or pending cases. This primarily involves the quantification of economic damages (e.g., economic losses from a breach of contract). Investigative accounting deals mostly with investigations of criminal matters such as employee theft, securities fraud, insurance fraud, kickbacks, and proceeds from criminal activities.

Forensic anthropology is the application of the science of physical anthropology to the legal process. Forensic anthropologists apply standard scientific techniques developed in physical anthropology to identify human remains and to assist in the detection of crime. In addition to assisting in the location and recovery of suspicious remains, forensic anthropologists work to suggest the age, sex, ancestry, stature, and unique features of a body from the skeleton. Forensic osteology, the foundation of forensic anthropology, specifically uses the information collected from the study of bones to determine such things as what types of trauma a body might have incurred, the age and gender of the decedent, and much more.

Forensic biology is a broad specialty involving the examination of insects (forensic entomology), soil, plant life, trees, seeds, and pollen (forensic botany). It also involves the subspecialty of forensic serology, which deals with the analysis, identification, and individualization of body fluids and tissues, secretions and excretions (such as blood, seminal fluid, and saliva).

According to Van Dommelen:

> Forensic botany is the application of plant science to the resolution of legal questions. The use of botanical evidence in legal investigations is relatively recent. Today, forensic botany encompasses numerous subdisciplines of plant science: anatomy, dendrochronology (the study of tree rings), palynology (the study of pollen, spores, and acid-resistant microorganisms), limnology (the study of freshwater ecology), systematics (required when the identity of suspected drug species, [notably] marijuana, is in question), ecology (useful to investigators in two main ways: to determine whether plant fragments recovered from a victim or object came from where it was found or from some other area, and in locating clandestine graves), and molecular biology. (2004)

Forensic chemistry is concerned with chemical testing of drugs and other substances found as evidence. This could include analysis of explosives, drugs, alcohol, or accelerants used in arson. A subspecialty of forensic chemistry is forensic toxicology, which

> is, quite literally, the use of toxicology in courts of law. This is most often understood to mean the analysis of alcohol, drugs, and poisons in body fluids and the interpretation of those analytical results for the benefit of the courts. There is considerable overlap between forensic toxicology and clinical toxicology, criminalistics, forensic psychology, employment drug testing, environmental toxicology, forensic pathology, pharmacology, sports medicine, and veterinary toxicology. Consequently there are few "pure" forensic toxicology sites on the Internet. (Barbour 2003)

Laboratory methods used in chemical toxicological analysis cover a wide range and may be broadly classified as: physical tests, crystal tests, chemical spot tests, spectrophotometric tests, and chromatographic tests.

Forensic DNA analysis relies on the key characteristic of DNA, that the configuration is the same in all cells of an individual. Each person carries around 20,000 to 30,000 genes in each cell, comprising three billion "base pairs" (the chemical building blocks of DNA). Forensic scientists focus on certain genetic sequences called markers, in which the arrangement of genetic information is highly variable and particular to each person. This area of specialization is often referred to as forensic molecular biology.

Forensic economics, or litigation economics, involves the application of the theory and methodology of economics to the measurement of damages and to the proof of liability in litigation. Typical situations would be the calculation of damages in a personal injury or wrongful death suit, business valuation in business interruption cases, or the proof of liability in employment discrimination cases.

Forensic engineering involves professional engineers who apply the art and science of engineering to the legal system. It may include investigating the physical causes of accidents, testimony at trials and/or hearings, the preparation of reports, or the rendering of advisory opinions regarding the resolution of disputes affecting life or property.

Forensic entomology refers to the investigation of insects and other arthropods that are recovered from crime scenes and corpses to uncover circumstances of interest to the law, often related to a crime. Insect evidence is used to approximate time lapsed since death. It is also useful for tracking the movement of a body after death.

Forensic linguistics refers to the scientific study of language as it is applied to forensic purposes and contexts. The discipline of forensic linguistics is evolving, but it currently includes several subspecialties such as auditory phonetics (the study of language sounds based on what is heard and interpreted by the human listener), acoustic phonetics (the study of the physical characteristics of speech sounds as they leave their source, move into the air, and gradually dissipate), semantics (the study of meaning as expressed by words, phrases, sentences, or texts), discourse and pragmatics (the study of units of language larger than the sentence, such as conversations), stylistics and questioned authorship (author identification of questioned writings), language and the law ("legalese"), language of the courtroom (discourse by witnesses, lawyers, and judges in the courtroom), and interpretation and translation (McMenamin 2002).

Forensic psychiatry is a medical subspecialty that involves the assessment and treatment of offenders. Forensic psychiatrists deal with legal issues relating to competency and criminal responsibility.

Forensic psychology is the application of the science of psychology to issues relating to law and the legal system. Forensic psychologists deal with the application of basic psychological processes to legal questions and research on legal issues. Examples of forensic psychology applications include profiling, emotional and behavioral questions, issues of intent, and even jury selection.

The Virginia Institute of Forensic Science and Medicine defines odontology as "the study of teeth. Forensic odontology is a specialized field of dentistry where, in a death investigation, identity has sometimes been established through analysis of the teeth and accompanying dental prosthetics, fillings and compounds" (2003).

Any material that conveys a message, whether visible, invisible, or partially visible, is a document. When such things as authorship or authenticity are questionable in a document, the document is considered a questioned document.

> The application of allied sciences and analytical techniques to questions concerning documents is termed forensic document examination. The examination of questioned documents consists of the analysis and comparison of questioned handwriting, hand printing, typewriting, commercial printing, photocopies, papers, inks, and other documentary evidence with known material in order to establish the authenticity of the contested material as well as the detection of alterations. (Document Examination Consultants, Inc. 2003)

Since "forensic" is typically defined as "pertaining to legal proceedings," the terms forensic document examinations (examiners) should be considered interchangeable with the terms questioned document examinations (examiners) (Mid-Atlantic Association of Forensic Scientists 2003).

Trace evidence analysis is meant to include a variety of types of small quantities of materials (such as paint chips, hair, and fibers) analyzed by experts who are sometimes identified as microanalysts. Microanalysts determine the nature of the trace evidence that was transferred at a crime scene and compare it with known materials for the purpose of determining its origin.

# Subject Classification Systems

Scientists and librarians use a number of classification systems for the forensic sciences. These systems are used to describe specific documents or concepts within a document. These descriptive terms, or metadata, can then be used for storage and retrieval purposes. The main systems are LC (Library of Congress), NLM (National Library of Medicine), and Dewey Decimal. Explanations of these three systems follow.

## LC Subject Classification

The most common subject heading classification system used by North American academic libraries for books is the Library of Congress (LC) Classification System. These subject headings have related call numbers that are used to organize books on the same topic next to each other on the shelf. Unfortunately, because forensic science is so interdisciplinary, there are several general subject headings and call numbers. The most useful subject headings in the LC system for forensic sciences are listed below.

*Forensic Sciences*  This subject heading is used extensively but has no single corresponding call number range. This heading is always used in conjunction with another subject heading and that heading determines the call number.

Graphology BF 889-905 (Psychology)
Anthropometry GN 51-59
Forensic anthropology GN 69.8
Identification GN 192 (Anthropology)
Dermatoglyphics GN 192
Hair GN 193 (Physical anthropology)
Counterfeits and counterfeiting HG 335-341
Forgery HG 1696-1698 (Checks)
Criminology HV 6001-7220.5
　Criminal anthropology HV 6035-6197
　Criminals-Identification HV 6055-6079
　Legal photography HV 6071 (Criminology)
　Fingerprints HV 6074
　Forgery HV 6675-85
Evidence preservation HV 7936 .E85
Criminal investigation HV8073-8079
　Chemistry, Forensic (General) HV 8073
　Identification HV 8073-8077.35 (Criminal investigation)
　Typewriting-Identification HV 8075
　Footprints-Identification HV 8077.5 .F6
　Writing-Identification HV 8074-8076

Firearms-Identification HV 8077
Forensic ballistics HV 8077
　Arson investigation HV 8079 .A7
　Computer crimes-Investigation HV 8079 .C65
Hair QL 942 (Comparative anatomy)
Hair QM 488 (Human anatomy)
Death-Proof and certification RA 405
Medical jurisprudence RA 1001-1171
　Identification RA 1055 (Medical jurisprudence)
　Chemistry, Forensic (Medical jurisprudence) RA 1057
DNA fingerprints RA 1057.55
Forensic genetics RA 1058-1058.2
Forensic radiography RA 1058.5
Forensic thermography RA 1058.7
Forensic dermatology RA 1061
Forensic hematology RA 1061-1061.5
Forensic serology RA 1061.6
Dental jurisprudence RA 1062
Forensic ophthalmology RA 1062.5
Forensic audiology RA 1062.8
Death-Causes RA 1063
Forensic pathology RA 1063.4
Forensic entomology RA 1063.45
Forensic taphonomy RA 1063.47
Forensic obstetrics RA 1064-1067

Psychological autopsy RA 1137
Forensic neurology RA 1147
Forensic neuropsychology RA 1147.5
Forensic psychology RA 1148
Forensic psychiatrists RA 1151
Forensic psychiatry RA 1151
Forensic nursing RA 1155
Forensic pharmacology RA 1160
Forensic epidemiology RA 1165
Forensic oncology RA 1170 .C35
Forensic cardiology RA 1170 .H4
Forensic toxicology RA 1228
Arsenic-Toxicology RA 1231 .A7
Drugs-Toxicology RA 1238
Body fluids-Analysis RB 52

Drugs-Analysis RB 56-56.5
  (Clinical pathology)
Graphology RC 473 .G7 (Psychiatry)
Gunshot wounds RD 96.3
Hallucinogenic drugs RM 324.8
Drugs-Analysis RS 189-190
  (Pharmacy)
Forensic engineering TA 219
Environmental forensics TD 193.4
Fire investigation TH 9180
Explosives TP 268-299
Ink TP 946-950
Legal photography TR 822
  (Applied photography)
Forgery Z 41 (Autographs)
Ink Z 112

The following subject headings are also related to the forensic sciences but have no corresponding call number range.

Crime laboratories
Crime scenes
Drugs-Physiological effects
Evidence, Criminal
Evidence, Demonstrative
Evidence, Documentary
Evidence, Expert
Forensic accounting
Forensic dentistry
Forensic economics
Forensic geology
Forensic gynecology
Forensic hypnotism
Forensic linguistics

Forensic orations
Forensic oratory
Forensic osteology
Forensic pathologists
Forensic phonetics
Forensic scientists
Forensic statistics
Forensics (Public speaking)
Mass spectrometry-Forensic
  applications
Medical examiners (Law)
Palmprints
Veterinary jurisprudence

## NLM Subject Classification

The National Library of Medicine (NLM) created the NLM Subject Classification to allow more specific classifications of medical publications than other classification systems were capable of providing. Items in the Medline database use this classification system.

Forensic Sciences (2004–)
Forensic Anthropology (1995–)
Forensic Ballistics (2004–)
Forensic Dentistry (1965–)
Forensic Medicine (1965–)
   Autopsy
   Blood Stains
   Dermatoglyphics
   DNA Fingerprinting (1991–)
   Lie Detection
   Paternity
   Forensic Psychiatry (1969–)
   Insanity Defense
Wounds, Gunshot (1966–2003)

## Dewey Decimal Subject Classification

The Dewey Decimal Subject Classification is used primarily in public and school libraries. It does not have the detailed subject headings that are found in the Library of Congress system.

340.6 Forensic medicine
347.075 Forensic orations
347.73 Forensic hypnotism
347.7367 Forensic engineering
363.232-363.25 Police procedures (includes police photography)
363.25 Crime scene investigation
363.24 Auxiliary services (includes evidence preservation)
363.25 Detection of crime (Criminal investigation) (also referred to as forensic sciences)
   Legal photography
363.252 Procurement of evidence
363.254 Interrogation of witnesses
363.256 Analysis of evidence (includes laboratories)
363.256 2 Physical evidence
363.256 5 Documentary evidence
363.258 Identification of criminals (includes fingerprints and voice prints)
364.1 Criminal offenses
364.12 Chemistry, Forensic
543 Analytical chemistry
614.1 Medical jurisprudence (includes forensic nursing and forensic pathology)
614.12 Forensic chemistry
614.13 Forensic toxicology

614.15 Forensic psychology and
  psychiatry
614.17 Forensic anthropology
  (includes forensic osteology)

614.18 Forensic dentistry
615.1901 Drug analysis
658.473 Forensic accounting
808.53 Forensics (Public speaking)

# References

Barbour, Alan D. 2003. The World Wide Web Virtual Library: Forensic Toxicology. http://home.lightspeed.net/~abarbour/vlibft.html (accessed July 28, 2004).

Brenner, John C. 2004. *Forensic science: An illustrated dictionary.* Boca Raton, FL: CRC Press. http://www.forensicnetbase.com/books/1244/1457_fm.pdf (accessed September 8, 2004).

Document Examination Consultants, Inc. Selecting a Forensic Document Examiner. http://www.decinc.ca/selecting/selecting.html (accessed September 10, 2004).

McMenamin, Gerald R. 2002. *Forensic linguistics: Advances in forensic stylistics.* Boca Raton, FL: CRC Press.

Mid-Atlantic Association of Forensic Scientists. Questioned Document Section. http://www.maafs.org/questioned%20documents.htm (accessed September 9, 2004).

Van Dommelen, Jennifer A. (October 22, 2004). [Online]. Available email: holt@gwu.edu Message: Re: Reprint permission request.

Virginia Institute of Forensic Science and Medicine. 2003. Glossary of forensic science terms related to a death investigation. http://www.vifsm.org/overview/glossary.html (accessed April 14, 2003).

# 1
# Bibliographic, Historical, and Biographical Sources

This chapter includes selective listings of published guides to the literature in the forensic sciences, the general sciences, medicine, and engineering, as well as history of the forensic sciences resources.

## Guides to the Literature

### Forensic Sciences

1.   Killoran, Katherine B. 1996. **Forensic science: A library research guide.** *RSR: Reference Services Review* 24(4): 15–30.

For many years this article has been the standard as an introduction to research resources in the forensic sciences. Although many of the resources still exist, they are often now out-of-date or newer editions have surpassed them. A large number of the Internet resources, although they may still exist, have changed URLs since the article appeared in 1996.

### General Science, Law, and Medicine

2.   Hurt, Charlie Deuel. 1998. *Information sources in science and technology.* 3rd ed. Englewood, CO: Libraries Unlimited, Inc. 346 p. $45. ISBN 1563085283 (cl.), 1563085313 (pbk.).

Unlike many other science and engineering subjects, forensic sciences does not have its own section in this book, although several resources in the multidisciplinary section and subject sections include resources of interest to researchers in the forensic sciences. Author/title and subject indexes are included.

3.   Malinowsky, H. Robert. 1994. *Reference sources in science, engineering, medicine, and agriculture.* Phoenix, AZ: Oryx Press. 355 p. $42.95. ISBN 0897747429 (cl.), 0897747453 (pbk.).

Similar to Hurt's book, but Part 1 includes some discourse on communication in science, types of reference sources, descriptions of the different sources of scientific and technical information, and the serial pricing crisis. Title, author, and subject indexes are included.

## Bibliographies and Catalogues

4.   Abel, Ernest, comp. 1987. *Homicide: A bibliography.* New York, NY: Greenwood Press. 169 p. $77.95 ISBN 0849386705.

This comprehensive, but by no means exhaustive, bibliography deals with various aspects of homicide, including forensics. Coverage includes references published prior to 1985 that were taken from the author's personal collection and from the reference lists included in these publications. Included are journal articles, books, conferences, and dissertations. Entries are arranged alphabetically by author and include bibliographic information with no abstracts. A subject index is included.

5.   Eckert, William G., ed. 1975. *Abortion.* Wichita, KS: International Reference Organization in Forensic Medicine and Sciences. 32 p.

Alternately titled *International bibliography on abortion: Medicolegal and forensic aspects.* This compilation brings together over 50 years of international literature on the medicolegal and forensic aspects of abortion. Brief bibliographic citations are arranged under 20 major subject headings. Subject and author indexes are included.

6.   Eckert, William G., ed. [1972?]. *Aircraft accidents: The medical aspects.* Wichita, KS: International Reference Organization in Forensic Medicine and Sciences. 89 p.

A compilation of the international literature on aviation pathology and aircraft accident investigation from the early years of aviation to 1970. Aviation pathology refers to correlating autopsy findings with the total environment of a fatal aircraft accident. The first section is a chronological list of fatal mass aircraft accidents. This is followed by a list of reference sources, then the bibliographic citations arranged by major subject headings. Subject and author indexes are included.

7.   Eckert, William G., ed. 1977. *Firearms examination.* Wichita, KS: International Reference Organization in Forensic Medicine and Sciences. 42 p.

A compilation of the international literature on firearms examination and law enforcement application of this specialty over several decades. The bibliography starts with a brief historical overview of the field. Brief citations are arranged by 39 major subject headings. Subject and author indexes are included.

8.   Eckert, William G., ed. 1972. *The medical, legal & law enforcement aspects of drugs & drug abuse; a bibliography of classic and current references.* Wichita, KS: International Reference Organization in Forensic Medicine and Sciences. 102 p.

A compilation of the international literature on drugs and drug abuse over several decades. The bibliography starts with a review of the forensic aspects of the drug problem. References appearing in the bibliography are drawn from the National Library of Medicine publications (the *Cumulative Index* and the *Toxicity Bibliography*), the *Selected Abstracts* published by Interpol, and the *Legal Index*. Brief citations are arranged by 36 major subject headings. Subject and author indexes are included. An interesting inclusion is a compilation of narcotic and dangerous drug laws of foreign nations.

9.   Eckert, William G., and Thomas T. Noguchi, eds. 1973. *Alcohol and alcoholism: The medical, legal and law enforcement aspects. Volume I— Alcohol.* Wichita, KS: International Reference Organization in Forensic Medicine and Sciences. 78 p.

This is alternately titled *A bibliography of classic and current references on alcohol and alcoholism: The medical, legal and law enforcement aspects. Volume I. Alcohol.* Volume I is a review of the international literature on the forensic aspects of alcohol, intended for use of workers in forensic medicine and sciences. The arrangement is topical (30 general headings), with a brief bibliographic citation for each entry. The bibliography starts with a general overview of the forensic aspects of alcohol and alcoholism. Subject and author indexes are included.

10.   Eckert, William G., and Thomas T. Noguchi, eds. 1974. *Alcohol and alcoholism: The medical, legal and law enforcement aspects. Volume II— Alcoholism.* Wichita, KS: International Reference Organization in Forensic Medicine and Sciences. 74 p.

This is alternately titled *A bibliography of classic and current references on alcohol and alcoholism: The medical, legal and law enforcement aspects. Volume II. Alcoholism.* Volume II is a companion to the first volume on alcohol. This volume reviews the international literature on the forensic aspects of alcoholism and is intended for use of workers in forensic medicine and sciences. Bibliographic citations are arranged under 26 general headings and are collected from the National Library of Medicine's *Cumulative Index*, the *Suggested Articles* publication of Interpol, the American Academy of Forensic Sciences publication *What's New in the Forensic Sciences*, and the *International Bibliography of Studies on Alcohol* publication from the Rutgers Center for Alcohol Studies. Subject and author indexes are included.

11.   Eckert, William G., and Thomas T. Noguchi, eds. 1977. *Aspects of toxicology*. Wichita, KS: International Reference Organization in Forensic Medicine and Sciences. 24 p.

Alternately titled *The forensic aspects of toxicology*. This compilation includes references from the international literature on the forensic aspects of toxicology. Bibliographic citations are arranged under 44 major subject headings. Coverage extends back to the 1940s, although the majority of the citations are from the 1970s. Subject and author indexes are included.

12.   Eckert, William G., and Thomas T. Noguchi, eds. 1972. *Autopsy*. Wichita, KS: International Reference Organization in Forensic Medicine and Sciences. 21 p.

A review of the literature on autopsy extending back to 1927. The first part of this publication is a five-page history covering 600 years of autopsies, written by Frederick Stenn, MD. The bibliography section itself consists of brief bibliographic citations and a subject index.

13.   Eckert, William G., and Thomas T. Noguchi, eds. 1972. *Battered child and infanticide*. Wichita, KS: International Reference Organization in Forensic Medicine and Sciences. 33 p.

Alternately titled *The bibliography of references on battered child & infanticide*. This bibliography brings together the international literature on battered children and infanticide from 1927 to 1971. It is a companion to the editors' compilation on Sudden Infant Death Syndrome. Topics covered include history and incidence, medical aspects, psychiatric and social aspects, and legal aspects. The references are pulled primarily from *Index Medicus*, the INTERPOL publication *Suggested Articles*, and *Legal Index*. Bibliographic citations are listed under 36 major subject headings. Subject and author indexes are included.

14.   Eckert, William G., and Thomas T. Noguchi, eds. 1974. *Cadaver*. Wichita, KS: International Reference Organization in Forensic Medicine and Sciences. 25 p.

Alternately titled *Bibliography of references on cadaver*. This compilation of the international literature in the field of pathology includes bibliographic citations back to 1926 on the subject from all standpoints, including historical and practical. A subject index is included.

15.   Eckert, William G., and Thomas T. Noguchi, eds. 1974. *Cold injury.* Wichita, KS: International Reference Organization in Forensic Medicine and Sciences. 19 p.

Alternately titled *International literature of cold injury.* This compilation is geared to practitioners and scholars. Brief bibliographic entries dating from 1843 are arranged under 34 major subject headings. A subject index is included.

16.   Eckert, William G., and Thomas T. Noguchi, eds. [1971?]. *Dangerous marine animals & foods.* Wichita, KS: International Reference Organization in Forensic Medicine and Sciences. 24 p.

This compilation covers more than 50 years of the literature on dangerous marine animals and foods. Brief bibliographic citations are arranged under 24 major subject headings. A subject index is included.

17.   Eckert, William G., and Thomas T. Noguchi, eds. 1974. *Drowning.* Wichita, KS: International Reference Organization in Forensic Medicine and Sciences. 10 p.

Alternately titled *The bibliography of references on drowning.* This compilation covers over 40 years of the literature on drowning. It is intended to assist the clinician as well as the pathologist who may be involved in the investigation of problems associated with deaths or near drownings. Brief bibliographic citations are arranged by major subject headings. A detailed subject index is included.

18.   Eckert, William G., and Thomas T. Noguchi, eds. 1974. *Electrical trauma.* Wichita, KS: International Reference Organization in Forensic Medicine and Sciences. 25 p.

This compilation brings together a collection of international references on electrical trauma spanning twenty years. Bibliographic citations are arranged under 22 major subject headings. Subject and author indexes are included.

19.   Eckert, William G., and Thomas T. Noguchi, eds. 1974. *Fat embolism.* Wichita, KS: International Reference Organization in Forensic Medicine and Sciences. 35 p.

This compilation brings together the world literature on the subject of fat embolism. It was compiled as a joint effort of the Kansas Medical Society and the Kansas Society of Pathology on the occasion of the International Seminar on Fat

Embolism. The compilation includes brief bibliographic citations from 1927 to 1974 arranged by subject. A short article on the Cryostat Test for fat embolism precedes the bibliography. Subject and author indexes are included.

20.   Eckert, William G., and Thomas T. Noguchi, eds. 1972. *Fingerprints.* Wichita, KS: International Reference Organization in Forensic Medicine and Sciences. 22 p.

This review of the international literature on fingerprints is intended for use by workers in the forensic sciences. The arrangement is topical (38 general headings), with a brief bibliographic citation for each entry. Subject and author indexes are included.

21.   Eckert, William G., and Thomas T. Noguchi, eds. 1975. *Firearm injuries.* Wichita, KS: International Reference Organization in Forensic Medicine and Sciences. 42 p.

Alternately titled *Firearms injury.* A compilation covering 40 years of the international literature on firearm injuries. The bibliography starts with a short historical overview of the field. Brief citations are arranged by 14 major subject headings. Subject and author indexes are included.

22.   Eckert, William G., and Thomas T. Noguchi, eds. 1973. *Forensic anthropology.* Wichita, KS: International Reference Organization in Forensic Medicine and Sciences. 56 p.

Alternately titled *The bibliography of references on forensic anthropology.* Eckert and Noguchi have compiled references in forensic anthropology covering 40 years of the international literature. The bibliographic citations section is preceded by an introduction by Dr. Clyde Snow, a leader in forensic anthropology in the United States in the time period when this was written and a founder of this specialty's section in the American Academy of Forensic Sciences. The citations are arranged under 14 major subject headings. Subject and author indexes are included.

23.   Eckert, William G., and Thomas T. Noguchi, eds. 1974. *The forensic aspects of blood: An international compilation of the literature.* Wichita, KS: International Reference Organization in Forensic Medicine and Sciences. 51 p.

This compilation of 1,320 bibliographic citations from the international literature on the forensic application of serologic examination of the blood is arranged under 29 major subject headings. An introductory overview article is included before the citations section. The earliest reference is 1901. Subject and author indexes are included.

24.    Eckert, William G., and Thomas T. Noguchi, eds. 1975. *The forensic aspects of explosives and explosions.* Wichita, KS: International Reference Organization in Forensic Medicine and Sciences. 27 p.

Alternately titled *The forensic aspects of explosives and firearms compilation.* This compilation brings together the international literature, starting in 1910, on the investigation of explosives and explosions. The intended audience is the practicing forensic scientist, law enforcement authorities, and students. Brief bibliographic citations are arranged under 21 major subject headings and are collected from law enforcement, medical, and legal sources such as Interpol's *Suggested Articles*, *Index Medicus*, and the *Legal Index*. Subject and author indexes are included.

25.    Eckert, William G., and Thomas T. Noguchi, eds. 1973. *Forensic odontology.* Wichita, KS: International Reference Organization in Forensic Medicine and Sciences. 59 p.

Alternately titled *Forensic dentistry.* This bibliography covers the international literature in forensic dentistry from the 1800s to 1972. Unlike others in this series, bibliographic citations are arranged alphabetically by author. A subject index is included.

26.    Eckert, William G., and Thomas T. Noguchi, eds. 1976. *Forensic photography.* Wichita, KS: International Reference Organization in Forensic Medicine and Sciences. 25 p.

This compilation of brief bibliographic citations is gathered from the international literature on forensic photography. It is intended for anyone in a criminalistic laboratory, the medicolegal investigator, and legal professionals. A three-page basic training manual for crime scene procedures precedes the bibliography. Citations are primarily from the fifties, sixties, and seventies, although the earliest citation is from 1930. Subject and author indexes are included.

27.    Eckert, William G., and Thomas T. Noguchi, eds. 1974. *Forensic psychiatry.* Wichita, KS: International Reference Organization in Forensic Medicine and Sciences. 52 p.

This compilation of international literature on forensic psychiatry is arranged in three parts: the subject index, the author index, and the bibliography of articles. Brief bibliographic citations, the earliest from 1940, are arranged under 42 major subject headings.

28.    Eckert, William G., and Thomas T. Noguchi, eds. 1976. *Hallucinogens.* Wichita, KS: International Reference Organization in Forensic Medicine and Sciences. 39 p.

Alternately titled *International literature compilation: Hallucinogens.* This compilation brings together the international literature on the use and abuse of hallucinogens. The intended audience for this bibliography is researchers, students, and forensic investigators. The bibliography is preceded by a brief review of hallucinogens. The earliest citation is from 1951. Subject and author indexes are included.

29.    Eckert, William G., and Thomas T. Noguchi, eds. 1974. *Heat injury.* Wichita, KS: International Reference Organization in Forensic Medicine and Sciences. 27 p.

Alternately titled *Thermal injury and related problems.* This compilation of the international literature on heat injuries spans 50 years. Brief bibliographic citations are arranged under 42 major subject headings. Subject and author indexes are included.

30.    Eckert, William G., and Thomas T. Noguchi, eds. 1969. *Homicide.* Wichita, KS: International Reference Organization in Forensic Medicine and Sciences. 26 p.

The third compilation in the INFORM bibliography series, this title covers 40 years of the homicide literature beginning in 1927. The compilation begins with a brief overview of the forensic aspects of homicide and continues with bibliographic citations for each reference. A subject index is included.

31.    Eckert, William G., and Thomas T. Noguchi, eds. 1972–1985. *The International bibliography of the forensic sciences: A collection of literature, world list of forensic centers, and activities in the forensic sciences, internationally.* Wichita, KS: International Reference Organization in Forensic Medicine and Sciences. ISSN 0098-2393.

An annual index to the forensics periodical literature, this publication is divided into a varying number of parts depending on the year. Generally there is an indexed collection of the current international forensics periodical literature. These bibliographic entries are grouped by major subject heading, although the headings themselves are not listed in the entries section. The articles can be accessed through the subject and author indexes. Another common part is a guide to the international scene. Always included is a section or sections that review the current state of the different forensic science disciplines. Another section deals with the historic aspects of the forensic sciences. A final section variously lists publications of forensic interest, including books, texts, proceedings, and new periodicals.

32.    Eckert, William G., and Thomas T. Noguchi, eds. 1978. *Legal medicine.* Wichita, KS: International Reference Organization in Forensic Medicine and Sciences. 32 p.

Alternately titled *International literature compilation: Legal medicine*. This compilation covers 5 years of literature on legal medicine. A previous work, *Index of legal medicine, 1940–1970: Annotated bibliography*, by William Nick, was published in 1970. Subject and author indexes are included.

33.   Eckert, William G., and Thomas T. Noguchi, eds. 1974. *Malpractice.* Wichita, KS: International Reference Organization in Forensic Medicine and Sciences. 48 p.

The intended audience for this compilation on malpractice is practicing physicians, attorneys, and insurance companies, as well as organizations and societies of law and medicine. Brief bibliographic citations are arranged under 27 major subject headings. The earliest citations are from 1941. Subject and author indexes are included.

34.   Eckert, William G., and Thomas T. Noguchi, eds. 1975. *Narcotic drugs.* Wichita, KS: International Reference Organization in Forensic Medicine and Sciences. 58 p.

Alternately titled *The international compilation on narcotic drugs*. This compilation brings together a large collection of references covering 40 to 50 years on narcotic drugs. Bibliographic citations are arranged under 22 major subject headings. It includes reference sources from the medical, legal, and law enforcement fields. It is meant to complement two other bibliographies in the series, *Forensic aspects of hallucinogens* and another on *Stimulant and depressant drugs*. Subject and author indexes are included.

35.   Eckert, William G., and Thomas T. Noguchi, eds. 1969. *On death.* Wichita, KS: International Reference Organization in Forensic Medicine and Sciences. 61 p.

This compilation is an entirely new edition of an earlier compilation on thanatology. It compiles 40 years of literature on all aspects of death that might interest the forensic practitioner. The publication begins with an overview of death and organ transplantation. The reference section includes brief bibliographic citations. A subject index is included.

36.   Eckert, William G., and Thomas T. Noguchi, eds. 1971. *Paleopathology.* Wichita, KS: International Reference Organization in Forensic Medicine and Sciences. 27 p.

This compilation—primarily covering the period between 1927 and 1970, but also including some references from the nineteenth century—covers the literature where medicine meets anthropology, commonly referred to as forensic anthropology in modern days. Bibliographic citations are arranged under 35 major subject headings.

37.    Eckert, William G., and Thomas T. Noguchi, eds. 1974. *Penetrating instruments*. Wichita, KS: International Reference Organization in Forensic Medicine and Sciences. 30 p.

Covering the medical and law enforcement aspects of non-firearm penetrating instruments back to the 1920s, this compilation includes bibliographic citations to both articles and books. A brief guide to the investigation of penetrating instrument cases precedes the reference section. A subject index is included.

38.    Eckert, William G., and Thomas T. Noguchi, eds. 1976. *Poisons and poisoning*. Wichita, KS: International Reference Organization in Forensic Medicine and Sciences. 33 p.

This bibliography covers poisons and poisoning as part of a general series on the field of toxicology. Brief bibliographic citations are arranged under 25 major subject headings. The earliest citation is from 1963. Subject and author indexes are included.

39.    Eckert, William G., and Thomas T. Noguchi, eds. 1977. *Questioned documents*. Wichita, KS: International Reference Organization in Forensic Medicine and Sciences. 42 p.

This compilation on questioned documents examination covers over 25 years of the international literature. References are gathered from Interpol publications, forensic periodicals, and from the American Academy of Forensic Sciences' *What's New in Forensic Sciences* series. Bibliographic citations are arranged under 43 major subject headings. Subject and author indexes are included.

40.    Eckert, William G., and Thomas T. Noguchi, eds. 1971. *Sex crimes*. Wichita, KS: International Reference Organization in Forensic Medicine and Sciences. 30 p.

This compilation of references covers the international literature on sex crimes from 1927 to 1970 primarily, although some classic texts and articles from before this time are also included. References are gathered from the National Library of Medicine's *Cumulative Index* and Interpol's *Suggested Articles*. The first section is a general overview of the forensic aspects of sex crimes and problems. This is followed by the bibliographic citations arranged under 34 major subject headings. Subject and author indexes are included.

41.    Eckert, William G., and Thomas T. Noguchi, eds. 1977. *Sudden death*. Wichita, KS: International Reference Organization in Forensic Medicine and Sciences. 27 p.

Alternately titled *Compilation of sudden death 1967–1976*. This compilation is a continuation of the 1967 compilation by the editors titled *On Death*. This work covers many aspects of sudden death, including age, sex, race, activity, international aspects by country, and the manner of death. Bibliographic citations are arranged under 5 major subject headings divided into 36 subheadings. Subject and author indexes are included.

42.   Eckert, William G., and Thomas T. Noguchi, eds. 1974. *Sudden infant death.* Wichita, KS: International Reference Organization in Forensic Medicine and Sciences. 44 p.
   Alternately titled *The bibliography of references on sudden death in infants.* This is a review of the international literature from 1927 to 1971 on sudden infant death syndrome, intended for use by organizations and scientists in this area. The arrangement is topical (36 general headings), with a brief bibliographic citation for each entry. Subject and author indexes are included.

43.   Eckert, William G., and Thomas T. Noguchi, eds. 1969. *Suicide.* Wichita, KS: International Reference Organization in Forensic Medicine and Sciences. 51 p.
   The second compilation in the INFORM bibliography series, this publication covers the literature on suicide from 1927 to 1968. It is primarily compiled from the National Library of Medicine's *Cumulative Index,* but it also includes a list of the classic texts on "suicidology." A subject index is included.

44.   Eckert, William G., and Thomas T. Noguchi, eds. 1968. *Thanatology.* Wichita, KS: International Reference Organization in Forensic Medicine and Sciences. 96 p.
   This compilation collates three previously published bibliographies in a series on the general subject of thanatology. The three bibliographies are *Autopsy, Cadaver,* and *Death.* Each section contains a subject index and a list of brief bibliographic citations on the topic. The bibliography covers 40 years of international literature on the subject of the medicolegal study of death and conditions affecting dead bodies.

45.   Eckert, William G., and Thomas T. Noguchi, eds. 1977. *Trace evidence.* Wichita, KS: International Reference Organization in Forensic Medicine and Sciences. 21 p.
   Alternately titled *International literature on trace evidence.* This compilation deals with criminalistics related to firearms, documents, chemistry, biology, and identification and photography. Bibliographic citations are arranged by major subject headings. Citations extend into the 1940s, although most are from the 1960s and 1970s. Subject and author indexes are included.

46.   Eckert, William G., and Thomas T. Noguchi, eds. 1975. *Traffic accidents.* Wichita, KS: International Reference Organization in Forensic Medicine and Sciences. 67 p.

Alternately titled *Traffic accident bibliography*. This compilation of articles extends back to the 1920s, bringing together the international literature on the medical, legal, and law enforcement aspects of traffic accidents. The bibliographic citations section, arranged under 42 keyword headings, follows a brief guide to the background on forensic aspects of vehicular accidents. Subject and author indexes are included.

47.    Eckert, William G., and Thomas T. Noguchi, eds. 1975. *War crimes: Medical-legal aspects*. Wichita, KS: International Reference Organization in Forensic Medicine and Sciences. 16 p.

This compilation is similar to others in this series but on the topic of medicolegal aspects of war crimes.

48.    Fraikor, Frederick, and William G. Eckert, eds. 1976. *Art forgery: The forensic detection of fakes and forgeries in art and archeology*. Wichita, KS: International Reference Organization in Forensic Medicine and Sciences. 20 p.

The bibliographic citations are preceded by a review of the general problem of art fraud and an outline of current techniques in detection. The bibliography, arranged alphabetically by author, provides a cross-section of the international literature on crimes in art and archaeology. Coverage includes popular and technical references. The earliest citation is from 1929. A subject index is included.

49.    Jerath, Bal K., and Rajinder Jerath. 1993. *Homicide: A bibliography*. 2nd ed. Boca Raton, FL: CRC Press. 788 p. $179.95. ISBN 0849386705.

This volume is aimed at researchers in all areas related to homicide, including sociologists, criminologists, homicide detectives, forensic pathologists, and attorneys, among others. This compendium contains more than 7,000 current and historical references back to the late 1800s from hundreds of journals and publications worldwide. Bibliographic citations are arranged into 12 chapters: introduction to homicide; statistics; the murderer; the victim; murder modes; causes of murder; investigation; case reports; homicide, suicide, and accidents; legal aspects; assassination; and prevention and control. Subject and author indexes are included.

50.    Nick, William V. 1970. *Index of legal medicine, 1940–1970: annotated bibliography*. Columbus, OH: Legal Medicine Press. 694 p.

This annotated bibliography covers the published English-language literature in legal medicine from 1940 to 1970. Citations include books, monographs, proceedings, and articles. The content is arranged under subject headings and includes cross-references. Within each subject section, book and monograph entries are listed first, followed by journal citations. Citations within each format (books and articles) are arranged chronologically and alphabetically within each year. There is also a useful list of journal abbreviations at the beginning of the bibliography.

51.    Vom Ende, Rudolf. 1982. *Criminology and forensic sciences: an international bibliography, 1950–1980 = Kriminologie und Kriminalistik: Eine internationale Bibliographie, 1950–1980.* New York, NY and München: Distributed by Gale Research Co. 3 v. ISBN 3598103743 (set).

The title is misleading because most of the entries in this bibliography focus on criminology, with very few on forensics. There is no subject index, so finding the forensics entries is like searching for a needle in a haystack. It is included because researchers might wonder at its absence from this list. It is not recommend for research in the forensic sciences.

52.    *What's new in forensic sciences.* 1965–1974. Kenosha, WI: Romantini Print Co.

An official publication of the American Academy of Forensic Sciences, this annual publication provides topical bibliographies arranged by broad areas of forensics: Forensic Criminalistics, Forensic Pathology (in later years, Forensic Pathology & Biology), Forensic Psychiatry, Forensic Questioned Documents, Forensic Toxicology, General, and Jurisprudence. Each area is compiled by a different expert and is subdivided into increasingly more specific subject headings. Citations include bibliographic information and sometimes abstracts. Abstracts in the forensic psychiatry section are quite extensive. In the early years, the jurisprudence section appeared at the end of each broad area. This section lists books and articles related to the law and forensics as well as select cases, some of which are annotated.

# Selective History of Forensic Science Resources

Robert Brittain and Jaroslav Nemec very thoroughly covered the literature of the history of the forensic sciences until 1972. References to their publications are annotated below. The remaining entries are a selective list of items published after 1972, with an occasional entry of particular note in the preceding years.

There are two archives of forensic science information in the United States: Michigan State University Library at East Lansing and the Bancroft Library at the

University of California at Berkeley. The **Michigan State University Archives and Historical Collections** has extensive collections in criminal justice and is in the process of organizing a large archive of forensic science materials. The most significant collection is the personal and professional papers of Ralph Turner, a founding member of the American Academy of Forensic Sciences. Of note is his research on alcohol and voiceprint identification. The library also holds the papers of LeMoyne Snyder, one of the first forensic scientists in the United States; Clarence Muehlberger, an internationally recognized expert in ballistics and firearm identification; William A. Wiltberger, who specialized in methods of investigation and interrogation; and J.H. Mathews, a pioneer in ballistics and firearms identification. Contact the Archives Department at msuarhc@msu.edu or 517-355-2330 for more details.

The **Bancroft Library at UC Berkeley** houses the papers of Edward Oscar Heinrich (1881–1953), a pioneer in the field of scientific crime detection. Dr. Heinrich, known as the "chemist of crime," laid the foundation for many of the scientific procedures used in crime laboratories today. Contact the reference department for more information, at bancref@library.berkeley.edu or 510-642-6481.

53.    Ackerknecht, Erwin H., and Frank L. Kozelka. 1950. *Early history of legal medicine*. Summit, NJ: Ciba Pharmaceutical Products. 31 p.

This symposium proceedings (*Ciba symposium*, v. 11, no. 7) consists of five separate articles: Early history of legal medicine [to the early 16th century]; Legal medicine in transition (16th–18th centuries); Legal medicine becomes a modern science (19th century); Legal medicine in the United States; and Translations of early reports by medical experts. Kozelka, an associate professor of toxicology, authored the article on the United States while Ackernecht, a professor of the history of medicine, authored the remaining four. The translations of early reports are especially fascinating.

54.    Benecke, Mark. 2001. **A brief history of forensic entomology.** *Forensic Science International* 120(1–2): 2–14.

A thorough account of the development of this subspecialty from medieval China to primarily 1950. It includes an extensive reference list.

55.    Brittain, Robert P. 1962. *Bibliography of medico-legal works in English*. London: Sweet & Maxwell Limited. 252 p.

Intended as a supplement to a larger project dealing with the history of legal medicine, this work focuses primarily on monographs, including pamphlets and theses. Only a few journal articles are referenced. English translations of foreign-language publications are included. Geographic areas covered include the United Kingdom, the Commonwealth, India, and the United States. Entries are arranged alphabetically by author name and include vital statistics of the author, their credentials, and detailed bibliographic information on the work. None of the entries is annotated. Cross-references are made from secondary authors to the primary author's entry for the work. Unlike other bibliographies, biographies are also included. Author and subject indexes are included.

56.    Brittain, Robert P., A. Saury, and M. R. Guidet. 1970. *Bibliographie des travaux français de médecine légale.* Paris: Masson. 188 p.

Similar to Brittain's bibliography of works in English, but this collection focuses on works in French. A subject index is included.

57.    Eckert, William G. 1980. *History of criminalistics.* Wichita, KS: INFORM. 19 p.

Not available for review because it is only available at John Jay College of Criminal Justice.

58.    Eckert, William G. 1990. *History forensic medicine.* Wichita, KS: IN-FORM. 2 vols.

This monograph is a compilation of historical writings, articles, cases, and activities in the forensic sciences. The full text of these articles has been reproduced in their entirety in this publication. There are no indexes included, only a table of contents. The quality of the images reproduced in the articles is quite poor, but the text is legible. Eckert originally wrote many of the articles. Some of the articles included are also listed separately in this chapter.

59.    Eckert, William G., and Neil Garland. 1984. **The history of the forensic applications in radiology.** *American Journal of Forensic Medicine and Pathology* 5(1): 53–56.

Includes a full report by Professor Arthur Schuster, involved in the earliest case using this method of detection, on the discovery of x-radiation by Professor Wilhelm Conrad Roentgen. This article includes a reference list.

60.    Eckert, William, and Thomas T. Noguchi. 1972. *History—medicolegal.* Wichita, KS: International Reference Organization in Forensic Medicine. 42 p.

This compilation is primarily that of Dr. Jaroslav Nemec, perhaps the world's most knowledgeable expert on legal and forensic medicine history. It consists of 1,375 bibliographic citations from the international literature arranged alphabetically by author. References are from the eighteenth, nineteenth, and twentieth centuries, although the majority are from the nineteenth and twentieth centuries. A subject index is included.

61.    Forbes, Thomas Rogers. 1985. *Surgeons at the Bailey: English forensic medicine to 1878.* New Haven: Yale University Press. 255 p. $57.69. ISBN 0300033389.

Although several histories of forensic medicine in Britain have been written over the years, this is one of the few that discusses the history of publications and university lectures in this time period.

62.    *Forensic Science Timeline.* http://www.forensicdna.com/Timeline020702 .pdf (accessed July 28, 2004).

Norah Rudin, a forensic consultant and expert witness in forensic DNA, compiles this "work in progress." It can also be found as an appendix in the book *Principles and Practice of Forensic Science: The Profession of Forensic Science* published by CRC Press in 2000 (Inman and Rudin, 2000).

63.    *Forensic Science Time Lines.* http://www.quincy.ca/TimeLine.cfm (accessed December 6, 2004).

Created by Shaunderson Communications Inc. (SCInc.), publishers of the the *International Journal of Document Examination*, this collection of time lines by forensic science fields includes computer forensics, anthropology, chemistry, document examination, engineering, entomology, firearms and tool marks, impression evidence, medicine and pathology, odontology, profiling, serology and DNA, toxicology, trace evidence, and crime scene. Each time line includes a list of references.

64.    Garland, A. Neil. 1987. **Forensic medicine in Great Britain. I. The beginning.** *American Journal of Forensic Medicine and Pathology* 8(3): 269–72.

This is the first of a two-part series on forensic medicine in Great Britain. The main focus is on the roll of Andrew Duncan, Sr., in medical jurisprudence. Included is Dr. Duncan's Memorial, an essay written by Duncan drawing attention to the need for a chair of medical jurisprudence at the Edinburgh University.

65.    Goddard, Calvin H. 1980. **A history of firearms identification to 1930.** *American Journal of Forensic Medicine and Pathology* 1(2): 155–168.

Calvin Goddard established firearm/tool mark examination as a discipline. Goddard traces the history of the discipline, interjecting case examples from his own experience, including the investigation of the St. Valentine's Day Massacre in Chicago.

66.   Lu Gwei-Djen, and Joseph Needham. 1988. **A history of forensic medicine in China.** *Medical History* 32(4): 357–400.

An extensive history of forensic medicine in China back to tenth century BC. Of particular value is the list of references at the end of the article, including old Chinese, Japanese, and Western references.

67.   MacDonell, Herbert Leon. 2000. *The literature of bloodstain pattern interpretation. Segment 00, Literature through the 1800s.* Corning, NY: Bloodstain Evidence Institute. 47 p.

Chronologically arranged from ancient times to 1900, entries summarize references to bloodstain pattern interpretation in the worldwide literature, often a description of a particular case. The sources of the information in the summaries are referenced as footnotes. The bibliography consolidates the sources but only lists works written before 1900. This is an updated version of an article by the author that appeared in the *Journal of Forensic Identification* in 1993, which was itself an update of a 1992 article in the *IAPBPA Newsletter.*

68.   MacDonell, Herbert Leon. 1992. **Segments in the documentation of bloodstain pattern interpretation. Segment 01: 1901–1910.** *IABPA Newsletter* 8(4): 5–22.

The second installment in a series of articles documenting the history of bloodstain pattern interpretation, this article is chronologically arranged from 1901 to 1910, with content similar to the first article in the series. Sources are referenced at the end of the articles.

69.   MacDonell, Herbert Leon. 1993. **The literature of bloodstain pattern interpretation. Segment 02: Literature from 1911 through 1920.** *IABPA Newsletter* 9(2): 4–10.

The third installment in a series of articles documenting the history of bloodstain pattern interpretation, this article is chronologically arranged from 1911 to 1920, with content similar to the first article in the series. Sources are referenced at the end of the articles.

70.   MacDonell, Herbert Leon. 1994. **The literature of bloodstain pattern interpretation. Segment 03: Literature from 1921 through 1930.** *IABPA Newsletter* 10(1): 6–14.

The fourth installment in a series of articles documenting the history of bloodstain pattern interpretation, this article is chronologically arranged from 1921 to 1930, with content similar to the first article in the series. Sources are referenced at the end of the articles.

71.   Mant, A. Keith, M.D. 1987. **Forensic medicine in Great Britain. II. The origins of the British medicolegal system and some historic cases.** *American Journal of Forensic Medicine and Pathology* 8(4): 354–361.

The second of two articles on forensic medicine in Great Britain, this gives a different perspective on British medicolegal history from that given in the Garland article. It details the development of the system, including discussions of a number of historical cases.

72.   Martin, Peter D., Hermann Schmitter, and Peter B. Schneider. 2001. **A brief history of the formation of DNA databases in forensic science within Europe.** *Forensic Science International* 119(2): 225–231.

The introduction of DNA analysis was a significant milestone in the forensic sciences. This article details the evolution of DNA databases in various European countries and the various legislations affecting them.

73.   McKnight, Brian, trans. 1981. *The washing away of wrongs: Forensic medicine in thirteenth-century China.* Ann Arbor: Center for Chinese Studies, University of Michigan. 181 p. $35.45 (cl.), $25.00 (pbk.). ISBN 0892648015 (cl.), 0892648007 (pbk.).

This is a translation of the oldest extant book on forensic medicine, *Hsi yuan chi lu*, written by Sung Tz'u in 1247. There have been several editions and translations of the *Hsi yuan chi lu*. McKnight includes marginal references to two early editions and to the first extended English translation. Figures are reproduced from the original work without translation. A subject index and bibliography are included.

74.   Nemec, Jaroslav. 1974. *International bibliography of the history of legal medicine.* Bethesda, MD: National Library of Medicine. 224 p. $17.45.

Annotated entries, arranged alphabetically by author or by title (for anonymous works), tracing the history of legal medicine worldwide from antiquity to 1972. Included are monographs, chapters or parts of monographs, journal articles, and dissertations. Each entry includes bibliographic information and a brief summary of the work. A subject index is included.

75.   Nemec, Jaroslav. 1976. *Highlights in medicolegal relations.* Rev. and enl ed. Bethesda, MD: National Library of Medicine. 166 p. $39.95.

Annotated chronological history of important events and publications in forensic medicine from ancient times to 1973. This publication is a revised and expanded version of an earlier work by the author. Each entry contains a description and/or evaluation of the event or publication in addition to a citation(s) for the source(s) of the information. The description or evaluation is based on published reviews or opinions if the author did not personally examine the text. Name and subject indexes, as well as an extensive bibliography of sources are included.

76.   Sachs, Hans. 1997. **History of hair analysis.** *Forensic Science International* 84(1–3): 7–16.
Sachs starts with a general overview of the history of hair analysis and proceeds to detail the history of various extraction methods, generally and then by drug groups.

77.   Salaçin, Serpil, M.D. 1982. **Forensic medicine in Turkey.** *American Journal of Forensic Medicine and Pathology* 3(2): 179–180.
A very brief introduction to forensic medicine in Hungary. Included is a short section on history.

78.   Somogyi, Endre, M.D. 1985. **The history of forensic medicine in Hungary.** *American Journal of Forensic Medicine and Pathology* 6(2): 145–147.
A brief overview of forensic medicine in Hungary from 1035 to 1985.

79.   Tabakman, Mark, M.D. 1980. **Forensic medical service in the U.S.S.R.** *American Journal of Forensic Medicine and Pathology* 1(3): 271–276.
The history of forensic medicine in the U.S.S.R. from 1716 to 1980.

80.   Tsunenari, Shigeyuki, M.D., and Hirofumi Suyama, M.D. 1986. **Forensic medicine in Japan.** *American Journal of Forensic Medicine and Pathology* 7(3): 219–223.
Primarily focused on the state of the Japanese medicolegal system in 1986, the first part of this article is devoted to the history of forensic medicine in Japan.

# Selective Biographical Forensic Sciences Resources

81.   Phillips, Charles, Alan Axelrod, and Kurt Kemper. 2000. *Cops, crooks, and criminologists: An international biographical dictionary of law enforcement.* Updated ed. New York, NY: Checkmark Books (an imprint of Facts On File, Inc.). 322 p. $50.00 (cl.), $18.95 (pbk.). ISBN 0816040761 (pbk.), 0816030162 (cl.).

An encyclopedic dictionary of major and significant figures who have shaped the history of law enforcement. Entries are alphabetically arranged by the person's surname. Birth and, where appropriate, death dates are included. Some entries include references to further reading. The introduction provides an overview of the historical background in which those included in the encyclopedia should be viewed. A subject/name index is included.

# 2
# Abstracting and Indexing Sources

Abstracting and Indexing (A&I) tools are intended to assist researchers in identifying relevant resources from a variety of primary and secondary information sources. There is no traditional tool in the forensic sciences because of its interdisciplinary nature. Indexes and catalogues to book materials are covered in Chapter 4. This chapter will identify and explain the coverage and utility of A&I tools.

## Journal A&I Tool Characteristics

To evaluate it properly, a researcher must determine whether the scope and search capabilities of a particular A&I tool matches the needs for their particular question. One tool may not meet the needs of an individual for all of their questions. The following are the primary characteristics of A&I tools that should be considered.

### Scope of Coverage

Every A&I tool covers only a portion of the literature, and it is important to understand exactly what is covered. Some tools are subject-specific, whereas others are interdisciplinary. A&I tools may also differ in the level of coverage: some focus on materials at the professional level, others focus on popular materials, and some attempt to cover both. Subject-specific tools tend to be more comprehensive in the coverage of materials in the subject area, indexing journals, books, conference proceedings, reports, and unpublished materials. They often cover materials in multiple languages as well. Some A&I tools focus on current information (current awareness services), whereas others take more time in production to add value to the content (e.g., abstracts and indexing). Some tools add value through metadata such as chemical indexing. Some A&I tools include coverage of preprints, Web sites, and other such information, whereas others focus on peer-reviewed materials. Some A&I tools provide access to the full text of sources, whether the full text is included in the index or through links to outside sources.

**Arrangement of the Search Options**

The majority of A&I tools, whether they are in print or online, provide access to information via basic searching of author names and some form of subject searching. Some use classification schemes, such as the NLM Subject Classification (see this book's introduction for more information on this classification scheme). Most online tools provide the capability to do keyword searching. Some online resources also include subject thesauri to improve search accuracy. The online platform often allows users to limit their searches by various criteria such as date, language, and publication type (e.g., journal, book, conference proceeding).

Online tools often allow the researcher to sort results in ways more useful to them (e.g., publication date, relevancy, alphabetical by title). Relevancy sorting is extremely useful to researchers because it allows users to see items at the beginning of their search results that, through various techniques such as word-frequency analysis, are more likely to be "on topic" for the researcher. An increasing number of tools now provide linking between citations within the index (e.g., related records, cited works lists). Many online tools also provide the ability to select specific citations for printing, saving to a disk, or emailing. Increasingly important to researchers is the ability to format results to be easily transferred to personal bibliographic database management software (e.g., End-Note, ProCite, RefWorks, Reference Manager). Unfortunately, there are so many proprietary search interfaces (e.g., Ovid, SilverPlatter, EBSCO*host*, ProQuest, ISI) on the market that learning the capabilities and search methods for each can become very confusing for users.

# Forensic Sciences–Related A&I Databases

There is no one index to the forensic sciences literature, making finding where a journal is indexed often a challenge. Several key forensic science journals are only listed in one index, are only available on the publisher's Web site, or are selectively listed by multiple indexes (e.g., in the journal *Science and Justice*, a publication of the Forensic Science Society, PubMed (http://www.ncbi.nlm. nih.gov/entrez/query.fcgi) indexes biological related articles such as DNA analysis, and Web of Science indexes non-biologically related articles such as firearms topics). Due to the interdisciplinary nature of the forensic sciences, researchers must branch out into A&I tools in multiple subject areas. The easiest way to approach choosing the most appropriate indexes to use is to first decide whether the topic is biological or physical. In this chapter, A& I tools have been categorized using the headings of General/Multidisciplinary, Biological, Physical, and Criminology/Legal.

## General/Multidisciplinary

82.  *Analytical Abstracts.* London, U.K.: Royal Society of Chemistry, 1954–.

A journal index focused on the specific needs of analytical scientists, *Analytical Abstracts* provides comprehensive coverage of new techniques and applications for the analyst. Areas of coverage includes chromatography; electrophoresis; spectrometry; radiochemical methods; clinical and biochemical analysis; pharmaceutical analysis; and environmental, agricultural, and food analysis.

Updates: Paper (monthly), online (monthly on Ovid and SilverPlatter; weekly on all others).

Paper: Includes free sitewide access to the companion Web site, *Analytical WebBase*.

Online: *Analytical Abstracts* (DataStar, 1978–present; Dialog, STN, Ovid, SilverPlatter, 1980–present); *Analytical WebBase* (1980–present).

83.  *Applied Science & Technology Index.* Bronx, NY: H.W. Wilson Company, 1958–.

Broad index to basic English-language applied science, engineering, and technology journals; trade and industrial publications; directories; buyers' guides; and conference proceedings. Disciplines covered include chemical, civil, electric and telecommunications, environmental, industrial, mining, mechanical, and nuclear engineering. It includes material of at least one column in length.

Updates: Paper (monthly except July with quarterly cumulations), online (daily on WilsonWeb; monthly all others), CD-ROM (monthly).

Paper: Main body of entries arranged by subject, followed by sections of book review citations and product review citations. Includes monthly subject index. Previous title: *Industrial Arts Index* from 1913–1957.

Online: Indexing from 1983, abstracts from 1993, and full text from 1997. *Applied Science & Technology Index* (WilsonWeb and WilsonDisc); *Applied Science & Technology Abstracts* (WilsonWeb and WilsonDisc); *Applied Science & Technology Full Text* (WilsonWeb and WilsonDisc); *Wilson Applied Science & Technology Index* (SilverPlatter); *Wilson Applied Science & Technology Abstracts* (Dialog, SilverPlatter, and Ovid); *Wilson Applied Science & Technology Full Text* (SilverPlatter).

84.   *ArticleFirst*. Dublin, OH: OCLC, 1990–.

An online index of articles from the contents pages of journals in multiple disciplines including business, humanities, medicine, popular culture, science, social science, and technology. Only bibliographic information is included. A list of libraries that have the journal title is provided for most entries.

Updates: Daily.

Host: OCLC FirstSearch.

85.   *CA Selects: Forensic Chemistry*. Columbus, OH: Chemical Abstracts Service (a division of the American Chemical Society), 1976–.

*CA Selects* is a biweekly current awareness service in which the most recent research( including journals, patents, and substance information) appearing in the *Chemical Abstracts* index on specific research topics is disseminated to subscribers. One of the research topic areas covered by *CA Selects* is forensic chemistry. Topics covered in the Forensic Chemistry edition include analytical techniques; trace analysis; drug abuse; the chemistry of investigative science; blood chemistry; biological fluid analysis and identification; rape; homicide; suicide; arson; forgery; counterfeiting; fiber, ink, and paint analysis and identification; breath analysis and drunkenness; and the chemical analysis of explosives and gunshot wounds. References included in each issue are abstracts formatted in an identical manner to those included in *Chemical Abstracts*. An enhanced version of this service is called *CA Selects Plus*. This service is an accelerated version of *CA Selects*, in that records from 1,500 core journals are included before they have been fully indexed. The remaining records come from the other non-core journals indexed in *Chemical Abstracts*.

Online: *CA Selects on the Web*.

86.   *Chemical Abstracts*. Columbus, OH: Chemical Abstracts Service (a division of the American Chemical Society), 1907–.

*CA* is the world's largest, most current collection of chemical information. Sources for *CA* include more than 9,000 major scientific journals, patents, technical reports, dissertations, conference proceedings, and books. *CA* is particularly useful for patent searching, covering over 50 active patent-issuing authorities around the world. Each abstract includes complete bibliographic information, commonly used chemical substance names and molecular formulas, chemical structure diagrams (when available), and patent references if applicable.

Paper: Weekly issues include abstracts arranged into 80 different subsections under 5 broad headings: Biochemistry, Organic, Macromolecular, Applied, and "Physical, Inorganic, and Analytical." Indexes by author, keyword, and patent are included, as well as biannual author, chemical substance, patent, formula, and general subject indexes. Also included: Decennial Indexes 1907/16–1947/56; Collective Indexes 1957/61–1997/2001.

Online: *SciFinder* and *SciFinder Scholar* (direct from the CAS); *Chemical Abstracts*, *STN* (*STN Express* interface, *STN on the Web* interface, *STN Easy* interface) (1967–present)—academic discount plan after 5 PM; *DataStar* (1967–present); CD-ROM direct from CAS (1977–present).

87.  *Conference Papers Index.* Bethesda, MD: Cambridge Scientific Abstracts, 1973–.

Citations to papers and poster sessions presented at major scientific meetings around the world. Emphasis is on the life sciences, environmental sciences, and aquatic sciences.

Updates: Paper (monthly plus annual index), online (bi-monthly).

Paper: Arranged by subject headings.

Online: *CONFSCI* (STN, 1973–present); *Conference Papers Index* (Cambridge Scientific Abstracts, 1982–present).

88.  *Dissertation Abstracts International.* Ann Arbor, MI: UMI, 1938–.

This is the most comprehensive information resource covering doctoral dissertations and master's theses. Virtually all accredited institutions in North America that award doctoral degrees are included. Subject coverage includes agriculture and food science, architecture, art, bioscience and biotechnology, business, chemistry, economics, education, history, geoscience, law and political science, mathematics, music, pharmaceuticals, psychology, social science, veterinary sciences, zoology, and more.

Paper: Divided into two sections: Humanities and Social Sciences, and Sciences and Engineering. Published monthly and cumulated annually. A third section covering non–North American materials is published quarterly as a separate volume. Abstracts are included from 1980 forward. Includes only titles submitted to ProQuest Information and Learning.

Online: *Dissertation Abstracts* (1861–present). Includes *Dissertation Abstracts International*, *American Doctoral Dissertations* (includes titles not published by ProQuest Information and Learning), *Masters Abstracts International* and *Comprehensive Dissertation Index.*

Hosts: Ovid, SilverPlatter, OCLC FirstSearch, ProQuest, Dialog, DataStar, STN (chemistry titles only).

89.    ***Forensic Science Abstracts.*** Amsterdam: Excerpta Medica (a subsidiary of Elsevier), 1974–.

This index is a subset of the medical database *Excerpta Medica*. This subset covers all aspects of biomedicine of relevance to criminal investigation. Coverage includes forensic pathology, forensic toxicology, lab techniques, crime scene investigation, and psychosocial problems with legal implications (such as child abuse).

Updates: Paper (bi-monthly), online (monthly on SilverPlatter; weekly on all others).

Paper: Citations with abstracts arranged by broad subject category. Includes author and subject indexes.

Online: *EMBASE—the Excerpta Medica Database* (Section 49 of *Excerpta Medica*).

Hosts: ScienceDirect, DataStar, Dialog, DIMDI, LexisNexis, STN (1974–present); Ovid, SilverPlatter (1980–present).

90.    ***FORS (Forensic Abstracts).*** London: Forensic Science Service, Information Services, 1976–.

Comprehensive coverage of the literature for forensic scientists and other professionals in criminal investigation, medical, and legal occupations relevant to the examination of evidential materials, analytical methods, and the presentation and interpretation of findings. Database coverage includes toxicology, forensic biology, forensic chemistry, forensic medicine and pathology, documents and firearms examination, arson investigation, image processing, fingerprints, safety, and quality and management aspects of running a forensic sciences lab. Citations and abstracts come from 30 core journals and 250 additional scientific, criminal justice, and trade journals. Also covered are books, conference proceedings, patents, and Web sites.

Updates: monthly.

Paper: *FORSight: The Forensic Abstracts Journal* (2002–present). The paper version of *Forensic Abstracts* serves as a comprehensive current awareness service for forensic scientists and other professionals in criminal investigation, medical, and legal occupations. Arranged by general subject categories. There are no subject or author indexes, although it includes a numerical index based on accession number that really serves no useful purpose.

Host: SilverPlatter.

91.  *General Science Index*. Bronx, NY: H.W. Wilson Company, 1978–.

Broad index to a limited number of basic English-language science journals, books, technical reports, and government reports. It includes material of at least one column in length in key popular science magazines and professional journals, including the *New York Times* Science section. It is useful for both the non-specialist and the expert.

Updates: Paper (monthly except June and December), online (daily on WilsonWeb; monthly all others), CD-ROM (monthly).

Paper: Main body of entries arranged by subject, followed by a section of book review citations. Includes monthly author and subject indexes.

Online: Indexing from 1984, abstracts from 1993, and full text from 1995. *General Science Index* (WilsonWeb and WilsonDisc); *General Science Abstracts* (WilsonWeb and WilsonDisc); *General Science Full Text* (WilsonWeb and WilsonDisc); *General Science Abstracts/Full Text* (Dialog); *Wilson General Science Index* (SilverPlatter); *Wilson General Science Abstracts* (SilverPlatter and Ovid); *Wilson General Science Abstracts Full Text* (SilverPlatter).

92.  *Index to Scientific & Technical Proceedings*. Philadelphia, PA: Thomson ISI, 1978–.

Comprehensive, multidisciplinary coverage of proceedings from international scientific and technology conferences, seminars, symposia, colloquia, conventions, and workshops. Coverage includes books, series, preprints, and journals in all disciplines in the sciences. Citations include author-supplied abstracts.

Updates: Paper (monthly with semi-annual cumulations), online (weekly), CD-ROM (quarterly).

Paper: Bibliographic descriptions of each proceedings is included in the "Contents of Proceedings" volumes. Entries are arranged in ascending order by a "proceedings number." Permuterm index (keyword in title), Category index (general topic), Author/Editor index (alphabetical by surname), Sponsor index (alphabetical), Meeting location index (alphabetical by country, state, and city), and Corporate index (divided into two sections—Geographic and Organization) are included.

Online: *Index to Scientific & Technical Proceedings* (ISI Web of Knowledge); *ISTPB + ISTP/ISSHP* (DIMDI).

93.  *NCJRS Abstracts Database*. Washington, DC: U.S. Department of Justice, early 1970s–.

The *Abstracts Database of the NCJRS* (National Criminal Justice Reference Service) indexes criminal justice publications, including journal articles, books, and reports. It comprehensively indexes items from the early 1970s and contains seminal works from the mid- to early 1960s. The NCJRS also has a Virtual Library of full text publications. These items are indexed in the *Abstracts Database* with links to the full text, but the *Abstracts Database* does not search the full text of these items. The separate Virtual Library search engine searches the full text of documents and spiders out to the Web sites of 11 sponsoring agencies. Coverage in the Virtual Library is from the mid-1990s to the present.

Hosts: NCJRS Web site (http://AbstractsDB.ncjrs.org/), Cambridge Scientific Abstracts (1975–present).

94.   *Science Citation Index.* Philadelphia: Thomson ISI, 1961–.

A multidisciplinary database of scientific and technical research covering more than 3,700 science and technical journals, but very few conference proceedings or books. The online versions cover more than 5,800 journals. This index provides the unique search feature of cited reference searching, which allows users to track the literature backward and forward. The online database includes a Related Records feature that allows researchers to conduct broad searches to discover subject relationships. The online versions include records from *Current Contents*; therefore it has good currency.

Updates: Paper (quarterly with annual cumulations); online (weekly).

Paper: Permuterm subject index (keyword in title), Source index (author), Corporate index, and Citation index (cited author name) are included. No subject heading indexing. Cumulative indexes for 1965–1969, 1970–1974, 1975–1979, and 1980–1984.

Online: *Science Citation Index Expanded* (part of the *Web of Science*, 1945–present); *SciSearch* (*Dialog*, *STN*, and *DIMDI*, 1974–present; *DataStar*, 1980–present).

Hosts: ISI Web of Knowledge, STN, Dialog, DataStar, DIMDI.

95.   *Social Sciences Citation Index.* Philadelphia: Thomson ISI, 1956–.

Current and retrospective bibliographic access to over 1,700 scholarly social sciences journals covering more than 50 disciplines. Select coverage of relevant items from 3,300 science and technology journals is also included. This index, like *Science Citation Index*, provides the unique search feature of cited reference searching, which allows users to track the literature backward and forward. The online versions include records from *Current Contents*; therefore it has good currency.

Updates: Paper (3 per year, with annual cumulations), online (weekly).

Paper: Permuterm subject index (keyword in title), Source index (author), Corporate index, and Citation index (cited author name) are included. No subject heading indexing. Cumulative indexes for 1966–1970, 1971–1975, 1976–1980, and 1981–1985.

Online: *Social Sciences Citation Index* (part of the *Web of Science*, 1956–present); *SocialSciSearch* (Dialog and DataStar, 1972–present; DIMDI, 1973–present).

Hosts: ISI Web of Knowledge, STN, Dialog, DataStar, DIMDI.

## Biological

96.   **Abstracts in Anthropology.** Amityville, NY: Baywood Publishing Company, Inc., 1970–.

Citation and abstract index arranged by broad subject categories. Coverage includes basic site reports, field techniques, analytical studies, and artifacts from around the world. Issues 1 and 3 include subject sections on Linguistics and Cultural Anthropology and issues 2 and 4 includes subject sections on Archaeology and Physical Anthropology. Subscriptions are sold in two volume groupings with four issues per volume. Includes author and subject indexes, with twice annual cumulative indexes. This index is not available online.

97.   **Agricola.** Washington, DC: National Agricultural Library, 1970–.

This bibliography includes citations to journal articles, monographs, theses, patents, software, audio-visual materials, and technical reports related to agriculture. This includes the allied disciplines of animal and veterinary sciences, entomology, plant sciences, and environmental sciences. This database is useful for forensic entomology, wildlife forensics, and forensic botany.

Updates: Online (quarterly on SilverPlatter; monthly on all others), CD-ROM (quarterly).

Paper: *Bibliography of Agriculture* (1940–2000).

Hosts: STN, Dialog, CSA, and the National Agricultural Library, 1970–present; Ovid, 1979–present; SilverPlatter, 1984–present.

98.   **The Anthropological Index.** London, U.K.: Royal Anthropological Institute, 1957–.

Bibliographic index arranged by geographical region, then subdivided into 5 categories: General, Physical Anthropology, Archaeology, Cultural Anthropology and Ethnography, and Linguistics.

Paper: Issues do not include indexes, although there is an annual cumulative author index.

Updates: Quarterly.

Online: *Anthropological Index Online* (updated 8–12 times per year—Royal Anthropological Institute); *Anthropology* Plus (updated monthly—RLG Eureka).

99.  ***Anthropological Literature.*** Cambridge, MA: Tozzer Library, Harvard University, 1979–.

Bibliographic index to articles in journals and edited works received by Tozzer Library, with more than 500,000 entries from the nineteenth century to the present. Coverage is international, although emphasis is on materials published in European languages. Articles, reports, commentaries, review essays, and obituaries are included.

Paper: Citations are arranged by 5 subject fields: Archaeology, Biological/ Physical Anthropology, Cultural/Social Anthropology, Linguistics, and Research in Related Fields and Topics of General Interest. A supplement of reviews is included where applicable. Includes subject and author indexes with annual cumulative indexes.

Updates: Quarterly.

Online: *Anthropological Literature* (updated quarterly); *Anthropology* Plus (updated monthly).

Host: RLG Eureka.

100.  ***Anthropology Plus.*** Mountain View, CA: RLG, late 19th century–.

This database brings together into one resource two highly respected anthropology indexes: *Anthropological Literature* from Harvard University and the *Anthropological Index* from the Royal Anthropological Institute in the United Kingdom. *Anthropology* Plus provides extensive worldwide indexing of journal articles, reports, commentaries, edited works, and obituaries in the fields of social, cultural, physical, biological, and linguistic anthropology; ethnology; archaeology; folklore; material culture; and interdisciplinary studies. The index offers excellent coverage of all core periodicals in the field, in addition to local and lesser-known journals.

101.  ***Biological Abstracts.*** Philadelphia, PA: Thomson BIOSIS, 1926–.

The world's most comprehensive index of journal literature for life sciences researchers. Coverage includes traditional areas of biology such as botany, biochemistry, microbiology, and zoology, as well as related fields such as ecology, pharmacology, forensic sciences, and plant sciences.

Updates: Paper (twice monthly), online (quarterly).

Paper: Entries are arranged by major concept headings. Author, biosystematic (taxonomic category), generic (genus and genus-species), and subject (title keyword in context) indexes are included in each issue. Cumulative indexes are provided twice yearly.

Online: *Biological Abstracts* (1969–present).

Hosts: SilverPlatter, EBSCO*host*, NISC; Ovid (1980–present).

102.  **Biological Abstracts/RRM.** Philadelphia, PA: Thomson BIOSIS, 1967–.

The RRM (Reports, Reviews, Meetings) index complements *Biological Abstracts* by compiling the non-journal literature for life sciences researchers, including symposia, meetings, conferences, books, software, literature reviews, and U.S. patents.

Updates: Paper (quarterly), online (bimonthly).

Paper: Similar to *Biological Abstracts* in print, this index has author, biosystematic, generic, and subject indexes. Cumulative indexes are provided twice yearly.

Online: *Biological Abstracts/RRM* (1969–present).

Hosts: SilverPlatter, Ovid.

103.  **BIOSIS Previews.** Philadelphia, PA: Thomson BIOSIS, 1969–.

This database combines the content of the *Biological Abstracts* and *Biological Abstracts/RRM* databases into one index.

Updates: Weekly.

Hosts: SilverPlatter, Ovid.

104.  **Index Medicus.** Bethesda, MD: U.S. Dept. of Health, Education, and Welfare, Public Health Service, National Institutes of Health, National Library of Medicine, 1941–.

The premier index covering the fields of medicine, nursing, dentistry, veterinary medicine, the health care system, and the preclinical sciences. This includes life sciences literature, including some aspects of biology, environmental science, marine biology, and plant and animal science, as well as biophysics and chemistry. Coverage includes over 4,600 worldwide journals.

Updates: Paper (monthly), online (weekly), CD-ROM (monthly).

Paper: Titles were *Current List of Medical Literature* to 1959 and *Monthly Bibliography of Medical Reviews* to 1977.

Online: *MEDLINE* (1966–present), *OLDMEDLINE* (1951–1965).

Hosts: Ovid, SilverPlatter, and ScienceDirect (1966–present); Cambridge Scientific Abstracts (1993–present); EBSCO*host* (1960–present); Dialog, DataStar, DIMDI, and PubMed (1951–present). PubMed is free direct from NLM. It includes access to bibliographic information from *MEDLINE*, *OLDMEDLINE*, articles from *MEDLINE*-covered journals that were considered out-of-scope for Medline, citations preceding the date that a journal was selected for *MEDLINE* indexing, and some additional life science journals that submit full text to PubMedCentral and receive a qualitative review by NLM.

105.  **Mathematical Reviews.** Providence, RI: American Mathematical Society, 1940–.

The leading indexing and abstracting tool in mathematics. Entries are arranged according to the Mathematics Subject Classification and cover journals, conferences, and technical reports. The abstracts are actually reviews by mathematicians.

Updates: Paper (weekly), online (weekly), CD-ROM (quarterly). *Note:* Subscription costs include a database fee and a platform fee.

Paper: Author and subject indexes in each issue, with annual cumulative indexes.

Online: *MathSciNet* (direct from AMS—http://www.ams.org/mathscinet/); *MathSci* (CD-ROM) from SilverPlatter and Ovid; *Mathematical Reviews* (Dialog and STN—includes *Current Index to Statistics* which is not in MathSci or MathSciNet). The online version covers *Mathematical Reviews* and *Current Mathematical Publications.* Citation searching is a recent enhancement to the online databases.

106.   *Psychological Abstracts.* Washington, DC: American Psychological Association, 1927–.

Provides access to the scholarly literature in the behavioral sciences and mental health. Coverage includes material of relevance to psychologists and those in related areas, such as psychiatry, education, neuroscience, business, social work, medicine, law, management, and social science. Close to 2,000 serials are monitored for inclusion. In addition, coverage includes books and technical reports. The online version also covers dissertations.

Updates: Paper (monthly), online (weekly), CD-ROM (monthly).

Paper: Organized by subject according to the *PsycINFO* Classification Codes. Monthly author, brief subject, and book title indices are included, with annual author and subject indices.

Online: *PsycINFO* (1887–present).

Hosts: SilverPlatter, Ovid, EBSCO*host,* Cambridge Scientific Abstracts, OCLC FirstSearch, Thomson ISI, Hogrefe & Huber (europsych.net), ProQuest, ScienceDirect, Dialog, DataStar, DIMDI.

107.   *Review of Medical and Veterinary Entomology* (formerly the *Review of Applied Entomology. Series B, Medical and Veterinary*). Wallingford, Oxfordshire, U.K.: CABI Publishing (a division of CAB International), 1913–.

An online citation and abstract index covering key English- and non-English-language journal articles, reports, conferences, and books about medical and veterinary entomology. Forensic entomology is an area of coverage.

Updates: Weekly. *Review of Medical and Veterinary Entomology* (1972–present). *CAB Abstracts Archive* (1913–1971; *Review of Medical and Veterinary Entomology* archival material is a part of the *CAB Abstracts Archive*).

108. **TOXLINE.** U.S. Dept. of Health, Education, and Welfare, Public Health Service, National Institutes of Health, National Library of Medicine, 19??–.

Citations plus abstracts from the core journal literature on biochemical, pharmacological, physiological, and toxicological effects of drugs and other chemicals. References are drawn from two parts, *TOXLINE Core* and *TOXLINE Special*. *TOXLINE Core* covers much of the standard journal literature in toxicology, whereas *TOXLINE Special* complements *TOXLINE Core* with an assortment of specialized journals and other sources, such as technical reports and research projects. The two parts can be searched individually or together.

109. **Zoological Record.** Philadelphia, PA: Thomson BIOSIS, 1865–.

The most comprehensive index to animal biology research, including journals, books, reports, and conference proceedings. From 1864–1869 the title was the *Record of Zoological Literature*. This index is useful for forensic entomology and wildlife forensics topics.

Updates: Print (annual), online and CD-ROM (monthly).

Paper: Bibliographic citations arranged in 27 sections: 25 taxonomic groups of animals, 1 comprehensive zoology section (general topics), and 1 list of new generic and subgeneric names. Includes an author index, detailed subject index, subject index, geographical index, palaeontological index, detailed systematic index, systematic index, and index to genera.

Online: 1978–present. Abstracts are included from 2001 forward. *Zoological Record* (SilverPlatter, Ovid, & NISC); *Zoological Record Plus* (Cambridge Scientific Abstracts); *Zoological Record Online* (Dialog).

**Physical**

110. **ABI/INFORM.** ProQuest, 1971–.

The premier source of business information, *ABI/INFORM* contains content from thousands of journals in all areas of business, including finance, accounting, economics, and management, among others. This database is useful for forensic accounting and forensic economics topics.

Updates: Online (daily), CD-ROM (monthly).

Hosts: ProQuest.

111. **Computer and Control Abstracts** (Science Abstracts, Section C). London: Institution of Electrical Engineers, 1966–.

Offers a comprehensive information service on all aspects of computer installations, applications, hardware, peripherals, software, and theory, as well as control engineering, robotics, systems theory, and artificial intelligence. Sources covered include journals, books, reports, dissertations, and conference proceedings. Useful for computer crime investigation and law enforcement technology topics, including photography.

Updates: Paper (monthly), online (weekly).

Paper: Title was *Control Abstracts* until 1969. Entries are arranged by subject classifications. Each issue has a subject guide and author index. Cumulated indexes are published twice yearly. Subsidiary indexes, such as a conference or book index, are included as appropriate.

Online: *Computer and Control Abstracts* is a portion of *INSPEC* (1969–present) and *INSPEC Archive* (1898–1968).

Hosts: Engineering Village 2, Ovid, and SilverPlatter (1898–present); ScienceDirect, STN, Dialog, DataStar, EBSCO*host*, ISI Web of Knowledge, OCLC, ProQuest (1969–present).

112.   ***EconLit.*** Nashville, TN: American Economic Association, 1969–.

*EconLit* is a comprehensive online index of journal articles, books, book reviews, collective volume articles, working papers, and dissertations in the area of economics. Until 2000 the print version, the *Journal of Economic Literature* (*JEL* - formerly the *Journal of Economic Abstracts*), included the items appearing in *EconLit* in an index section. Starting in 2000 these items appeared online-only in a database called *e-JEL* (for individual subscribers). Institutional subscribers can receive CD-ROM versions of the *e-JEL*, but most institutions opt for a subscription to *EconLit*. *EconLit*, in addition to containing the content of *e-JEL*, contains the Cambridge University Press *Abstracts of Working Papers in Economics* and recent *JEL* book reviews. This index is the premier index to economics literature.

Updates: Monthly.

Hosts: EBSCO*host*, CSA, Dialog, OCLC FirstSearch, ScienceDirect, Ovid, SilverPlatter.

113.   ***Engineering Index.*** Hoboken, NJ: Engineering Information (a subsidiary of Elsevier), 1884–.

*Engineering Index* covers the engineering literature, including citations and abstracts from over 5,000 journals and conference proceedings. Useful for forensic engineering topics.

Paper: Title was *Index Notes* until 1892, when it changed to *Journal of the Association of Engineering Societies*. In 1896 it took its present name.

Online: *Compendex* (1969–present); *Engineering Index Backfile* (1884–1968).

Host: Engineering Village 2 (from Ei); ScienceDirect (1969–present); DataStar (1976–present).

114. **MLA International Bibliography.** New York, NY: Modern Language Association, 1921–.

An index of books, articles, and dissertations published on modern languages, literatures, folklore, and linguistics. The majority of records are from English-language publications. This index is useful for forensic linguistics topics.

Updates: Print (annual), online (10 times per year).

Paper: Two printed versions of the bibliography appear annually: a clothbound version for libraries and a paperbound version for individual purchasers. The library edition consists of two books. The first contains all 5 classified volumes, along with an index to authors and editors of articles and books; the second contains a list of subject terms that refer to the classified entries. The third classified volume contains the articles on linguistics.

Online: *MLA International Bibliography* (1963–present).

Hosts: EBSCO*host*, Gale (InfoTrac and Literature Resource Center), OCLC FirstSearch, CSA.

## Criminology/Legal

115. **Criminal Justice Abstracts.** Thousand Oaks, CA: Sage Publications, 1968–.

A comprehensive index of the literature of criminology and related disciplines covering current books, journal articles, and reports published worldwide. Prepared in cooperation with the Criminal Justice Collection of Rutgers University Library.

Updates: Print (quarterly); online (quarterly or annual).

Print: Citations and abstracts arranged by broad categories: Crime, the Offender, and the Victim; Juvenile Justice and Delinquency; Police; Courts and Legal Process; Adult Corrections; and Crime Prevention and Control Strategies. Includes subject, author, and geographic indexes. Title from 1968–1976 was *Crime and Delinquency Literature.*

Online: *Criminal Justice Abstracts.*

Hosts: SilverPlatter and Ovid.

116. **Current Law Index.** Farmington Hills, MI: Thomson Gale, 1980–.

This monthly index provides coverage of more than 900 key law journals, legal newspapers, and specialty publications from the United States, Canada, the United Kingdom, Ireland, Australia, and New Zealand. Topics include interpretation and analysis of laws, cases, statutes, and legal trends. Divided into four sections with entries arranged under subject headings. Within subject headings, entries are chronologically arranged. Quarterly and annual cumulations. There is no online equivalent for this index.

117. *Index to Legal Periodicals & Books.* New York, NY: H.W. Wilson Company, 1929–.

An index to English-language legal periodicals, symposia, books, legislation, court decisions, and jurisdictional surveys published or edited in the United States, Canada, Great Britain, Ireland, Australia, and New Zealand. Articles must be at least one-half page in length.

Updates: Print (monthly except September), online (daily on WilsonWeb; monthly all others), CD-ROM (monthly).

Paper: Citations are arranged in a common subject and author index under the most specific subject used and further subdivided by jurisdiction where appropriate. Includes a Table of Cases (listed alphabetically under both plaintiff and defendant's name), a Table of Statutes (by jurisdiction, then alphabetically by name), and an index to Book Reviews (alphabetically by author or title as appropriate). Includes an annual cumulation.

Online: *Index to Legal Periodicals & Books* (indexing only 1981–present; WilsonDisc and WilsonWeb); *Index to Legal Periodicals Full Text* (indexing from 1981–1993, and full text from 1994; Wilson Web); *Wilson Index to Legal Periodicals* (Ovid); *Index to Legal Periodicals & Books (Wilson)* (SilverPlatter); *Index to Legal Periodicals Retrospective* (1918–1981; WilsonWeb).

118. *ProQuest Criminal Justice Periodical Index (CJPI).* Ann Arbor, MI: ProQuest, 1981–.

*CJPI* was a print index from 1975 to 1998, when it ceased publication in print and went to online only. The online index provides excellent coverage of criminal justice, including forensic science. The practical nature of *CJPI* makes this index especially suitable for undergraduates. Coverage is primarily American, with some British and Canadian content. The online database includes some full text content.

# Search Services: Hosts to Multiple Databases

119. *Cambridge Scientific Abstracts.* CSA. http://www.csa.com/ (accessed November 17, 2004).

CSA's Internet Database Service provides access to more than 50 databases in a variety of subject areas. The search interface is Web based, is Z39.50 compliant, and allows for command searching and "fill-in-the-box" searching. Interestingly, the interface best suited to novice searchers (fill-in-the-box) is the advanced search option. Subscriptions are negotiated on a case-by-case basis.

120. **DataStar.** Thomson Dialog. http://www.dialog.com/products/productline/
datastar.shtml (accessed November 17, 2004).

*Dialog DataStar* provides access to over 350 databases of business and technical information. Access options are not as plentiful but include a *Classic* and *Classic on the Web* versions similar to *Dialog*. There is no guided search mode for novices. It was the first online service in Europe.

121. **Dialog.** Thomson Dialog. http://www.dialog.com/products/productline/
dialog.shtml (accessed November 17, 2004).

*Dialog* is a host to more than 1,200 scientific, technical, medical, business, news, and patent databases. There are a plethora of access options through the Web, desktop, telnet, email, and intranet, featuring interfaces for all levels of users from the novice to the power searcher. Most of these options require a pre-arranged account for searching, often with monthly minimums to maintain the account.

For the experienced searcher, there is *DialogClassic*. This command-language interface allows the user to directly connect to the mainframe for fast and highly flexible searches.

*DialogWeb* is the most flexible of all, offering a command search mode for the power user (*DialogClassic*, but in the Web environment) and a guided search mode for the novice, all through a Web browser.

*Dialog Open Access* is an alternative to the subscription services above and requiring only a credit card to receive instant access.

122. **DIMDI.** German Institute of Medical Documentation and Information. http://www.dimdi.de/dynamic/en/index.html (accessed November 17, 2004).

*DIMDI* was founded in 1969 within the scope of the German Federal Ministry of Health and Social Security. Its main task is to provide the public with quick and easy access to the latest information in the life sciences. To that end, it provides users with access to more than 70 databases focusing on health care, medicine, and related fields such as toxicology, pharmacology, and biology.

123. **FirstSearch.** OCLC. http://www.oclc.org/firstsearch/default.htm (accessed November 17, 2004).

OCLC's *FirstSearch* provides access to more than 75 online databases, including more than 10 million full text and full-image articles. *FirstSearch* offers several document delivery options, including email and interlibrary loan.

*FirstSearch*'s interface is Web based and Z39.50 compliant. Subscriptions are available exclusively to individual libraries or groups of libraries on a subscription basis or for a per-search fee (purchased in blocks of 500 searches).

124.   ***STN International*** (Scientific & Technical Information Network). http://
www.stn-international.de/ (accessed November 17, 2004).

This network is cooperatively operated by FIZ Karlsruhe, the American
Chemical Society (ACS), and the Japan Science and Technology Corporation
(JST). It concentrates on databases in science and technology, with more than
220 databases. There are basically 3 interfaces to access *STN*: *STN Express*, *STN
Easy*, and *STN on the Web*. *STN Express* with Discover! provides desktop access
through locally installed software. Searching is done using command language.
*STN Easy* provides a Web-based guided search mode to over 90 *STN* databases
for the occasional searcher. There is no subscription or monthly fee for this
interface. *STN on the Web* is a Web-based interface with command-language
searching of all *STN* databases. Some databases have reduced-cost evening
academic options.

# 3
# Journals

This chapter identifies some of the journal sources that provide the most current information in the forensic sciences. This chapter strives to introduce researchers to not only a list of the resources, but also tools and methods for evaluation of these resources. A caveat to this is that most of these evaluative resources are for traditional paper journals—not for those distributed electronically.

## History of Journal Publishing

It was not until 1956, with the publication of the *Journal of Forensic Sciences*, that journals devoted to the publication of scholarly articles in the forensic sciences became more prevalent. Soon after, *Journal (Forensic Science Society)*, now *Science and Justice*, published its first issue. Until that point, most forensics articles were published in medical (e.g., *American Journal of Clinical Pathology*), legal (e.g., *Journal of Criminal Law and Criminology*), chemistry (e.g., *Acta Pharmacologica et Toxicologica*), and criminology/police methods (e.g., *FBI Law Enforcement Bulletin*) journals. Although there were two forensic science journals publishing before this time—the *Deutsche Zeitschrift für die Gesamte Gerichtliche Medizin* began in 1922 and *Hoigaku No Jissai To Kenyku* began in 1954—neither was in English. They are now *International Journal of Legal Medicine* and *Research and Practice in Forensic Medicine*, respectively.

Another trend in society/association periodical publishing in the forensic sciences is to have two publications: one, a journal for scholarly articles and the other, more of a newsletter for member news and case updates. An example of this is the Forensic Science Society, which publishes *Science and Justice* (their scholarly article journal) and *INTERfaces* (their member newsletter).

Currently there are many journals in the forensic sciences, most published by societies and associations. This history of societal publishing has greatly affected the speed of new format adoption for publishing these journals. Most associations and societies are volunteer-based organizations, or have very small permanent staffs. With limited resources, most have had neither the time nor the manpower to create and maintain online publications. It has only been recently that there has been a push for online access, resulting in the outsourcing of the online publication of these journals to commercial, or larger societal/association, publishers. Forensic journals published by commercial publishers, such as *Forensic Science International* and the *International Journal of Legal Medicine*, were online well before the association publications.

# Journal Bibliographies

Identifying journals of interest to researchers in the forensic sciences can sometimes be difficult because of the many sub-disciplines. Journal bibliographies can help in this identification process. The major tools available currently for this are *Ulrich's Periodicals Directory*, *The Serials Directory*, and *PubList*. Other sources for this information are metasites, such as Zeno's Forensic Site (see Chapter 5), and resource links on various association Web sites (see Chapter 6).

125.   *Ulrich's Periodicals Directory.* New Providence, NJ: R.R. Bowker LLC, 1932–. Annual. 42nd ed. 4 vols. $749. ISBN 0835245918.

For years *Ulrich's* has been the standard source of information on serials published around the world. Information included in each entry includes the title, the language(s) of the publication text, the year publication started, the frequency of the publication, subscription price information, descriptive information on special features, the ISSN, the document type, a brief description, title changes, related editions, abstracting and indexing, and publisher information. Not every entry includes all pieces of information, and some of the information is unverified.

Paper: Entries are arranged alphabetically by subject category in 3 volumes. The fourth volume includes a cross-index to subjects, a list of ceased titles, an ISSN index, a title index, a list of producers of serials on CD-ROM, a list of producers of online serials, an index to publications of international organizations, and an index to U.S. newspapers.

Online: The online equivalent is **Ulrichsweb.com**. Updated weekly, Ulrichsweb.com also links out to the full text of journals.

126.  *The Serials Directory.* Birmingham, AL: EBSCO, 1986. Quarterly. Available via EBSCOhost online service, http://www.epnet.com/ (accessed January 23, 2005). Price is determined on a case-by-case basis.

This standard source for journal information went online-only in 2000. It contains bibliographic information, including current pricing, for over 184,000 titles. Coverage also includes newspapers, both U.S. and international.

127.  *PubList.* http://www.publist.com/ (accessed August 18, 2004).

Owned by Infotrieve, a document delivery service, this Internet-based reference contains publication information for over 150,000 domestic and international print and electronic publications, including magazines, journals, e-journals, newsletters, and books. It is not as complete as *Ulrich's* or *The Serials Directory*, but it is easy to use and free.

# Key Publishers

Most journals in the forensic sciences are not published by commercial publishers but are instead published by associations and societies. Unlike other subject areas, there are really no key publishers of journals in forensic sciences. There are, however, publishers of key journals in forensics.

128.  **American Society for Testing and Materials (for the American Academy of Forensic Sciences)**, 100 Barr Harbor Drive, West Conshohocken, PA 19428-2959. Tel.: 610-832-9585. Fax: 610-832-9555. Web: http://www.astm.org/ (accessed February 22, 2005).

129.  **American College of Forensic Psychology**, P.O. Box 5870, Balboa Island, CA 92662. Tel.: 949-673-7773. Fax: 949-673-7710. Web: http://www.forensicpsychology.org/ (accessed February 22, 2005).

130.  **American Society of Questioned Document Examiners, Inc.**, P.O. Box 18298, Long Beach, CA 90807. Fax: 562-907-3378. Web: http://www.asqde.org/ (accessed February 22, 2005).

131.  **The Association of Firearm and Tool Mark Examiners**, c/o Matthew L. Noedel (Editor), Washington State Patrol Crime Lab-Tacoma, 2502 112th Street East, 2nd Floor, Tacoma WA 98445-5104. Email: editor@afte.org. Web: http://www.afte.org/ (accessed February 22, 2005).

132. **Australian Academy of Forensic Sciences**, P.O. Box 2192, Clovelly, New South Wales 2031, Australia. Tel.: +61 2 9665 5909. Fax: +61 2 9664 5909. Web: http://justaus.net/forensicQ/ (accessed February 22, 2005).

133. **The British Psychological Society**, St. Andrews House, 48 Princess Road East, Leicester, LE1 7DR, United Kingdom. Tel.: +44 (0) 0116 254 9568. Fax: +44 (0) 0116 247 0787. Web: http://www.bps.org.uk/ (accessed February 22, 2005).

134. **Elsevier**, Sara Burgerhartstraat 25, 1055 KV Amsterdam, The Netherlands. Tel.: +31 20 485 3911. Fax: +31 20 485 2457. Web: http://www.elsevier.com/ (accessed February 22, 2005).

135. **Federal Bureau of Investigation**, J. Edgar Hoover Building, 935 Pennsylvania Avenue, NW, Washington, DC 20535-0001. Tel.: 202-324-3000. Web: http://www.fbi.gov/ (accessed February 22, 2005).

136. **The Fingerprint Society**, 2nd Floor, Norwich House, Water Street, Liverpool, L2 9XR, United Kingdom. Web: http://www.fpsociety.org.uk/ (accessed February 22, 2005).

137. **The Forensic Science Society**, 18A Mount Parade, Harrogate, North Yorkshire, HG1 1BX, United Kingdom. Tel.: +44 (0) 1423 506 068. Web: http://www.forensic-science-society.org.uk/ (accessed February 22, 2005).

138. **International Association for Identification**, 2535 Pilot Knob Road, Suite 117, Mendota Heights, MN 55120-1120. Tel.: 651-681-8566. Fax: 651-681-8443. Web: http://www.theiai.org/ (accessed February 22, 2005).

139. **The International Association of Forensic Toxicologists.** Email: info@tiaft.org. Web: http://www.tiaft.org/ (accessed February 22, 2005).

140. **Lippincott, Williams & Wilkins (for the National Association of Medical Examiners)**, 16522 Hunters Green Parkway, Hagerstown, MD 21740. Tel.: 301-223-2300. Fax: 301-223-2398. Web: htpp://www.lww.com/ (accessed February 22, 2005).

141. **Pavilion Publishing Ltd. (for the Forensic Psychiatric Nurses Association)**, The Ironworks, Cheapside, Brighton, East Sussex, BN1 4GD, United Kingdom. Tel.: +44 (0) 1273 623 222. Fax: +44 (0) 1273 625 526. Web: http://www.pavpub.com/ (accessed February 22, 2005).

142.    **Preston Publications, Inc.**, 6600 West Touchy Avenue, Niles, IL 60714. Tel.: 847-647-2900. Fax: 847-647-1155. Web: http://www.prestonpub.com/ (accessed February 22, 2005).

143.    **Springer (Springer-Verlag).** Heidelberger Platz 3, 14197 Berlin, Germany. Tel.: +49 (0) 30 827 870. Fax: +49 (0) 30 821 4091. Web: http://www.springer.de/ (accessed February 22, 2005).

# Evaluation of Journals

## By Journal Title

Quite often a researcher needs to determine the quality of a journal. This is sometimes necessary for determining essential journals for a personal or library collection, to determine where to publish, or as a tool to determine the quality of a scientist's work. Ideally this should be determined by careful review of each individual publication, but quantitative analysis tools can provide data that relate the overall quality of specific journals. Bibliometric analysis is not without faults. It must be used cautiously, as it depends on the underlying effectiveness of the peer review process, as well as authors' use of self-citation and methods of citation selection.

The most common measure of quality used by many researchers is the impact factor. The impact factor is a calculated value relating the average number of annual citations to an article in a specific journal. This value is calculated by Thomson Scientific, Inc., also the producers of *Science Citation Index* (SCI®). The impact factors, calculated annually, are arranged alphabetically by journal name and by discipline, and are published in the *ISI Journal Citation Reports* (JCR®). This tool can serve as a measure of the prestige and importance of particular journals. Journals can be listed in multiple disciplines, which helps identify those journals with interdisciplinary coverage. The JCR® does not cover all of the journals for the many forensic science specialties, only the legal medicine–related journals. Below are the impact factors for these select journals.

**ISI Impact Factors from the 2003 JCR® Science Edition for
    "Medicine, Legal" Category** (Thomson Scientific, Inc. 2003).
2.093 *International Journal of Legal Medicine*
1.642 *Expert Opinion on Therapeutic Patents*
1.616 *Forensic Science International*
1.440 *Regulatory Toxicology and Pharmacology*

1.372 *Journal of Law, Medicine & Ethics*
1.237 *Journal of Forensic Sciences*
0.791 *Science & Justice*
0.527 *American Journal of Forensic Medicine and Pathology*
0.360 *Medicine, Science and the Law*

### By Specific Article

The quality and impact of specific journal articles can be determined by using *Science Citation Index* (SCI®) (see Chapter 2). SCI® includes citation counts for each article. The impact of the work can ideally be correlated to the number of citations (after removing self-citations).

*Science Citation Index*® can be used to generate reports such as: (1) most productive authors in an institution, and (2) most cited authors and articles in an institution.

SCI® has a useful Related Records feature that allows users to determine the impact and influence of a particular article. This is determined using bibliometric analysis, mainly the frequency of similar citations among articles, to find related articles that have not cited each other. It is a useful method of locating articles related to an area but that may not use the terminology from the original search.

# Journals in the Forensic Sciences

The list of journals provided is intended to assist subject selectors in creating a collection to meet the needs of their user community. Other local factors need to be considered to customize the collection for the specific user community.

Entries include publication frequency and currency information using the following abbreviations:

| a. | annual | q. | quarterly |
| s-a. | semi-annual | $ | U.S. dollars |
| bi-e. | bi-ennial | GBP | pound (U.K.) |
| bi-m. | bi-monthly | AUD | Australian dollar |
| m. | monthly | CDN | Canadian dollar |
| irreg. | irregular | JPY | Japanese yen |
| w. | weekly | | |

Note: Only the U.S. price is listed when available. The price is the institutional price, not the personal subscription price, except where indicated.

Indexing and abstracting services are abbreviated as follows:

| | |
|---|---|
| Abstr. Anthropol. | *Abstracts in Anthropology* |
| ABI/INFORM | *ABI/INFORM* |
| Acad. Search Elite | *Academic Search Elite* |
| Acad. Search Prem. | *Academic Search Premier* |
| Adol. Ment. Hlth. Abstr. | *Adolescent Mental Health Abstracts* |
| AgeL. | *AgeLine* |
| Agricola | *Agricola (Bibliography of Agriculture)* |
| AMED | *AMED (Allied and Complementary Medicine Database)* |
| Anal. Abstr. | *Analytical Abstracts* |
| Anim. Behav. Abstr. | *CSA Animal Behavior Abstracts* |
| Anthropol. Ind. | *Anthropological Index* |
| Anthropol. Lit. | *Anthropological Literature* |
| Appl. Sci. & Tech. Ind. | *Applied Science & Technology Index* |
| Appl. Soc. Sci. Ind. & Abstr. | *A.S.S.I.A.: Applied Social Science Index & Abstracts* |
| Aquat. Sci. & Fish. Abstr. | *Aquatic Sciences and Fisheries Abstracts* |
| Art & Archaeol. Tech. Abstr. | *Art and Archaeology Technical Abstracts* |
| Aust. P.A.I.S. | *A.P.A.I.S.: Australian Public Affairs Information Service* |
| Biochem. Abstr. | *Biochemical Abstracts* |
| Biol. Abstr. | *Biological Abstracts* |
| Biol. & Agric. Ind. | *Biological & Agricultural Index* |
| Biol. Dig. | *Biology Digest* |
| BIOSIS Prev. | *BIOSIS Previews* |
| Biostat. | *Biostatistica* |
| Brit. Nurs. Ind. | *British Nursing Index* |
| Bus. Source Elite | *Business Source Elite* |
| Bus. Source Prem. | *Business Source Premier* |
| Cal. Tiss. Abstr. | *Calcium and Calcified Tissue Abstracts* |
| Chem. & Erth. Sci. | *Chemical & Earth Sciences* |
| Chem. Abstr. | *Chemical Abstracts* (online equivalent *SciFinder*) |
| Chem. Cit. Ind. | *Chemistry Citation Index* |
| Chem. Titles | *Chemical Titles* |
| Chrom. Abstr. | *Chromatography Abstracts* |
| CINAHL | *Cumulative Index to Nursing & Allied Health Literature* |

| | |
|---|---|
| Civ. Eng. Abstr. | *Civil Engineering Abstracts* |
| CMCI | *Compumath Citation Index* |
| Comp. & Info. Syst. Abstr. | *Computer and Information Systems Abstracts Journal* |
| Comp. Rev. | *Computing Reviews* |
| Crim. Just. Abstr. | *Criminal Justice Abstracts* |
| Crim. Just. Per. Ind. | *ProQuest Criminal Justice Periodical Index* |
| Crim. Pen. & Pol. Sci. Abstr. | *Criminology, Penology & Police Science Abstracts* |
| Curr. Adv. Ecol. & Environ. Sci. | *Current Advances in Ecological and Environmental Sciences* |
| Curr. Adv. Gen. & Molec. Biol. | *Current Advances in Genetics and Molecular Biology* |
| Curr. Chem. Reac. | *Current Chemical Reactions* |
| Curr. Cit. | *Current Citations* |
| Curr. Cont. | *Current Contents* |
| Curr. Ind. Stat. | *Current Index to Statistics* |
| Curr. Law Ind. | *Current Law Index* |
| Dent. Abstr. | *Dental Abstracts* |
| Ecol. Abstr. | *Ecology Abstracts* |
| EconLit | *EconLit* |
| Electr. & Comm. Abstr. J. | *Electronics and Communications Abstracts Journal* |
| Eng. Ind. | *Engineering Index Monthly* (online equivalent *Compendex*) |
| Eng. Mat. Abstr. | *CSA Engineered Materials Abstracts* |
| Entomol. Abstr. | *Entomology Abstracts* |
| Environ. Abstr. | *Environment Abstracts* |
| Environ. Sci. & Pollut. Mgmt. | *Environmental Science and Pollution Management* |
| e-psyche | *E-psyche* |
| Excerp. Med. | *EMBASE: Excerpta Medica Abstract Journals (Section 49: Forensic Science Abstracts)* |
| Exp. Acad. Ind. | *Expanded Academic Index* |
| Food Sci. & Tech. Abstr. | *Food Science and Technology Abstracts* |
| For. Abstr. | *Forensic Abstracts* (online equivalent *FORS*) |

| | |
|---|---|
| Genet. Abstr. | *Genetics Abstracts* |
| Gen. Sci. Ind. | *General Science Index* |
| GEOBASE | *GEOBASE* |
| GeoRef | *Bibliography and Index of Geology* (online equivalent *GeoRef*) |
| TRIS | *TRIS Electronic Bibliographic Data Base* (Transportation Research Information Services) |
| IBZ | *IBZ: International Bibliography of Periodical Literature* |
| Ind. Can. Leg. Per. Lit. | *Index to Canadian Legal Periodical Literature* |
| Ind. Chem. | *Index Chemicus* |
| Ind. Dent. Lit. | *Index to Dental Literature* |
| Ind. Leg. Per. | *Index to Legal Periodicals* |
| Ind. Med. | *Index Medicus* (online equivalent *Medline*) |
| Ind. Per. Art. Rel. Law | *Index to Periodical Articles Related to Law* |
| Ind. U.S. Gov. Per. | *U.S. Government Periodicals Index* |
| Ind. Vet. | *Index Veterinarius* |
| INIS Atomind. | *I N I S Atomindex* |
| Inpharma | *Inpharma Weekly* |
| Intl. Bibl. Soc. Sci. | *International Bibliography of the Social Sciences* |
| Intl. Nurs. Ind. | *International Nursing Index* (available online as a subset of *Medline*) |
| Intl. Pharm. Abstr. | *International Pharmaceutical Abstracts* |
| Lab Haz. Bull. | *Laboratory Hazards Bulletin* |
| Leg. Cont. | *Legal Contents* |
| Leg. Per. | *Legal Periodicals* |
| LegalTrac | *LegalTrac (Online)* |
| Mass Spectr. Bull. | *Mass Spectrometry Bulletin* |
| Mat. Sci. Cit. Ind. | *Materials Science Citation Index* |
| Math. Rev. | *Mathematical Reviews* (online equivalent *MathSciNet*) |
| Mech. Eng. Abstr. | *Mechanical Engineering Abstracts* |
| Mech. &Transp. Eng. Abstr. | *CSA Mechanical & Transportation Engineering Abstracts* |
| Microbiol. Abstr. | *Microbiology Abstracts* |
| NCJRS | *NCJRS Abstracts Database* |

| | |
|---|---|
| Neuro. Abstr. | *CSA Neurosciences Abstracts* |
| Nuc. Acids Abstr. | *Nucleic Acids Abstracts* |
| Nurs. Abstr. | *Nursing Abstracts* |
| Nutr. Abstr. & Rev. | *Nutrition Abstracts and Reviews* |
| P.A.I.S. | *P.A.I.S. International* |
| Pollut. Abstr. | *Pollution Abstracts* |
| ProQuest Res. Lib. | *ProQuest Research Library* |
| Protozool. Abstr. | *Protozoological Abstracts* |
| Psychol. Abstr. | *Psychological Abstracts* (online equivalent *PsycInfo*) |
| Qual. Cont. & Appl. Stat. | *Quality Control and Applied Statistics* |
| Reac. | *Reactions Weekly* |
| Reac. Cit. Ind. | *Reaction Citation Index* |
| Ref. Zh. | *Referativnyi Zhurnal* |
| Res. Alert | *Research Alert* |
| Rev. Med. & Vet. Entomol. | *Review of Medical and Veterinary Entomology* |
| Rev. Med. & Vet. Mycol. | *Review of Medical and Veterinary Mycology* |
| Risk Abstr. | *Risk Abstracts (Online Edition)* |
| Russ. Acad. Sci. Bibl. | *Russian Academy of Sciences Bibliographies* |
| Sci. Cit. Ind. | *Science Citation Index* |
| Soc. Abstr. | *Sociological Abstracts* |
| Soc. Serv. Abstr. | *Social Services Abstracts* |
| SocInd. | *SocIndex* |
| Soc. Work Abstr. | *Social Work Abstracts* |
| Soc. Sci. Cit. Ind. | *Social Sciences Citation Index* |
| Soc. Sci. Ind. | *Social Sciences Index* |
| Soils & Fert. | *Soils and Fertilizers* |
| Tox. Abstr. | *Toxicology Abstracts* |
| Vet. Bull. | *Veterinary Bulletin* |
| Viol. & Abuse Abstr. | *Violence & Abuse Abstracts* |
| Wat. Res. Abstr. | *Water Resource Abstracts* |
| WESTLAW | *WESTLAW Journals & Law Reviews* |
| Wild. Rev. | *Wildlife Review Abstracts* |
| Zent. Math | *Zentralblatt MATH* |
| Zoo. Rec. | *Zoological Record* |

## Core Forensics Journals

144.  *AFTE Journal*, Association of Firearm and Tool Mark Examiners, 1972–, q., $150/yr. ISSN 1048-9959. http://www.afte.org/ExamResources/journal-index.htm (accessed February 21, 2005).

Indexed: For. Abstr.

145.  *American Journal of Forensic Medicine and Pathology*, National Association of Medical Examiners, Lippincott Williams & Wilkins (subsidiary of Wolters Kluwer N.V.), 1980–, q., $509/yr. ISSN 0195-7910 (print), ISSN 1533-404X (online). http://www.amjforensicmedicine.com/ (accessed February 21, 2005).

Some whole issues are available free in full text for non-subscribers from 2001 to the present.

Indexed: Abstr. Anthropol., Biol. Abstr., BIOSIS Prev., Crim. Just. Abstr., Curr. Cont., Curr. Law Ind., Excerp. Med., For. Abstr., Ind. Med. (1980–), INIS Atomind., Inpharma, Intl. Nurs. Ind., Reac., Rev. Med. & Vet. Entomol., Soc. Sci. Cit. Ind.

146.  *American Journal of Forensic Psychiatry*, American College of Forensic Psychology, 1978–, q., $85/yr. ISSN 0163-1942.

Indexed: e-psyche, Excerp. Med., Psychol. Abstr. (1983–).

147.  *American Journal of Forensic Psychology*, American College of Forensic Psychology, 1983–, q., $85/yr. ISSN 0733-1290.

Indexed: Crim. Just. Abstr., e-psyche, Excerp. Med. (1996–), Psychol. Abstr.

148.  *American Journal of Pathology*, American Society for Investigative Pathology, 1925–, m., $550/yr. ISSN 0002-9440.

Indexed: Chem. Abstr., Curr. Cit., Curr. Cont., Excerp. Med., Ind. Med., Ind. Vet., Nutr. Abstr. & Rev., Sci. Cit. Ind., Soc. Sci. Cit. Ind.

149.  *Canadian Society of Forensic Science Journal* (formerly *Canadian Society of Forensic Science. Newsletter*), Canadian Society of Forensic Science, 1968–, q., CDN 105/yr. ISSN 0008-5030. http://www.csfs.ca/journal/journal.htm (accessed February 21, 2005).

The full text of all book reviews is available online.

Indexed: Art & Archaeol. Tech. Abstr., Chem. Abstr., Chem. Titles, Crim. Pen. & Pol. Sci. Abstr., Curr. Cit., Excerp. Med., For. Abstr., Russ. Acad. Sci. Bibl.

150.  *FBI Law Enforcement Bulletin*, Federal Bureau of Investigation, 1932–, m., $36/yr. ISSN 0014-5688. http://www.fbi.gov/publications/leb/leb.htm (accessed February 21, 2005).

The full text of articles from 1989 to the present is available on the FBI site. Issues from 1989–1995 are in Zip format.

Indexed: AgeL., Crim. Just. Per. Ind., Crim. Just. Abstr., Crim. Pen. & Pol. Sci. Abstr., For. Abstr., Ind. U.S. Gov. Per., P.A.I.S., Soc. Sci. Ind. (Jan. 1983–).

151.  *Forensic Examiner*, American College of Forensic Examiners International, 1993–, bi-m., $130/yr. ISSN 1084-5569. http://www.acfei.com/forensic_ examiner.php (accessed February 21, 2005).

Indexed: Comp. & Info. Syst. Abstr., Civ. Eng. Abstr., Electr. & Comm. Abstr. J., Eng. Mat. Abstr., Mech. & Transp. Eng. Abstr.

152.  *Forensic Science International* (formerly *Forensic Science; and Journal of Forensic Medicine*), Elsevier Science Ltd., 1972–, 24/yr., $2,393/yr. ISSN 0379-0738. http://www.sciencedirect.com/science/journal/03790738 (accessed February 21, 2005).

Indexed: Abstr. Anthropol., Anal. Abstr., Biol. Abstr., BIOSIS Prev., Cal. Tiss. Abstr., Chem. Abstr., Chem. Titles, Crim. Just. Abstr., Curr. Crim. Pen. & Pol. Sci. Abstr., Cont., Curr. Law Ind., Environ. Sci. & Pollut. Mgmt., Excerp. Med., For. Abstr., Genet. Abstr., GeoRef, Ind. Med. (1978–), Inpharma, L.R.I. (Jan. 1980–), Mass Spectr. Bull., Nutr. Abstr. & Rev., Pollut. Abstr., Reac., Rev. Med. & Vet. Entomol., Rev. Med. & Vet. Mycol., Risk Abstr., Russ. Acad. Sci. Bibl., Sci. Cit. Ind., Tox. Abstr., TRIS.

153.  *Forensic Science Review*, University of Alabama, Department of Justice Sciences, 1989–, s-a., $80/yr. ISSN 1042-7201.

Indexed: Curr. Cit., Envron. Sci. Pollut. Mgmt, For. Abstr., Genet. Abstr., Pollut. Abstr., Tox. Abstr.

154.  *Human Biology: The International Journal of Population Biology and Genetics*, Wayne State University, 1929–, bi-m., $200/yr. ISSN 0018-7143.

Indexed: Abstr. Anthropol., Acad. Search Prem., Anthropol. Lit., Biol. Abstr., Biol. & Agric. Ind., Chem. Abstr., Curr. Cit., Curr. Cont., Ind. Med., Exp. Acad. Ind., Gen. Sci. Ind., Nutr. Abstr. & Rev., Sci. Cit. Ind., Soc. Cit. Cit. Ind., Soc. Abstr.

155.  *International Journal of Law and Psychiatry*, Elsevier, 1978–, bi-m., $1,065/yr. ISSN 0160-2527. http://www.sciencedirect.com/science/journal/ 01602527 (accessed February 21, 2005).

Indexed: Adol. Ment. Hlth Abstr., Appl. Soc. Sci. Ind. & Abstr., Crim. Just. Abstr., Curr. Cont., Curr. Law. Ind., Excerp. Med., Ind. Med., Leg. Cont., Leg. Per., Psych. Abstr., Res. Alert, Soc. Abstr.

156. *International Journal of Legal Medicine* (formerly *Zeitschrift für Rechtsmedizin—Journal of Legal Medicine; and Deutsche Zeitschrift für die Gesamte Gerichtliche Medizin*), International Academy of Legal Medicine, Springer, 1922–, bi-m., $1,064/yr. ISSN 0937-9827 (print) 1437-1596 (on-line). http://springerlink.metapress.com/openurl.asp?genre=journal&eissn=1437-1596 (accessed February 21, 2005).

The online site includes electronic supplementary material that does not appear in the print publication.

Indexed: Biol. Abstr., BIOSIS Prev., Chem. Abstr., Curr. Cont., Curr. Law Ind., Excerp. Med., Ind. Med. (1990–), For. Abstr., Inpharma, LEGALTRAC, Reac., Rev. Med. & Vet. Entomol., Sci. Cit. Ind.

157. *The International Journal of Speech, Language and the Law: Forensic Linguistics* (formerly *Forensic Linguistics*), University of Birmingham Press, 1994–, s-a., $130/yr. ISSN 1350-1771. http://www.js-ijsll.bham.ac.uk/editor/welcome.asp (accessed February 21, 2005).

Indexed: Ind. Leg. Per., Soc. Sci. Cit. Ind.

158. *Journal of Analytical and Applied Pyrolysis*, Elsevier, 1979–, bi-m., $2,585/yr. ISSN 0165-2370.

Indexed: Anal. Abstr., Biol. Abstr., Chem. Abstr., Chem. & Erth. Sci., Curr. Cit., Curr. Cont., Eng. Ind., GeoRef, Mass Spectr. Bull., Sci. Cit. Ind.

159. *Journal of Analytical Toxicology*, Preston Publications, Inc., 1977–, 8/yr., $445/yr. ISSN 0146-4760. http://www.jatox.com/ (accessed February 21, 2005).

Indexed: Anal. Abs., Aquat. Sci. & Fish. Abstr., Chem. Abstr., Chem. Cit. Ind., Chem. Titles, Chrom. Abstr., Cur. Cont., Environ. Sci. Poll. Mgmt., Excerp. Med., Food Sci. & Tech. Abstr., For. Abstr., Ind. Med. (1977–), Ind. Vet., INIS Automind., Inpharma, Mass Spectr. Bull., Microbiol. Abstr., Nutr. Abstr. & Rev., Pollut. Abstr., Reac., Ref. Zh., Rev. Med. & Vet. Entomol., Rev. Med. & Vet. Mycol., Sci. Cit. Ind., Tox. Abstr., TRIS, Vet. Bull., Weed Abstr.

160. *Journal of Clinical Forensic Medicine*, The Association of Forensic Physicians; Australia and New Zealand Forensic Medicine Society Inc.; and the British Association in Forensic Medicine, Harcourt Publishers Ltd. (subsidiary of Elsevier Science), 1972–, q., $410/yr. ISSN 1353-1131. http://www.harcourt-international.com/journals/jcfm/ (accessed February 21, 2005).

Indexed: Cal. Tiss. Abstr., Crim. Just. Abstr., Environ. Sci. & Pollut. Mgmt., Excerp. Med., For. Abstr., IBZ, NCJRS, Pollut. Abstr., Risk Abstr.

161. *Journal of Forensic Accounting*, R.T. Edwards, Inc., 2000–, s-a., $239/yr. ISSN 1524-5586. http://www.edwardspub.com/journals/JFA/ (accessed February 21, 2005).
Indexed: Not indexed in traditional indexes.

162. *Journal of Forensic Document Examination*, Association of Forensic Document Examiners, 1987–, a., $33/yr. ISSN 0895-0849. http://www.afde.org/journal.html (accessed February 21, 2005).
Indexed: WESTLAW.

163. *Journal of Forensic Economics* (absorbed *Litigation Economics Review* in 2005), National Association of Forensic Economics, 1987–, 3/yr., $110/yr. ISSN 0898-5510.
Indexed: Bus. Source Prem., Curr. Law Ind., EconLit, Exp. Acad. Ind., IBZ, Intl. Bibl. Soc. Sci., L.R.I. (Mar. 1993–)

164. *Journal of Forensic Identification* (formerly *Identification News*), International Association for Identification, 1960–, bi-m., $135/yr. ISSN 0895-173X. http://www.theiai.org/publications/jfi.html (accessed February 21, 2005).
Only volumes from 1998 to 1999 are indexed online presently although the full text of all issues from 1988 to the present are available on CD-ROM in PDF format.
Indexed: Crim. Just. Per. Ind., Excerp. Med. (1996–), For. Abstr., NCJRS.

165. *Journal of Forensic Neuropsychology*, (Neuropsychology Center, Dallas) Haworth Press, Inc., 1998–, q., $125/yr. ISSN 1521-1029. http://www.haworthpress.com/web/JFN/ (accessed February 21, 2005).
Indexed: e-psyche, Excerp. Med., IBZ, Ref. Zh.

166. *Journal of Forensic Nursing*, International Association of Forensic Nurses, 2005–, q., $175/yr. ISSN TBA.
Indexed: Acad. Search Prem., CINAHL, Ind. Med., Nurs. Abstr.

167. *The Journal of Forensic Odonto-Stomatology* (formerly *International Journal of Forensic Dentistry*), International Organisation for Forensic Ondonto-Stomatology, 1983–, s.a., $50/yr. ISSN 0258-414X. http://www.dentistry.adelaide.edu.au/forensic/Journalwebpage.htm (accessed February 21, 2005).
Indexed: Excerp. Med., Ind. Med.

168. *Journal of Forensic Psychology Practice*, Haworth Press, Inc., 2001–, q., $225/yr. ISSN 1522-8932 (paper), ISSN 1522-9092 (online). http://www. haworthpress.com/web/JFPP/ (accessed February 21, 2005).

Indexed: Crim. Just. Abstr., e-psyche, Excerp. Med., IBZ, Ind. Per. Art. Rel. Law, Ref. Zh., SocInd., Viol. & Abuse Abstr.

169. *The Journal of Forensic Psychiatry & Psychology (formerly Journal of Forensic Psychiatry)*, Brunner-Routledge (subsidiary of Taylor & Francis Ltd.), 1990–, 3/yr., $370/yr. ISSN 1478-9949 (paper), ISSN 1469-9478 (online).

Indexed: AgeL., Appl. Soc. Sci. Ind. & Abstr., Biol. Dig., Crim. Just. Abstr., Curr. Cont., e-psyche, Excerp. Med. (1996–), Intl. Bibl. Soc. Sci., Psychol. Abstr., Soc. Sci. Cit. Ind.

170. *Journal of Forensic Sciences*, American Academy of Forensic Sciences, American Society for Testing and Materials, 1956–, bi-m., $374/yr. ISSN 0022-1198. http://www.aafs.org/?section_id=journal_of_fs&page_id=searchable_index (accessed February 21, 2005).

The online comprehensive index covers 1981–present.

Indexed: Abstr. Anthropol., Anal. Abstr., Art & Archaeol. Tech. Abstr., Biol. Abstr., BIOSIS Prev., Chem. Abstr., Chem. Cit. Ind., Chem. Titles, CMCI, Comp. & Info. Syst. Abstr., Crim. Just. Abstr., Crim. Just. Per. Ind., Crim. Pen. & Pol. Sci. Abstr., Curr. Cont., Curr. Law Ind., Electr. & Comm. Abstr. J., Eng. Mat. Abstr., e-psyche, Excerp. Med., For. Abstr., Ind. Med. (1956–), INIS Atomind., Inpharma, Lab. Haz. Bull., Mass Spectr. Bull., Mech. & Transp. Eng. Abstr., NCJRS, Protozool. Abstr., Psychol. Abstr. (1989–), Reac., Rev. Med. & Vet. Entomol., Rev. Med. & Vet. Mycol., Russ. Acad. Sci. Bibl., Sci. Cit. Ind., Soils & Fert., TRIS, Wild. Rev., Zoo. Rec.

171. *Journal of Legal Economics*, American Academy of Economic and Financial Experts, 1991–, 3/yr., $65/yr. ISSN 1054-3023.

Indexed: ABI/Inform, Acad. Search Prem., Bus. Source Elite, Bus. Source Prem., Curr. Law Ind., EconLit, L.R.I.

172. *Journal of the American Society of Questioned Document Examiners*, American Society of Questioned Document Examiners, 1998–, s-a., $100/yr. ISSN 1524-7287. http://www.asqde.org/ (accessed February 21, 2005).

Indexed: For. Abstr.

173. *Journal of the American Academy of Psychiatry and the Law* (formerly the *Bulletin of the Academy of Psychiatry and the Law*), American Academy of

Forensic Psychiatry and the Law, 1973–, q., $140/yr. ISSN 1093-6793. http://www.aapl.org/journal.htm (accessed February 21, 2005).

Indexed: Excerp. Med., Ind. Med., LEGALTRAC, Psychol. Abstr., Soc. Sci. Cit. Ind.

174. *Journal of the National Association of Document Examiners*, National Association of Document Examiners, 1980–, q., $50/yr. ISSN 8755-1020.

Indexed: *QDE Index—A Guide to Periodical Articles in English on Document Examination, Handwriting Expertise and Expert Testimony* on CD-ROM available from the Association.

175. *Law Enforcement Technology*, Cygnus Business Media, 1984–, m., $66/yr. ISSN 0747-3680.

Indexed: NCJRS.

176. *Legal and Criminological Psychology*, British Psychological Society, 1996–, s-a., $148/yr. ISSN 1355-3259. http://www.bps.org.uk/publications/journals/lcp/lcp_home.cfm (accessed February 13, 2005).

Indexed: Appl. Soc. Sci. Ind. & Abstr., Crim. Just. Abstr., Excerp. Med., IBZ, Psychol. Abstr., Soc. Abstr., Soc. Serv. Abstr.

177. *Legal Medical Quarterly*, Jonah Publications, 1977–, bi-m., $135/yr. ISSN 0703-1211.

Indexed: CINAHL, Curr. Law. Ind., Ind. Can. Leg. Per. Lit., Intl. Pharm. Abstr.

178. *Legal Medicine*, Japanese Society of Legal Medicine, Elsevier Science, 1999–, q., $281/yr. ISSN 1344-6223.

Indexed: Environ. Sci. Pollut. Abstr., Excerp. Med., Ind. Med., Risk Abstr., Tox. Abstr.

179. *Medicine and Law: An International Journal*, Yozmot Heiliger Ltd., 1982–, q., $160/yr. ISSN 0723-1393.

Indexed: Crim. Pen. & Pol. Sci. Abstr., e-psyche, Excerp. Med., Ind. Med. (1982–), Psychol. Abstr. (1992–)

180. *Medicine, Science and the Law*, Chiltern Publishing, 1960–, q., GBP 85/yr. ISSN 0025-8024.

Indexed: Chem. Abstr., Crim. Just. Abstr., Curr. Cit., Curr. Cont., Curr. Law Ind., Ind. Dent. Lit., Ind. Med., LEGALTRAC, Sci. Cit. Ind., Soc. Sci. Cit. Ind.

181.    *Science & Justice* (formerly *Journal of the Forensic Science Society*), Forensic Science Society, 1960–, q., $104/yr. ISSN 1355-0306. http://www. forensic-science-society.org.uk/journal.html (accessed February 21, 2005).

Articles can be searched through a keyword searchable index (http:// www.forensic-science-society.org.uk/publications/ls.html—accessed July 28, 2004). Book reviews from 1996 to 2001 are available full text through a searchable index (http://www.forensic-science-society.org.uk/publications/ br.html—accessed July 28, 2004).

Indexed: Chem. Abstr., Chem. Titles, Crim. Just. Abstr., Crim. Pen. & Pol. Sci. Abstr., Curr. Adv. Ecol. & Environ. Sci., Curr. Adv. Gen. & Molec. Biol., Curr. Cont., Curr. Law Ind., Excerp. Med., For. Abstr., Ind. Med. (1995–), Ind. Vet., INIS Atomind., Inpharma, L.R.I. (Jan. 1980–Oct. 1994, Mar. 1995–), Mass. Spectr. Bull., Reac., Ref. Zh., Russ. Acad. Sci. Bibl., Sci. Cit. Ind., Vet. Bull.

## Secondary/Specialized Forensic Science Journals

182.    *American Journal of Clinical Pathology*, ASCP Press (a division of the American Society for Clinical Pathology), 1931–, m., $480/yr. ISSN 0002-9173. http://ajcp.metapress.com/openurl.asp?genre=journal&issn=0002-9173 (accessed February 21, 2005).

Indexed: Abstr. Anthropol., Acad. Search Prem., Biol. Abstr., Chem. Abstr., Curr. Cit., Curr. Cont., Ind. Med., Excerp. Med., Ind. Dent. Lit., Ind. Vet., Sci. Cit. Ind.

183.    *American Journal of Physical Anthropology*, John Wiley & Sons (for the American Association of Physical Anthropolgists), 1918–, q., $1,895/yr. ISSN 0002-9483 (print), 1096-8644 (online).

Indexed: Biol. Abstr., Curr. Cont., Excerp. Med., Exp. Acad. Ind., Ind. Med., Sci. Cit. Ind., Soc. Sci. Cit. Ind.

184.    *Australian Journal of Forensic Sciences*, Australian Academy of Forensic Sciences, 1968–, 2/yr., AUD 60. ISSN 0045-0618.

Indexed: Aus. P.A.I.S., Chem. Abstr., Curr. Law Ind., Excerp. Abstr., For. Abstr., INIS Atomind., L.R.I. (Mar. 1980–).

185.    *The British Journal of Forensic Practice*, Forensic Psychiatric Nurses Association, Pavilion Publishing Ltd., 1999–, q., GBP 135. ISSN 1463-6646.

Indexed: Brit. Nurs. Ind., CINAHL, Soc. Work Abstr.

186. ***Bulletin of the International Association of Forensic Toxicologists***, International Association of Forensic Toxicologists, 1970–, q., free with membership. ISSN 1080-9945.
    Indexed: For. Abstr.

187. ***Digital Investigation: The International Journal of Digital Forensics & Incident Response***, Elsevier Advanced Technology, 2004–, q., $650/yr. ISSN 1742-2876.
    Indexed: Inclusion under consideration by several traditional indexes.

188. ***Evidence Technology Magazine***, Wordsmith Publishing, 2003–, bi-m., $24/yr. http://www.evidencemagazine.com/default.htm (accessed February 21, 2005).
    Indexed: NCJRS.

189. ***Fingerprint Whorld: The International Journal of the Fingerprint Society***, The Fingerprint Society, 1974–, q., $73/yr (free with membership). ISSN 0951-1288.
    Indexed: For. Abstr.

190. ***Forensic Accounting Review and Computer Security Digest*** (formed by merger of *Forensic Accounting Review* and *Computer Security Digest*), Computer Protection Systems Inc., 1980s–, m., $110/yr. ISSN 8756-8888.
    Indexed: ABI/INFORM, Crim. Just. Per. Ind., ProQuest Res. Lib.

191. ***The Forensic Drug Abuse Advisor***, Forensic Drug Abuse Advisor, Inc., 1989–, 10/yr., $197/yr. ISSN 1048-8731. http://www.fdaa.com/ (accessed February 21, 2005).
    Indexed: Indexed on the journal Web site.

192. ***Forensic Science Communications*** (formerly ***Crime Laboratory Digest***), Federal Bureau of Investigation, 1999–, q., free online. ISSN 1528-8005. http://www.fbi.gov/hq/lab/fsc/current/index.htm (accessed February 21, 2005).
    Indexed: Indexed online at http://www.fbi.gov/hq/lab/fsc/current/search.htm

193. ***Fraud Magazine***, Association of Certified Fraud Examiners, 1987–, bi-m., $55/yr. ISSN 1097-8216.
    Indexed: Currently not indexed in traditional indexes.

194. ***IABPA Newsletter***, International Association of Bloodstain Pattern Analysts, 1984–, q., Free with membership. http://www.iabpa.org/newslett.htm (accessed February 21, 2005).

Indexed: Currently not indexed in traditional indexes.

195. *Information Bulletin for Shoeprint/Toolmark Examiners*, Marks Working Group, European Network of Forensic Science Institutes (ENFSI), 1995–, q., free online. http://www.intermin.fi/intermin/hankkeet/wgm/home.nsf/ pages/47A43E6C3D552B2CC2256C8E003C04D0 (accessed February 21, 2005).

Indexed: Currently not indexed in traditional indexes. Indexes and abstracts are included as PDF files in online site.

196. *Japanese Journal of Forensic Toxicology (Hochudoku)*, Hamamatsu University School of Medicine, Department of Legal Medicine, Japanese Association of Forensic Toxicology, 1983–, 3/yr., JPY 5,000. ISSN 0915-9606.

Indexed: Chem. Abstr., Chem. Titles, Excerp. Med. (1993–), Mass Spectr. Bull.

197. *Journal of Evidence Photography* (variant title *E P I C Journal; formerly Evidence Photography*), Evidence Photographers International Council, 1968–, s.a. $175/yr.http://www.epic-photo.org/ (accessed February 21, 2005).

Indexed: Currently not indexed in traditional indexes.

198. *Journal of Psychoactive Drugs*, Haight-Ashbury Publications, 1967–, q., $160/yr. ISSN 0279-1072.

Indexed: Biol. Abstr., Chem. Abstr., Crim. Just. Abstr., Curr. Cit., Curr. Cont., Ind. Med., Excerp. Med., Pscyhol. Abstr., Soc. Sci. Cit. Ind.

199. *Journal of Threat Assessment*, Haworth Press, Inc., 2001–, q., $200/yr. ISSN 1533-2608.

Indexed: Environ. Sci. & Pollut. Mgmt., Ref. Zh., Risk Abstr.

200. *Pediatric Trauma and Forensic Newsletter*, Pediatric Trauma & Forensic, 1993–, a., $195/yr. ISSN 1090-9970.

Indexed: Currently not indexed in traditional indexes.

201. *Research and Practice in Forensic Medicine (Hoigaku No Jissai To Kenkyu)*, Tohoku Daigaku, 1954–, a., JPY 5,000. ISSN 0289-0755.

Indexed: Biol. Abstr., BIOSIS Prev.

202. *Romanian Journal of Legal Medicine (Revista de Medicina Legala)*, Romanian Legal Medicine Society—Societatea de Medicina Legala din Romania, Bucura Mond Prod Com S R L, 1993–, q., $110/yr. ISSN 1221-8618.

Indexed: Excerp. Med. (1995–).

203.  *Scientific Sleuthing Review* (formerly *Scientific Sleuthing Newsletter; Science in Criminal Law Newsletter; and Scientific Sleuthing Newsletter*), Scientific Sleuthing, Inc., 1976–, q., $35/yr. ISSN 1043-4224.
    Indexed: Currently not indexed in traditional indexes.

204.  *TIAFT Bulletin*, The International Association of Forensic Toxicologists, 1970–, q., free with membership. ISSN 1080-9945.
    Indexed: Currently not indexed in traditional indexes.

## Interdisciplinary Journals Covering Forensic Science Topics

205.  *American Journal of Human Genetics*, University of Chicago Press (for The American Society of Human Genetics), 1948–, m., $995/yr. ISSN 0002-9297. http://www.journals.uchicago.edu/AJHG/ (accessed February 8, 2005).
    Indexed: Abstr. Anthropol., Anthropol. Ind., Biol. Abstr., Biol. & Agric. Ind., Biostat., Chem. Abstr., Chem. Titles, CINAHL, Curr. Ind. Stat., Excerp. Med., Genet. Abstr., Gen. Sci. Ind., Ind. Med., Inpharma, Reac., Sci. Cit. Ind.

206.  *American Scientist*, Sigma Xi, The Scientific Research Society, 1913–, bi-m., $28/yr (personal), $65/yr (institutional). ISSN 0003-0996 (print), ISSN 1545-2786 (online). http://www.americanscientist.org/template/Index/ (accessed February 8, 2005).
    Indexed: Abstr. Anthropol., Acad. Search Elite, Acad. Search Prem., Agricola, Appl. Sci. & Tech. Ind., Aquat. Sci. & Fish. Abstr., Art & Archaeol. Tech. Abstr., Curr. Cit., Curr. Cont., Environ. Abstr., Exp. Acad. Ind., Gen. Sci. Ind., GeoRef, Ind. Med., Math. Rev., Nutr. Abstr. & Rev., Pollut. Abstr., Sci. Cit. Ind., Soc. Abstr., Soc. Sci. Cit. Ind.

207.  *The Analyst*, Royal Society of Chemistry, 1876–, m., $1,645/yr. ISSN 0003-2654 (print), 1364-5528 (online). http://www.rsc.org/is/journals/current/analyst/anlpub.htm (accessed March 9, 2005).
    Indexed: Aquat. Sci. & Fish. Abstr., Art & Archaeol. Tech. Abstr., Anal. Abstr., Anim. Behav. Abstr., Biol. Abstr., Comp. & Info. Sci. Abstr., Chem. Cit. Ind., Chem. Abstr., Chem. Titles, Chrom. Abstr., Civ. Eng. Abstr., Curr. Cont., Electr. & Comm. Abstr. J., Eng. Mat. Abstr., Excerp. Med., Food Sci. & Tech. Abstr., For. Abstr., Intl. Pharm. Abstr., Ind. Med., Ind. Vet., Mech. & Transp. Eng. Abstr., Mass Spectr. Bull., Mat. Sci. Cit. Ind., Nutr. Abstr. & Rev., Protozool. Abstr., Reac. Cit. Ind., Ref. Zh., Rev. Med. & Vet. Mycol., Soils & Fert., Sci. Cit. Ind., Vet. Bull.

208.  *Analytical Chemistry* (formerly *Industrial and Engineering Chemistry*), American Chemical Society, 1929–, s-m., $1,374/yr. ISSN 0003-2700. http://pubs.acs.org/journals/ancham/index.html (accessed February 8, 2005).

Indexed: Acad. Search Elite, Acad. Search Prem., Appl. Sci. & Tech. Ind., Aquat. Sci. & Fish. Abstr., Art & Archaeol. Tech Abstr., Biol. Abstr., Chem. Abstr., Curr. Cit., Curr. Cont., Electr. & Comm. Abstr. J., Excerp. Med., Exp. Acad. Ind., Food Sci. & Tech. Abstr., Gen. Sci. Ind., GeoRef, Ind. Dent. Lit., Ind. Med., INSPEC, Intl. Pharm. Abstr., Mass Spectr. Bull., Nutr. Abstr. & Rev., Pollut. Abstr., Sci. Cit. Ind.

209.  *European Journal of Human Genetics*, Nature Publishing Group (for the European Society of Human Genetics), 1993–, m., $1,276/yr. ISSN 1018-4813. http://www.nature.com/ejhg/index.html (accessed February 8, 2005).

Indexed: Biol. Abstr., BIOSIS Prev., Chem. Abstr., Chem. Titles, Curr. Cont., Excerp. Med., Ind. Med., Inpharma, Reac., Sci. Cit. Ind.

210.  *Journal of AOAC International* (formerly *Association of Official Analytical Chemists Journal*), AOAC International, 1915–, bi-m., $433/yr. ISSN 1060-3271. http://www.aoac.org/pubs/pubjaoac.html (accessed February 8, 2005).

Indexed: Agricola, Anal. Abstr., Aquat. Sci. & Fish. Abstr., Biol. Abstr., Biol. & Agric. Ind. (Mar. 1983–Nov. 1991, Jan. 1992–), BIOSIS Prev., Chem. Abstr., Chem. Cit. Ind., Chrom. Abstr., Curr. Cont., Eng. Ind., Environ. Abstr., Environ. Sci. Pollut. Abstr., Food Sci. & Tech. Abstr., GeoRef, INIS Automind., Ind. Med. (1992–), Ind. Vet., Inpharma, Intl. Pharm. Abstr., Lab Haz. Bull., Mass Spectr. Bull., Microbiol. Abstr., Nutr. Abstr. & Rev., Pollut. Abstr., Protozool. Abstr., Reac., Rev. Med. & Vet. Entomol., Rev. Med. & Vet. Mycol., Sci. Cit. Index, Soils & Fert., Tox. Abstr., Vet. Bull., Zoo. Rec.

211.  *Journal of Chromatography A*, Elsevier, 1958–, 78/yr., $12,992/yr. ISSN 0021-9673. http://www.sciencedirect.com/science/journal/00219673 (accessed February 8, 2005).

Indexed: Anal. Abstr., Biochem. Abstr., BIOSIS, Chem. Abstr., Chem. Titles, Chrom. Abstr., Curr. Cont., Excerp. Med., Ind. Med., Mass Spectr. Bull., Ref. Zh., Res. Alert, Sci. Cit. Ind.

212.  *Nature*, Nature Publishing Group, 1869–, w., $159/yr. (personal), $1,526/yr (institutional). ISSN 0028-0836. http://www.nature.com/nature/ (accessed February 8, 2005).

Indexed: Acad. Search Elite, Acad. Search Prem., Agricola, Aquat. Sci. & Fish. Abstr., Art & Archaeol. Tech. Abstr., Biol. Abstr., Biol. & Agric. Ind., Chem.

Abstr., Curr. Cit., Curr. Cont., Electr. & Comm. Abstr. J., Eng. Ind., Environ. Abstr., Excerp. Med., Exp. Acad. Ind., Food Sci. & Tech. Abstr., For. Abstr., Gen. Sci. Ind. (1984–), GeoRef, Ind. Dent. Lit., Ind. Med., Ind. Vet., INSPEC, Microbiol. Abstr., Nutr. Abstr. & Rev., Pollut. Abstr., Psych. Abstr., Sci. Cit. Ind.

213.  *PNAS: Proceedings of the National Academy of Sciences of the United States of America*, National Academy of Sciences of the United States of America, 1914–, bi-w., $275/yr (personal), $1,395/yr (institutional). ISSN 0027-8424 (print), ISSN 1091-6490 (online). http://www.pnas.org/ (accessed February 8, 2005).

Indexed: Agricola, Anim. Behav. Abstr., Aquat. Sci. & Fish. Abstr., Biol. & Agric. Ind. (Aug. 1989–), Biol. Abstr., BIOSIS Prev., Cal. Tiss. Abstr., Chem. Abstr., Chem. Cit. Ind., Chem. Titles, CMCI, Curr. Cont., Curr. Ind. Stat., Ecol. Abstr., Eng. Ind., Entomol. Abstr., Environ. Sci. & Pollut. Mgmt., Excerp. Med., Food Sci. & Tech. Abstr., For. Abstr., Genet. Abstr., Gen. Sci. Ind. (June 1992–), GeoRef, Ind. Med. (1915–), Ind. Vet., INIS Atomind., Inpharma, Mass Spectr. Bull., Mat. Sci. Cit. Ind., Microbiol. Abstr., Nuc. Acids Abstr., Nutr. Abstr. & Rev., Protozool. Abstr., Reac., Ref. Zh., Rev. Med. & Vet. Entomol., Rev. Med. & Vet. Mycol., Russ. Acad. Sci. Bibl., Sci. Cit. Ind., Soils & Fert., Vet. Bull., Wild. Rev., Zent. Math, Zoo. Rec.

214.  *Science (Weekly)*, American Association for the Advancement of Science (AAAS), 1883–, w., $550/yr. ISSN 0036-8075. http://www.sciencemag.org/ (accessed February 8, 2005).

Indexed: Abstr. Anthropol., AgeL., Agricola, AMED, Anim. Behav. Abstr., Anal. Abstr., Appl. Sci. & Tech. Ind. (Sept. 1983–), Aquat. Sci. & Fish. Abstr., Art & Archaeol. Tech. Abstr., Biol. Abstr., Biol. & Agric. Ind. (Jan. 1996–), Biol. Dig., BIOSIS Prev., Biostat, Cal. Tiss. Abstr., Chem. Abstr., Chem. Cit. Ind., CMCI, Comp. & Info. Syst. Abstr., Comp. Rev., Crim. Just. Abstr., Curr. Adv. Ecol. & Environ. Sci., Curr. Chem. Reac., Curr. Cont., Curr. Ind. Stat., Ecol. Abstr., Electr. & Comm. Abstr. J., Entomol. Abstr., Environ. Abstr., Environ. Sci. & Pollut. Mgmt., e-psyche, Excerp. Med., Food Sci. & Tech. Abstr., For. Abstr., Gen. Sci. Ind. (1984–), GEOBASE, GeoRef, Ind. Chem., Ind. Med. (1883–), Ind. Vet., INIS Atomind, Inpharma, INSPEC (1968–), Intl. Nurs. Ind., Lab Haz. Bull., LEGALTRAC, Mass Spectr. Bull., Math. Rev., Mech. & Transp. Eng. Abstr., Mech. Eng. Abstr., Microbiol. Abstr., Neuro. Abstr., Nutr. Abstr. & Rev., Pollut. Abstr., Protozool. Abstr., Psychol. Abstr. (1925–), Reac. Cit. Ind., Ref. Zh., Rev. Med. & Vet. Entomol., Rev. Med. & Vet. Mycol., Reac., Russ. Acad. Sci. Bibl., Sci. Cit. Ind., Soils & Fert., Vet. Bull., Wat. Res. Abstr., Wild. Rev., Zoo. Rec.

215. *Scientific American*, Scientific American, 1845–, bi-m., $24.97/yr. (personal), $39.95/yr (institutional). ISSN 0036-8733. http://www.sciam.com/ (accessed February 8, 2005).

Indexed: Abstr. Anthropol., AgeL., Agricola, Appl. Sci. & Tech. Ind. (Nov. 1983–), Aquat. Sci. & Fish. Abstr., Biol. Abstr., Biol. & Agric. Ind. (Jan. 1996–), Biol. Dig., BIOSIS Prev., Biostat, Brit. Nurs. Ind., Cal. Tiss. Abstr., Can. Per. Ind. (Jan. 1988–), Chem. Abstr., Chem. Titles, CINAHL, Civ. Eng. Abstr., Comp. Lit. Ind., Curr. Adv. Ecol. & Environ. Sci., Curr. Cont., Dent. Abstr., Ecol. Abstr., Eng. Ind., Environ. Abstr., Environ. Sci. & Pollut. Mgmt., Food Sci. & Tech. Abstr., For. Abstr., Gen. Sci. Ind. (Apr. 1984–), GEOBASE, GeoRef, Ind. Med. (1845–), Ind. Vet., INIS Atomind., Inpharma, INSPEC (1969–), Mass Spectr. Bull., Math. Rev., Mech. & Transp. Eng. Abstr., Neuro. Abstr., Pollut. Abstr., Qual. Cont. & Appl. Stat., Reac., Ref. Zh., Rev. Med. & Vet. Entomol., Russ. Acad. Sci. Bibl., Sci. Cit. Ind., Wat. Res. Abstr., Wild. Rev., Zoo. Rec.

## Free Full Text Online Forensics Newsletters and Journals

Many forensic science–related journals are published by associations; therefore they have been slow to appear full text on the Web or are only available full text online to members. Below are some publications that are available free to all.

216. *Anil Aggrawal's Internet Journal of Forensic Medicine and Toxicology*, Anil Aggrawal, 2000–, bi-en., free online. ISSN 0972-8074 (online), 0972-8066 (CD). http://www.geradts.com/~anil/ij/indexpapers.html (accessed December 10, 2004).

Indexed: Chem. Abstr., Excerp. Med., NCJRS.

217. *Crime and Clues: The Art and Science of Criminal Investigation*, 2000–, irreg., free. http://www.crimeandclues.com/index.htm (accessed July 28, 2004).

Edited by Daryl W. Clemens, a crime scene technician, this collection contains articles in various fields of forensic sciences written by experts.

218. *In the Spotlight: Forensic Science*, National Criminal Justice Reference Service (NCJRS), bi-m., free. http://www.ncjrs.org/forensic/summary.html (accessed July 28, 2004).

This title focuses on crime, public safety, and drug policy.

219. *Indian Internet Journal of Forensic Medicine & Toxicology*, Indian Congress of Forensic Medicine & Toxicology, 2003–, q., free. http://www.icfmt .org/online.htm (accessed January 30, 2005).

Indexed: Currently not indexed in traditional indexes.

220.   *INTERfaces*, The Forensic Science Society, 1995–, q., free. ISSN 1359-0820. http://www.forensic-science-society.org.uk/publications/interfaces.html (accessed February 21, 2005).

221.   *International Journal of Digital Evidence*, Economic Crime Institute (ECI) at Utica College, 2002–, q., free. http://www.ijde.org/index.html (accessed February 4, 2005).
    Indexed: Currently not indexed in traditional indexes.

222.   *International Journal of Drug Testing*, Florida State University School of Criminology and Criminal Justice, 1995–, irreg., free. http://www.criminology.fsu.edu/journal/ (accessed February 4, 2005).
    Indexed: Currently not indexed in traditional indexes.

223.   *Scientific Testimony: An Online Journal*, University of California, Dept. of Criminology, Law and Society, m., free. http://www.scientific.org/ (accessed February 21, 2005).

## Selected Forensic Sciences Journals by Subdiscipline

Below are lists of selected titles in subdisciplines of forensic sciences. They are not arranged in order of importance.

### General
*American Journal of Forensic Medicine and Pathology*
*American Scientist*
*Australian Journal of Forensic Sciences*
*American Journal of Pathology*
*Canadian Society of Forensic Science Journal*
*Crime and Clues: The Art and Science of Criminal Investigation*
*FBI Law Enforcement Bulletin*
*Forensic Examiner*
*Forensic Science Communications*
*Forensic Science International*
*Forensic Science Review*
*In the Spotlight: Forensic Science*
*Indian Internet Journal of Forensic Medicine & Toxicology*
*Institute of Criminology & Forensic Sciences Bulletin*
*International Journal of Legal Medicine*
*Journal of Clinical Forensic Medicine*
*Journal of Forensic Sciences*
*Legal Medical Quarterly*
*Legal Medicine*
*Medicine and Law: An International Journal*
*Medicine, Science and the Law*

Nature

Pediatric Trauma and Forensic
    Newsletter

PNAS: Proceedings of the National
    Academy of Sciences of the United
    States of America

Research and Practice in Forensic
    Medicine

Romanian Journal of Legal Medicine

Science

Science & Justice

Scientific American

Scientific Sleuthing Review

## Accounting and Economics

Forensic Accounting Review and
    Computer Security Digest

Fraud Magazine

Journal of Forensic Accounting

Journal of Forensic Economics

Journal of Legal Economics

## Anthropology

American Journal of Physical
    Anthropology

## Chemistry, Serology, and
    Toxicology

Analytical Chemistry

Anil Aggrawal's Internet Journal of
    Forensic Medicine and Toxicology

Bulletin of the International
    Association of Forensic
    Toxicologists

Forensic Drug Abuse Advisor

Forensic Serology News

International Journal of Drug Testing

Japanese Journal of Forensic
    Toxicology

Journal of Analytical and Applied
    Pyrolysis

Journal of Analytical Toxicology

Journal of AOAC International

Journal of Chromatography A

Journal of Psychoactive Drugs

TIAFT Bulletin

## Computer Forensics/Technology

Digital Investigation: The
    International Journal of Digital
    Forensics & Incident Response

Evidence Technology Magazine

Forensic Accounting Review and
    Computer Security Digest

International Journal of Digital
    Evidence

Law Enforcement Technology

## Criminalistics

Fingerprint Whorld: The
    International Journal of the
    Fingerprint Society

International Bulletin for Shoeprint/
    Toolmark Examiners

Journal of Forensic Identification

IABPA Newsletter

## DNA

American Journal of Human Genetics

European Journal of Human Genetics

Human Biology

## Environmental

Journal of Threat Assessment

## Firearms

AFTE Journal

## Linguistics

International Journal of Speech,
    Language and the Law: Forensic
    Linguistics

## Nursing

British Journal of Forensic
    Practice

Journal of Forensic Nursing

**Odontology**

*Journal of Forensic Odonto-*
*Stomatology*

**Photography**

*Journal of Evidence Photography*
(variant title *E P I C Journal*)

**Psychology and Psychiatry**

*American Journal of Forensic*
*Psychiatry*
*American Journal of Forensic*
*Psychology*
*International Journal of Law and*
*Psychiatry*
*Issues in Forensic Psychology*
*Journal of Forensic Neuropsychology*
*Journal of Forensic Psychology*
*Practice*

*Journal of Forensic Psychiatry &*
*Psychology*
*Journal of the American Academy*
*of Psychiatry and the Law*
*Legal and Criminological*
*Psychology*

**Questioned Documents**

*Journal of Forensic Document*
*Examination*
*Journal of the American Society*
*of Questioned Document*
*Examiners*
*Journal of the National Association of*
*Document Examiners*

**Scientific Testimony**

*Scientific Testimony: An Online*
*Journal*

# Document Delivery Services

It is virtually impossible for libraries in today's fiscal climate to collect every-thing published in a given subject area. With increased specialization and the explosion in publishing of niche journals, libraries are finding that they can fill customer needs more cost-effectively through interlibrary loan and document delivery services. Services in academic libraries may be free for users or avail-able for a reduced fee. The document delivery services listed below are the most useful for forensic science documents. Some journal aggregators also offer pay-per-view services.

224. **CISTI (Canada Institute for Scientific and Technical Informa-tion).** http://cisti-icist.nrc-cnrc.gc.ca/docdel/docdel_e.shtml (accessed December 1, 2004).

CISTI is one of the world's major sources for document delivery in science, technology, medicine, and agriculture. Registration for this service is free, but registration for an account number and password is required to use the service. Fees for documents are dependent on the method of order and delivery. Appli-cable copyright fees are added to the document delivery fee. The most common method for delivery is via Ariel (a document transmission system), but fax, courier, and PDF delivery are also options. Most documents are supplied within 24–48 hours.

Documents not held by CISTI can be obtained through their Link Service for a small additional fee. CISTI's Link Service is a network of formal arrangements with several international libraries that allow CISTI to retrieve items from outside their collection. Documents retrieved through the Link Service are delivered within 72 hours.

225. **Infotrieve.**    http://www4.infotrieve.com/products_services/document_ delivery/default.asp (accessed December 1, 2004).

Infotrieve specializes in scientific, technical, and medical content. Infotrieve supplies documents through its network of partnerships and alliances with publishers and content producers. Registration for an account is free. Orders can be submitted online, via email, or by fax. Delivery is available via Ariel, PDF, fax, email, regular mail, and courier. The fee includes the article fee, copyright royalties, and the delivery method fee. Most delivery methods are free, except fax, email, and courier, which incur an additional cost.

226. **Thomson ISI Document Solution.** http://www.isinet.com/products/doc-delivery/ids/ (accessed December 9, 2004).

Document Solution provides access to any publicly available document from within select ISI databases or from outside sources. Coverage includes journals, conference proceedings, books, technical and government reports, standards, and patents. Delivery is available electronically, via fax, by mail, or by courier. Orders are processed within 24 hours of receipt. Fees are dependent on the method of delivery. Registration for the service is free.

# Abbreviations

Many journal references use abbreviations. These abbreviations are not standardized across fields, so it is often necessary to consult abbreviation lists/guides for the full and complete title.

There is no primary tool for forensics. For chemistry-related titles, researchers can consult the **Chemical Abstracts Service Source Index (CASSI)**. This set is arranged alphabetically by the full journal names, with the abbreviation letters in bold. For medicine/health-related titles, researchers can consult the **List of Serials Indexed for Online Users** [of *Medline*] (http://www.nlm.nih.gov/tsd/serials/

lsiou.html—accessed December 9, 2004) from the National Library of Medicine. It is arranged alphabetically by abbreviated title. Researchers can also consult the **List of Journals Indexed in Index Medicus** (http://www.nlm.nih.gov/tsd/serials/lji.html—accessed December 9, 2004), also from the National Library of Medicine. It lists journals indexed in *Medline* and their abbreviations. Titles are listed alphabetically by abbreviation, alphabetically by full title, alphabetically by subject, and alphabetically by country of publication. For titles in engineering, researchers can consult the **Publications in Engineering (PIE)** list by Engineering Information. For titles in the biological sciences, researchers can consult the **BIOSIS Serial Sources** from BIOSIS. Titles are listed alphabetically by full title. For titles in psychology, researchers can consult the online **Journal Coverage List** (http://www.apa.org/psycinfo/about/covlist.html) from the American Psychological Association. For titles in economics, researchers can consult the *Journal of Economic Literature* **Journal Abbreviation List** (http://www.aeaweb.org/journal/abbrev.html—accessed December 11, 2004). For titles in other areas, researchers can consult the **ISI Master Journal List** (http://www.isinet.com/cgi-bin/jrnlst/jloptions.cgi?PC=master—accessed December 9, 2004).

For older titles, researchers can consult the following:

**1700–1949**

227.    *Union List of Serials in Libraries in the United States and Canada.* 3rd ed. Titus, Edna Brown, ed. New York: H.W. Wilson, 1965. 5 v.

228.    *Union List of Serials in Libraries in the United States and Canada.* 3rd ed. Gregory, Winifred, ed. New York: H.W. Wilson, 1943. 5 v.

229.    *Union List of Serials in Libraries in the United States and Canada.* Gregory, Winifred, ed. New York: H.W. Wilson, 1927. 4 v.

**1950–1999**

230.    *New Serial Titles.* Prepared under the sponsorship of the Joint Committee on the Union List of Serials. Washington, DC: Library of Congress.

This title began January 1953. It consists of 8 monthly issues, 4 quarterly issues, and annual cumulations that are semi-cumulative through periods of 5 or 10 years.

# References

Thomson Scientific, Inc. 2003. Medicine, Legal. *ISI Journal Citation Reports®, 2003 JCR Science Edition.* http://jcr02.isiknowledge.com/ (accessed December 9, 2004).

# 4
# Books

This chapter discusses important books in the forensic sciences. Included is an annotated list of selected reference books (e.g., dictionaries, encyclopedias, handbooks, directories), a list of key monographic series, a list of key forensics book publishers, tools to help researchers identify recently published books, book review sources, a description of the book selection/buying process in many academic research libraries, and a selective bibliography of subject books. This chapter also introduces researchers to useful book searching techniques and databases that cover multiple library catalogues.

## Historical Overview of Book Publishing

The oldest extant book on forensic medicine, *Hsi yuan chi lu*, was written in 1247 by Sung Tz'u, a Chinese "coroner" (see Chapter 1). There have been several editions and translations of the *Hsi yuan chi lu*, which translates to "The washing away of wrongs." Since then, there have been several milestone books published in the forensic sciences. In 1814, Matthieu Orfila, considered the father of modern toxicology, published the two-volume set *Traité des poisons tirés des règenes minéral, végétal, et animal, ou Toxicologie générale, considerée sous les rapports de la physiologie, de la pathologie et de la médicine légale* (published in English from 1816–1817 as *A general system of toxicology, or, a treatise on poisons, drawn from the mineral, vegetable, and animal kingdoms: Considered as to their relations with physiology, pathology and medical jurisprudence*). In 1893, Hans Gross, an examining magistrate and professor of criminal law at the University of Graz in Austria wrote *Handbuch für Untersuchungsrichter*

**69**

("Handbook for examining magistrates," published in English in 1907 as *Criminal investigation: A practical handbook for magistrates, police officers, and lawyers*), the first comprehensive description of the uses of physical evidence in solving a crime. In 1892, Sir Francis Galton published *Fingerprints*, the first comprehensive publication on the nature of fingerprints and their use in solving crimes. Following on this, Sir Edward Richard Henry developed a classification system for fingerprints and published it as *Classification and uses of finger prints* in 1900. This system was used in Europe and North America. In 1910, Victor Balthazard, a professor of forensic medicine at the Sorbonne, and Marcelle Lambert published *Le poil de l'homme et des animaux: applications aux expertises médico-légales et aux expertises des fourrures* ("The hair of man and animals"), the first comprehensive hair study. In the same year, Albert Sherman Osborn, an influential document examiner, published *Questioned documents: A study of questioned documents with an outline of methods by which the facts may be discovered and shown*. In 1922, Leone Lattes published *L'individualità del sangue nella biologia, nella clinica, nella medicina, legale* (published in English in 1932 as *Individuality of the blood in biology and in clinical and forensic medicine*), dealing with blood group typing, including heritability, paternity, typing of dried stains, and clinical issues. In 1920, Edmond Locard published *L'enquête criminelle et les méthodes scientifique* ("Criminal investigation and scientific methods"). In this book is the first reference to the forensic precept that every contact leaves a trace. In 1953, Paul Leland Kirk, leader of the criminology program at the University of California, Berkeley, published *Crime investigation; physical evidence and the police laboratory*, a comprehensive criminalistics and crime investigation text encompassing theory and practice. In 1972, Bryan J. Culliford of the British Metropolitan Police Laboratory and co-developer of the immunoelectrophoretic technique for haptoglobin typing of bloodstains, published *The examination and typing of bloodstains in the crime laboratory*. This publication is generally accepted as the vehicle for disseminating reliable polymorphic protein and enzyme marker typing protocols worldwide. Most recently in 1996, the second National Research Council Committee on Forensic DNA convened and published *The evaluation of DNA evidence*, to respond to concerns about the statistical interpretation of forensic DNA evidence.

# Key Publishers

Recent years have seen an explosion in book publishing in the forensic sciences. Where only a few years ago there were but a couple of key publishers, now it seems like every publisher is publishing some sort of book on forensics. The following are some of the more important book publishers in the forensic sciences.

231.   **Elsevier Academic Press**, 30 Corporate Drive, Suite 400, Burlington, MA 01803. Tel: 781-221-2212. Fax: 781-221-1615. http://books.elsevier.com/ (accessed December 12, 2004).

*232.   **Addison-Wesley** (a division of Pearson Education), 75 Arlington Street, Suite 300, Boston, MA 02116. Tel: 617-848-7500. http://www.awbc.com/ (accessed December 12, 2004).

*233.   **Artech House**, 685 Canton Street, Norwood, MA 02062. Tel: 800-225-9977, 781-769-9750. Fax: 781-769-6334. http://www.artechhouse.com/ (accessed December 12, 2004).

*234.   **Auerbach**, 29 West 35th Street, New York, NY 10001. Tel: 800-272-7737 ext. 6407. Fax: 800-374-3401. http://www.auerbach-publications.com/ home.asp (accessed December 12, 2004).

235.   **Elsevier Butterworth-Heinemann**, 30 Corporate Drive, Suite 400, Burlington, MA 01803, USA. Tel: 781-221-2212. Fax: 781-221-1615. http://books.elsevier.com/ (accessed December 12, 2004).

236.   **Charles C Thomas**, 2600 South First Street, Springfield, IL 62704. Tel: 800-258-8980. Fax: 217-789-9130. http://www.ccthomas.com/ (accessed December 12, 2004).

237.   **CRC Press**, 2000 NW Corporate Blvd., Boca Raton, FL 33431. Tel: 800-272-7737, 561-994-0555. Fax: 800-374-3401, 561-989-9732. http://www.crcpress.com/ (accessed December 12, 2004).

**238.   **Hodder & Stoughton Educational** (a division of Hodder Arnold), 338 Euston Road, London, NW1 3BH, United Kingdom. Tel: +44(0)20 7873 6000. Fax: +44(0)20 7873 6024. http://www.hodderheadline.co.uk/ (accessed December 12, 2004).

239.   **Humana Press**, 999 Riverview Drive, Suite 208, Totowa, NJ 07512. Tel: 973-256-1699. Fax: 973-256-8341. http://humanapress.com/ (accessed December 12, 2004).

240.   **John Wiley & Sons**, 111 River Street, Hoboken, NJ 07030-5774. Tel: 201-748-6000. Fax: 201-748-6088. http://www.wiley.com/ (accessed December 12, 2004).

**241.   **Jossey-Bass Publishers** (an imprint of Wiley), 10475 Crosspoint Blvd., Indianapolis, IN 46256. Tel: 877-762-2974. Fax: 800-597-3299. http://www.josseybass.com/WileyCDA/ (accessed December 12, 2004).

*242.   **McGraw-Hill/Osborne Media**, 2100 Powell Street, 10th Floor, Emeryville, CA 94608. Tel: 800-227-0900. http://shop.osborne.com/cgi-bin/osborne/ (accessed December 12, 2004).

243.   **Springer Science + Business Media**, 233 Spring Street, New York, NY 10013. Tel: 212-460-1500. Fax: 212-460-1575. http://www.springeronline.com/ (accessed December 12, 2004).

244.   **Prentice Hall** (a division of Pearson Education), One Lake Street, Upper Saddle River, NJ 07458. Tel: 800-922-0579. http://vig.prenhall.com/ (accessed December 12, 2004).

245.   **Taylor & Francis**, 270 Madison Avenue, New York, NY 10016. Tel: 212-216-7800. Fax: 212-564-7854. http://www.tandf.co.uk/books/ (accessed December 12, 2004).

*Computer Forensics
**Psychology and Psychiatry

# Types/Uses of Sources

There are several types of books, and each type can have multiple uses that may never have been imagined by the original creator. Librarians can act as mediators in the information-seeking process to find the best source for a researcher's needs. Below are some types of books commonly used by researchers.

**Fact books:** encyclopedias, dictionaries, almanacs, and handbooks. These books provide quick facts or general overviews of a subject area.

**Contact information:** directories and biographical sources. These books provide information about an individual, groups, or organizations. They often provide subject linking to find similar entries.

**Reading sources:** texts and textbooks. These sources provide information through reading material.

**Verification sources:** local library catalogues, *Books in Print*, OCLC WorldCat, amazon.com. These tools provide bibliographic information to verify the publication information for books.

# Ordering Books

Researchers can order books through bookstores, online Web sites, or directly from publishers. Books that are still in print can be identified using a tool such as *Books in Print*.

246.   **Books in Print.** New Providence, NJ: R.R. Bowker LLC. Annual.

This tool provides bibliographic and ordering information for books published by many of the major publishers in the United States. Books are arranged by title and by author. There is also a volume that provides contact and ordering information for more than 76,000 publishers. Subject indexing is available in a companion product, the *Subject Guide to Books in Print*. A complementary product, *Forthcoming Books*, is published three times a year. Most libraries have these tools in some format. *Books in Print* is available in print, on CD-ROM, and online through several vendors.

247.   **GlobalBooksInPrint.com.** New Providence, NJ: R.R. Bowker LLC. http://www.globalbooksinprint.com/ (accessed January 23, 2005).

This tool includes the content of most Bowker print book–related products (*Books in Print*, *Australian Books in Print*, *Forthcoming Books*, *Subject Guide to Books in Print*, *Children's Books in Print*, *Subject Guide to Children's Books in Print*, *Books Out Loud: Bowker's Guide to Audiobooks*, *Law Books and Serials in Print*, *Medical and Health Care Books and Serials in Print*, *Large Print Books and Serials*, and *Publishers, Distributors & Wholesalers of the U.S.*), and a CD-ROM product *Canadian Books in Print*. It allows the user to search by market, review source, vendor, and price range, in addition to the usual bibliographic and subject search options. Price comparisons are provided with availability information from international vendors. Value-added information includes professional reviews, tables of contents, and previews of full text. The online version is updated weekly. A CD-ROM version called *Global Books in Print ON DISC* is available with monthly updates.

## Online Bookstores

There are several online bookstores that allow researchers to look for books from many publishers in a single search and order these items. The most popular of these are the following.

248.    **amazon.com**, http://www.amazon.com/ (accessed November 17, 2004).

249.    **Barnes and Noble**, http://www.barnesandnoble.com/ (accessed November 17, 2004).

250.    **Borders**, http://www.borders.com/ (accessed November 17, 2004).
    Borders has teamed with amazon.com for delivery of online orders.

## Out-of-Print Dealers

Out-of-print titles can be ordered through out-of-print dealers, many of whom have online sites where you can search the inventory of a network of booksellers and order the items. The most popular is the following one-stop search site.

251.    **Bookfinder.com**, http://www.bookfinder.com/ (accessed November 17, 2004).
    This site aggregates the inventories of many of the big out-of-print dealers, such as Alibris, Abebooks, and many others into one search.
    Another popular site is the following.

252.    **BuyUsed.co.uk**, http://www.usedbooksearch.co.uk/ (accessed May 11, 2005).
    This is a meta-search site of out-of-print dealers (Alibris, AbeBooks, AbeBooks (U.K.), Amazon.com, Amazon.co.uk, Barnes & Noble, BiblioQuest, Biblio.com, Gemm, WHSmith, Biblion, Chapters.Indigo, Books&Collectibles, Choosebooks, Powells, and Half.com).

## Library Approval Plans and Firm Orders

Libraries buy books in several ways. Sometimes they purchase directly from a publisher, but most often they use vendors, enabling them to take advantage of discounts. Libraries can purchase books through vendors by directly requesting a particular title, often after viewing a publisher's catalogue or flyer. This is also how libraries tend to procure difficult-to-find items. This method is generally called a firm order.

Another method used by libraries with vendors is the use of approval plans. Approval plans created through vendors deliver books or book order forms based on collection profiles. These profiles are most often subject based and allow libraries to automatically receive, or be notified of, the latest books from publishers. Using approval plans helps libraries to optimize their book-buying process.

## Book Reviews

Book reviews are a great way to discover the truly useful research sources. Many key journals in the forensic sciences include book review sections. The key scientific journals that contain book reviews in the forensic sciences are the *Canadian Society of Forensic Science Journal* (http://www.csfs.ca/journal/BookReports/bookreps.htm, accessed January 12, 2005), the *Journal of Forensic Sciences* (http://www.astm.org/cgi-bin/SoftCart.exe/jforensicsci/search.html? E+mystore—search on "review of"—accessed January 12, 2005), *Anil Aggrawal's Internet Journal of Forensic Medicine and Toxicology* (http://www.geradts.com/~anil/ij/sundry/reviews/subject/technical/technical_subject_001.html—accessed January 12, 2005), the Forensic Science Society's Book Reviews from *Science & Justice* and *INTERfaces* (http://www.forensic-science-society.org.uk/publications/br.html—accessed January 12, 2005), *Science*, *Scientific American*, *New Scientist*, *American Scientist*, and *Nature*. There are also two library journals that contain book reviews: *CHOICE: Current Reviews for Academic Libraries* and *Booklist*. *CHOICE* is also available online as a searchable database of reviews called *ChoiceReviews.online* (http://www.choicereviews.org/—accessed February 3, 2005).

There are also several indexes that identify book reviews in many subject areas. They are the following.

253. **Book Review Digest.** New York, NY: H.W. Wilson, 1906–.

*Book Review Digest* is a bibliographic index that cites and provides excerpts of reviews of current English-language fiction and nonfiction books for children and adults. An abstract of each book is also provided. Periodical coverage includes leading magazines from the United States, Canada, and Great Britain. An electronic version of this index is available with expanded full text from H.W. Wilson. Online coverage is from 1983 to the present.

Updates: Paper (monthly), online (daily on WilsonWeb; quarterly on Silver-Platter), CD-ROM (monthly).

Online: ***Book Review Digest Plus*** (WilsonWeb); ***Book Review Digest*** (WilsonDisc); ***Wilson Book Review Digest*** (SilverPlatter).

254.   ***Book Review Index.*** Farmington Hills, MI: Thomson Gale, 1965–.

*Book Review Index* is a bibliographic index to reviews of books, periodicals, books on tape, and electronic media. Coverage includes popular, academic, and professional publications. The online edition provides full text linking for subscribers to *InfoTrac OneFile* or *Expanded Academic ASAP*.

Updates: Paper (3/yr.), online (daily).

Online: ***Book Review Index Online***.

## Library Catalogues

A useful method for identifying books in the forensic sciences is to locate an academic institution with a strong forensic sciences program (http://www.aafs .org/default.asp?section_id=resources&page_id=colleges_and_universities— accessed February 3, 2005) and search that institution's library catalogue. Most library catalogues can be found on the Web. A convenient gateway to libraries worldwide is found at http://sunsite3.berkeley.edu/Libweb/ (accessed December 10, 2004).

## Book Indexing/Consortial Gateways

There is no one book catalogue that contains all books published. Researchers need to use multiple resources for a comprehensive search (e.g., publisher Web sites, *Books in Print*, online bookstores).

Some libraries subscribe to book catalogues that provide information on books and resources in other formats in multiple subject areas. The two major databases are the following.

255.   **WorldCat.** http://www.oclc.org/worldcat/default.htm (accessed December 10, 2004).

This is an OCLC FirstSearch database that has worldwide coverage of the holdings of its 9,000 member institutions. It contains millions of records spanning thousands of years, covering books, recordings, Web sites, serials, historical documents, and numerous other publications.

256.   **RLG Union Catalog.** http://www.rlg.org/en/page.php?Page_ID=174 (accessed December 10, 2004).

This is a database of holdings of the Research Libraries Group's member institutions. It contains over 45 million titles in a multitude of languages, making it a truly global catalogue. Coverage includes books, computer files, photographs and graphics, serials, historical documents, maps and globes, and recordings and music.

# Selected Reference Book Bibliography

Below are listed some representative forensic sciences reference titles in various categories. This is a selective list and is not intended to be comprehensive. Included are selected core materials and some newer materials not listed in earlier bibliographies (see Chapter 1). Consulting a librarian for more suggestions is recommended. In addition to these paper sources, consult the many online tools listed in Chapter 5.

### Dictionaries and Encyclopedias

257.    Lee, C. C., ed. *Dictionary of environmental legal terms.* New York, NY: McGraw-Hill, 1997. 818 p. $79.95. ISBN 0070381135.

This extensive dictionary provides access to 10,000 statutory definitions, regulatory definitions, health-related environmental definitions, radioactive waste–related environmental definitions, common environmental engineering definitions, and 3,500 environmental acronyms and abbreviations. References and major environmental laws and environmental regulations are included.

258.    Palmer, Louis J., Jr. *Encyclopedia of DNA and the United States criminal justice system.* Jefferson, NC: McFarland & Company, 2004. 464 p. $95. ISBN 0786417358.

Useful quick reference for the layperson on DNA in the U.S. criminal justice system. The full text of several related federal and state laws is welcome, although the index is not very useful for finding case references related to particular topics.

259.    Payne-James, Jason, Roger W. Byard, Tracey S. Corey, and Carol Henderson. *Encyclopedia of forensic and legal medicine.* San Diego, CA: Elsevier Academic Press, 2005. 4 v. 2084 p. $740. ISBN 0125479700.

This set is similar in structure to the *Encyclopedia of forensic sciences* (entry 261), but with a broader geographical coverage. Comprehensive coverage of forensics and legal medicine for researchers in the forensic, medical, healthcare, legal, judicial, and investigative fields. Emphasis is global, multidisciplinary, and multijurisdictional. Diagrams, tables, and full-color images are included throughout. Articles range from the topic of age progression to war crimes. Further reading references are included for each article, as well as cross-references to related entries. One minor annoyance with the set is that the index to all volumes is included only in volume four.

260.    Bell, Suzanne. *Encyclopedia of forensic science.* New York, NY: Facts on File, 2003. 376 p. $75. ISBN 0816048118.

Intended for the beginner, this single-volume encyclopedia provides a comprehensive overview of the core areas of forensic science. There are some discrepancies in the entries that might mislead novices, so read with care. Some entries are several pages long, but most are much briefer. Entries are enhanced by the inclusion of 14 relevant essays interspersed among the entries. An appendix—arranged by forensic discipline—of bibliographies and Web resources is included at the end of the encyclopedia.

261.    Siegel, Jay A., Pekka J. Saukko, and Geoffrey C. Knupfer, eds. *Encyclopedia of forensic sciences.* San Diego, CA: Academic Press, 2000. 3 v. 1440 p. $995. ISBN 0122272153 (set), 0122272161 (v.1), 012227217X (v.2), 0122272188 (v.3).

This encyclopedia was the first of its kind in the forensic sciences. This comprehensive reference work covers a broad range of scientific disciplines, with separately authored sections on topics ranging from accident investigation to wood analysis. It is distinguished by the qualifications of the editors and contributing authors as well as by the diversity of nationalities of these authors. This diversity gives this encyclopedia a strong international perspective. The depth of the articles varies, with some areas covered extensively and others barely touched or non-existent.

262.    Gardner Conklin, Barbara, Robert Gardner, and Dennis Shortelle. *Encyclopedia of forensic science: A compendium of detective fact and fiction.* Westport, CT: Oryx Press, 2002. 329 p. $64.95. ISBN 1573561703.

This encyclopedia for the armchair enthusiast provides information about various aspects of forensic science pertaining primarily to events that occurred and people who lived during the nineteenth and twentieth centuries in the United States, although there are topics from other countries. Major scientific techniques and devices that forensic scientists use in analyzing evidence collected at a crime scene are covered. Topics also include crimes and criminals. None of the authors is a forensic scientist.

263.   Resh, Vincent H., and Ring T. Cardé, eds. *Encyclopedia of insects*. New York, NY: Academic Press, 2003. 1266 p. $99.95. ISBN 0125869908.

This encyclopedia bills itself as the complete source of information on insects. Its intended audience is insect biologists and scientists, students, and the general public. As such, it offers information at many levels. There are 271 separate articles, with each article providing an overview of a topic and a further reading section at the end. There is a detailed table of contents arranged into 12 general subject areas: (1) anatomy, (2) physiology, (3) behavior, (4) evolution, (5) reproduction, (6) development and metamorphosis, (7) major groups and notable forms, (8) interactions with other organisms, (9) interactions with humans, (10) habitats, (11) ecology, and (12) history and methodology. A subject index is included, as well as a glossary of specialized terms found in the articles.

264.   Tranter, George E., John L. Holmes, and John C. Lindon, eds. *Encyclopedia of spectroscopy and spectrometry*. San Diego, CA: Academic Press, 2000. 3 v. 2581 p. $1,075. ISBN 0122266803 (set), 0122266811 (v.1), 012226682X (v.2), 0122266838 (v.3).

The encyclopedia provides comprehensive coverage of the whole topic of spectroscopy, from theory to applications. Each topic includes a short article with a list of further readings. Articles are arranged alphabetically. Each article is flagged as to which area of spectroscopy it covers ("Mass Spectroscopy," "Atomic Spectroscopy," etc.) and whether it covers theory, methods and instrumentation, or applications. There are 3 sections specifically related to forensic sciences: (1) Forensic Science Applications of Atomic Spectroscopy, (2) Forensic Science Applications of IR Spectroscopy, (3) and Forensic Science Applications of Mass Spectrometry (very short article). A subject index is included.

265.   Morrison, Robert D. *Environmental forensics: A glossary of terms*. Boca Raton, FL: CRC Press, 1999. $49.95. ISBN 0849300010.

This companion guide to *Environmental forensics: Principles and applications* is intended for practicing environmental attorneys and environmental consultants/engineers. The intent of the glossary is to define terms that researchers might find in environmental reports, regulatory correspondence, testimony, and interrogations. Acronyms and abbreviations are included in a separate section before the alphabetically arranged glossary of terms and definitions.

266.   Brenner, John C. *Forensic science: An illustrated dictionary*. Boca Raton, FL: CRC Press, 2004. $79.95. ISBN 0849314577.

This update to the author's 1999 *Forensic Science Glossary* introduces terms commonly used in the field of forensic science. The intended audience is the law enforcement community, students in forensic science or criminal justice, and attorneys involved in criminal court cases. Some entries are too brief to accurately define the term, but for the most part, entries are helpful as a quick reference.

## Handbooks and Atlases

267.    Dix, Jay, Michael Graham, and Randy Hanzlick. *Asphyxia and drowning: An atlas*. Boca Raton, FL: CRC Press, 2000. 110 p. $39.95. ISBN 084932369X.

Third in the *Causes of Death Atlas Series* from CRC Press. An overview of the different types, mechanisms, and physical findings associated with deaths involving asphyxia, this atlas is intended to serve as a reference for death investigators, law enforcement personnel, and others involved in the investigation of such deaths. The text presenting these topics is accompanied by pictorial representations of findings associated with these types of deaths.

268.    Hearle, John W. S., Brenda Lomas, and William D. Cooke. *Atlas of fibre fracture and damage to textiles*. 2nd ed. Boca Raton, FL: CRC Press, 1998. 480 p. $539. ISBN 0849338816.

One of the most comprehensive compilations dealing with textile damage, this updated second edition contains two new sections on forensic and medical studies and is a much-needed addition to the forensics literature. The atlas contains over 1,500 scanning electron micrographs with explanatory text on fracture mechanics to help forensic scientists to identify the causes of failure.

269.    Robert R. Ogle, Jr., and Michelle J. Fox. *Atlas of human hair: Microscopic characteristics*. Boca Raton, FL: CRC Press, 1998. 84 p. $89.95. ISBN 0849381347.   http://www.forensicnetbase.com/ejournals/books/book_summary/ summary.asp?id=554

This atlas provides photographic examples for human hair variations that are intended to provide for uniform descriptors for these variations. It also partitions the microscopic characteristics into classes for determination of frequency data for each of the variations. A scoring system is introduced that is intended to allow examiners to easily and rapidly score the variations seen in a study hair. Macroscopic characteristics of human hair are also included. A reference list, an extensive bibliography pertaining to forensic hair examination, and a glossary of terms used in the atlas are included.

270.    Finkbeiner, Walter E., Philip C. Ursell, and Richard L. Davis. *Autopsy pathology: A manual and atlas*. Philadelphia, PA: Churchill Livingstone, 2004. 412 p. $125. ISBN 0443076766.

A manual covering a range of specific autopsy procedures followed by an atlas of autopsy findings organized by body system and illustrated by full-color photos. Useful for students in forensic pathology.

271.   Petraco, Nicholas, and Thomas Kubic. *Color atlas and manual of microscopy for criminalists, chemists, and conservators.* Boca Raton, FL: CRC Press, 2003. 313 p. $199.95. ISBN 0849312450.

This illustrated book is arranged into 14 chapters, including one of case studies. Topics covered include basic light microscopy, stereomicroscopy, chemical microscopy and microtechnique, identification and comparison of human hair, animal hair identification, synthetic fiber identification, textile examination, soil and mineral examination, gemstone identification, and dust examination. Appendices include a human hair atlas, animal hair atlas, a compendium of photomicrographs of synthetic fibers, and a compendium of paint and pigment photomicrographs. Glossaries and reference lists are included at the end of each chapter.

272.   Dix, Jay. *Color atlas of forensic pathology.* Boca Raton, FL: CRC Press, 1999. 192 p. $239.95. ISBN 0849302781.

Essentially a collection of photographs illustrating postmortem changes, this atlas should prove useful to death investigators, attorneys, medical examiners, coroners, and law enforcement officers. Each chapter has a brief discussion on the topic area, and captions beneath the photos explain the feature the photo is illustrating.

273.   Wagner, Scott A. *Color atlas of the autopsy.* Boca Raton, FL: CRC Press, 2004. 264 p. $199.95. ISBN 0849315204.

An illustrated guide to autopsy procedures and protocols from start to finish, suitable for all audience levels. Each chapter discusses basic terms, principles, and techniques related to the autopsy process.

274.   Davis, Joseph A. *Conducting research: A preparation guide for writing and completing the research project or thesis in criminal justice, criminology, forensic science and related fields.* Lido Beach, NY: Whittier Publications, 1995. 123 p. $19.50. ISBN 1878045773 (pbk.).

This guide describes the steps for planning and developing an outline for a research project or paper, dissertation, or thesis. Topics covered include library privileges, form and style, different types of projects and methods, the proposal, and then a chapter-by-chapter development of a research paper/project. Sample pages for each step of the process are included.

275.   Douglas, John E., Ann W. Burgess, Allen G. Burgess, and Robert K. Ressler. *Crime classification manual: A standard system for investigating and*

*classifying violent crimes.* New York, NY: Lexington Books, 1992. 374 p. $48. ISBN 0669246387.

The CCM standardizes terminology within the criminal justice field, develops a database for investigative research, and facilitates communication within the field of criminal justice and between mental health and criminal justice. The classification is based on the primary intent of the criminal (criminal enterprise, personal cause, sexual intent, and group cause). Crime definitions are taken from the FBI's Uniform Crime Reporting Program. The manual itself is organized into two major parts: (1) the classifications, and (2) crime scene analysis. The second part is of most interest to forensic scientists. It addresses the decision process for classifying a crime, the detection of staging and personation (unusual behavior by a perpetrator beyond what is needed to commit the crime) at the crime scene, the modus operandi and the signature aspects of violent crime, crime scene photography, and prescriptive interviewing. This book is highly recommended for those interested in learning more about the perpetrators of crimes.

276.    Mauriello, Thomas P. *Criminal investigation handbook.* New York, NY: LexisNexis Matthew Bender, 1990–. $166. ISBN 0820516732.

Formerly the *Police investigation handbook*, which was first published in 1990. This loose-leaf volume, useful for practical guidance through each element of a criminal investigation, has periodic updates with revisions. Coverage includes aspects of an investigation as well as pertinent legal analysis, including crime scene investigation, forensic interviewing, documenting the investigation, and testifying and use of evidence in court, as well as a section on specific crimes.

277.    Karch, Steven B., ed. *Drug abuse handbook.* Boca Raton, FL: CRC Press, 1998. 1138 p. $139.95. ISBN 0849326370.

Steven Karch is the author of *Karch's pathology of drug abuse*, the authoritative guide on the analysis of drugs of abuse. In this outstanding handbook for professionals, he has brought together an impressive array of information from many experts in the field.

278.    Saferstein, Richard, ed. *Forensic science handbook.* 2nd ed. Upper Saddle River, NJ: Prentice Hall, 2002–. 767 p. (v.1), 528 p. (v.2). $166.67 (v.1), $166.67 (v.2). ISBN 0130910589 (v.1), 013112434X (v.2).

An update of Saferstein's classic 1982 edition, this three-volume set is designed to familiarize the reader with the latest techniques and methods available to forensic scientists. Chapters are devoted to the legal aspects of forensic science, DNA analysis, fiber analysis, drug identification, firearm examination, the microscopic examination of physical evidence, trace evidence analysis, questioned document examination, mass spectrometry, high-performance liquid chromatography and capillary electrophoresis, and the characterization of biological stains. Reference lists appear at the end of each chapter, along with suggested reading lists. The first edition of volume three, published in 1993, is still available in print (432 p., $166.67, ISBN 0133253902).

279.   Laing, Richard R., ed. *Hallucinogens: A forensic drug handbook.* San Diego, CA: Academic Press, 2003. 290 p. $89.95. ISBN 0124339514.

A comprehensive reference for those involved in the forensic analysis of hallucinogenic drugs. A substantial background in physiology and chemistry is needed to best use this handbook.

280.   Bogusz, Maciej J., ed. *Handbook of analytical separations. Volume 2, Forensic Science.* Amsterdam: Elsevier, 2000. 742 p. $302.95. ISBN 0444829989.

The second volume of this three-part handbook, the bulk of the content is devoted to forensic toxicology. The purpose of the book is to present the most critical, current information on separation methods in various disciplines of forensics. Forensic toxicologists are the practitioners who will get the most use from this publication.

281.   Ellison, Hank. *Handbook of chemical and biological warfare agents.* Boca Raton, FL: CRC Press, 1999. 507 p. $99.95. ISBN 0849328039.

This book is formatted into a series of indices for rapid access to information on chemical, biological, and toxin agents. Indices are cross-referenced to connect related entries. A glossary and reference list is included at the end of the book. This book will be useful for forensic toxicologists.

282.   Liu, Ray H., and Daniel E. Gadzala. *Handbook of drug analysis: Applications in forensic and clinical laboratories.* Washington, DC: American Chemical Society, 1997. 367 p. ISBN 0841234485.

This book was written with the intention of bridging the gap between instrumental and analytical texts. The intended audience is both new analysts and experienced practitioners, and it is highly recommended to both groups.

283.   Hess, Allen K., and Irving B. Weiner, eds. *Handbook of forensic psychology.* 2nd ed. New York, NY: John Wiley, 1999. 756 p. $145. ISBN 0471177717.

This handbook is divided into 25 chapters. Of particular use for research are chapters 3 and 18. Chapter 3 discusses accessing the legal literature, whereas

Chapter 18 provides guidance on writing forensic reports. All chapters will be useful for researchers intent on finding discussion of relevant issues, as well as for those who just want to expand their knowledge of this rapidly expanding area. All chapters include a reference list at the end, some quite extensive. Author and subject indexes are included.

284.    O'Donohue, William T., and Eric R. Levensky, eds. *Handbook of forensic psychology: Resource for mental health and legal professionals.* San Diego, CA: Elsevier Academic Press, 2004. 1064 p. $149.95. ISBN 0125241968.

The intent of this handbook is to be a source of current, practical, and empirically based information. Each of the 37 chapters is separately authored. The handbook itself is divided into four broad parts: (I) Basic Issues, (II) Assessment, (III) Mental Disorders and Forensic Psychology, and (IV) Special Topics. Chapter 4 covers forensic report writing. Subject and author indexes are included. This handbook was designated a *CHOICE* Outstanding Book.

285.    *Handbook of forensic services.* Washington, DC: Federal Bureau of Investigation, 2003. 180 p. $12 (paper; free online). ISBN 0160515823 (paper), 0932115187 (online). http://www.fbi.gov/hq/lab/handbook/forensics.pdf (accessed December 10, 2004).

Formerly called the *Handbook of forensic sciences*, the purpose of the handbook is to provide guidance and procedures for safe and efficient methods for collecting, preserving, packaging, and shipping evidence, and to describe forensic examinations done by the FBI's Laboratory and Investigative Technology Divisions. Chapters cover submitting evidence, evidence examinations, crime scene safety, and crime scene search.

286.    Goldstein, Alan M., ed. *Handbook of psychology. Vol. 11.* New York, NY: John Wiley & Sons, 2003. 606 p. $150. ISBN 047138321X.

This handbook is divided into seven independently authored parts. The whole volume is of use to researchers in learning more about this field and the differences between civil and criminal forensic psychology. Chapter 1, written by Goldstein, is particularly useful in distinguishing between the different areas in which forensics and psychology intersect. Each chapter has a table of contents at the beginning and an extensive reference list at the end.

287.    Matshes, Evan W., Brent Burbridge, Belinda Sher, Adel Mohamed, and Bernhard H. Juurlink. *Human osteology & skeletal radiology: An atlas and guide.* Boca Raton, FL: CRC Press, 2005. 448 p. $99.95. ISBN 0849319013.

A valuable addition to the reference library of every forensic anthropologist, the marriage of radiological images and traditional photographs and graphics makes this a unique tool in skeletal recognition.

288.    Dix, Jay, Michael Graham, and Randy Hanzlick. *Investigation of road traffic fatalities: An atlas.* Boca Raton, FL: CRC Press, 2000. $39.95. ISBN 0849323681.

Second in the *Causes of Death Atlas Series* from CRC Press. This atlas is written for medical examiners and coroners, medicolegal death investigators, and law enforcement personnel who work with medical examiners and coroners during the investigation of road traffic fatalities. Much like other atlases in this series, the text covers the issues involved in determining the nature and extent of injuries, as well as the cause, manner, and circumstances of death. An extensive assemblage of photographs depicting the various aspects of road traffic fatality injuries follows.

289.    Eastaugh, Nicholas, Valentine Walsh, Tracey Chaplin, and Ruth Siddall. *Pigment compendium.* Oxford: Elsevier Butterworth-Heinemann, 2004. 2 v. 950 p. $365. ISBN 0750664614 (set), 0750657499 (*Dictionary . . .*), 0750645539 (*Optical . . .*).

This two-volume set consists of the *Dictionary of historical pigments* and *Optical microscopy of historical pigments*. It draws together the illustrative manual dedicated to optical microscopy of historical pigments and the essential dictionary of pigment names and synonyms, providing the reader with a thorough guide to historical pigments. This is particularly useful to questioned document examiners.

290.    Brogdon, Byron Gilliam, Hermann Vogel, and John D. McDowell, eds. *A radiologic atlas of abuse, torture, terrorism, and inflicted trauma.* Boca Raton, FL: CRC Press, 2003. 323 p. $139.95. ISBN 0849315336.

This atlas provides a radiologic exploration of the results of violence and aggression on the human body. It is edited by two radiologists and a board-certified forensic odontologist, all well known in their fields. In addition to editing the work, they also contribute several chapters. The atlas is divided into seven sections: Abuse, Torture, Terrorism, Missile-Firing Personal Weapons, Inflicted Trauma, Radiologic Identification and Evaluation, and Border Control and Internal Security. Each section consists of separately authored chapters from a variety of contributors. Chapters discuss a topic within the scope of the section, including references, and radiographs illustrating the topic of discussion. A subject index is included.

291.   Dix, Jay, and Michael Graham. *Time of death, decomposition and identification: An atlas.* Boca Raton, FL: CRC Press, 1999. 112 p. $49.95. ISBN 0849323673.

First in the *Causes of Death Atlas Series* from CRC Press. The intended audience is death investigators, law enforcement professionals, attorneys, and others who might be involved in forensic death cases. This book deals with the determination of the time of death, postmortem changes, and identification. An abundance of photographs illustrates the concepts in this atlas. A reference list and section on cases are included.


## Data Tables/Books

292.   *Instrumental data for drug analysis.* 2nd ed. Boca Raton, FL: CRC Press, 1992–1996. 7 v. $1,395. ISBN 0849395267 (set), 0849395216 (v.1), 0849395224 (v.2), 0849395232 (v.3), 0849395240 (v.4), 084939516X (v.5), 0849381142 (v.6), 0849381150 (v.7).

Volumes 1–4: Terry Mills III, and J. Conrad Roberson

Volume 5: Terry Mills III, J. Conrad Roberson, H. Horton McCurdy, and William H. Wall

Volumes 6–7: Terry Mills III, J. Conrad Roberson, William H. Wall, Kevin L. Lothridge, William D. McDougall, and Michael W. Gilbert

The second edition of this essential title includes accurate instrumental data on 1,200 drug-related compounds. Data for each compound includes the formula, molecular weight, synonyms, trade names, use, and a structure diagram. Also included are data from ultraviolet (UV) spectrophotometry, infrared (IR) spectrophotometry, proton nuclear magnetic resonance (NMR) spectrometry, mass spectrometry (MS), gas chromatography (GC), and high-pressure liquid chromatography (HPLC). Data in volumes 1–3 are arranged alphabetically by compound name. Volume 4 includes appendices of standard KBr Infrared Spectra and Standard NMR Solvent Spectra, Supplemental IR Spectra, Supplemental NMR Spectra, Ultraviolet Absorption Maxima and indices for Mass Spectra, Infrared Peak table index, Gas Chromatographic Data, Molecular Formula, and Compound Name. All of the NMR data has been revised in the second edition using a 300 MHz FTNMR system. Volume 5 includes the same data for derivatized drugs. An additional index is included of retention times. Volume 6 includes a special section of analytical data especially designed for toxicologists. It also contains mass spectra of over 200 pesticides. In addition, there are over 600 GC/FTIR spectra for many of the drugs found in Volumes 1–5. Volume 7 contains cumulative indices for the first six volumes.

## Standards

293.   *Annual Book of ASTM Standards. Volume 14.02 General Test Methods; Forensic Psychophysiology; Terminology; Conformity Assessment; Statistical Methods.* West Conshohocken, PA: ASTM International, 1970–. $210. ISBN 0803140290 (paper), 0803140304 (CD-ROM). Online access is available at two levels: Online Basic ($252) and Online Plus ($294). http://www.astm.org/ (accessed February 3, 2005).

For the forensic sciences, there are two important parts within this section: Forensic Sciences and Forensic Psychophysiology. The Forensic Sciences section provides test methods, practices, and guides for forensic investigations that cover criminalistics, engineering, questioned documents, interdisciplinary issues, and terminology. The Forensic Psychophysiology part examines guides and practices relating to polygraph training and education, and recommended factors in the design, conduct, and reporting of research on psychophysiological detection of deception (polygraph).

## Key Textbooks

294.   Kirk, Paul L., and Thornton, John I., ed. *Crime investigation.* 2nd ed. New York, NY: Wiley, 1974. 508 p. $66.50. ISBN 0471482471.

This classic text for the criminal investigator covers the essential techniques for the examination of physical evidence at the crime scene. Chapters include fingerprints, hair, blood, fibers, tracks and trails, firearms, and vehicular accidents.

295.   White, Peter C., ed. *Crime scene to court: The essentials of forensic science.* 2nd ed. Cambridge, U.K.: Royal Society of Chemistry, 2004. 473 p. $59.95. ISBN 0854046569.

This book is intended primarily for teaching and training purposes in forensic science courses in the United Kingdom. It provides nontechnical coverage of crime scene and forensic examination techniques and methods. Although intended for a U.K. audience, it is widely used by forensic scientists around the world.

296.   Saferstein, Richard. *Criminalistics: An introduction to forensic science.* 8th ed. Upper Saddle River, NJ: Prentice Hall, 2004. 580 p. $97.60. ISBN 0131118528.

This is the eighth edition of this classic introductory text. It is intended to depict the role of the forensic scientist in the criminal justice system. Chapters cover an introduction to forensic science; the crime scene; physical evidence; glass and soil; organic analysis; inorganic analysis; the microscope; hairs, fibers, and paints; drugs; toxicology; arson and explosion investigations; serology; DNA; fingerprints; firearms and tool marks; document and voice examination; and the forensic science on the Internet. There are some useful guides and instructions for evidence collection and chemical formulas for various tests in the appendices. A subject index is included to facilitate access to topics of interest.

297.    Saukko, Pekka, and Bernard Knight. *Knight's forensic pathology.* 3rd ed. London: Arnold, 2004. 671 p. $225. ISBN 0340760443.

The definitive, English-language manual for forensic pathologists and graduate students. *Knight's* has become the standard for practicing pathologists. The third edition has been fully revised and updated, including coverage of the European Autopsy Protocol.

298.    Geberth, Vernon J. *Practical homicide investigation: Tactics, procedures, and forensic techniques.* 3rd ed. Boca Raton, FL: CRC Press, 1996. 961 p. $89.95. ISBN 0849381568.

Considered the bible in crime investigation, this textbook walks the investigator through the crime scene, including photography, sketches, the search, time of death estimation, identifying the deceased, death notifications, modes of death, suicide investigation, collection of evidence, the autopsy, the media, suspect identification, criminal personality profiling, and supervision and management of the investigation. The intended audience of this book is the practitioner.

299.    Spitz, Werner U., ed. *Spitz and Fisher's medicolegal investigation of death: Guidelines for the application of pathology to crime investigation.* 3rd ed. Springfield, IL: Charles C Thomas, 1993. 856 p. $105.95. ISBN 0398058180.

Pathologists around the world know this book as the bible of forensic pathology. The text is oriented to forensic pathologists, criminal investigators, and attorneys. It covers all aspects of the pathology of trauma as it is witnessed daily by law enforcement officers, interpreted by pathologists of varying experience and expertise in forensic pathology, and used by lawyers involved in the prosecution and defense in criminal cases as well as those engaged in civil litigation.

300.    Fisher, Barry A. J. *Techniques of crime scene investigation.* 7th ed. Boca Raton, FL: CRC Press, 2004. 507 p. $89.95. ISBN 084931691X.

This is the latest revision of a classic text written by Svensson and Wendel. Fisher joined Svensson and Wendel with the third edition, eventually assuming full responsibility for it with the fifth edition. It is written for the nonspecialist and introduces concepts, procedures, and technical information on crime scene investigation. Some of the topics included in this edition are professional ethics, expert witness testimony, forensic DNA testing, forensic databases, forensic science and terrorist acts, and health and safety issues at crime scenes, in addition to the traditional crime scene investigation topics.

## Key Book Series

301. *Issues in Forensic Psychology* (formerly *Issues in Criminological Psychology*). Division of Forensic Psychology, The British Psychological Society, 1996–, irreg., ISSN 1468-4748. Free to members; GBP7 per issue for nonmembers.
    Indexed: Crim. Just. Abstr., e-psyche, Psychol. Abstr.

302. *Causes of Death Atlas Series.* Boca Raton, FL: CRC Press, 1999–, irreg.

303. *Forensic and Police Science Series.* Boca Raton, FL: CRC Press, 1992–, irreg.

304. *Forensic Pathology Reviews.* Totowa, NJ: Humana Press, 2004–, irreg.
    Each volume contains a collection of review articles on narrow topics in forensic pathology suitable to practicing forensic pathologists.

305. *Forensic Science Series* (formerly *Taylor & Francis Forensic Science Series*). Boca Raton, FL: CRC Press, 2004–, irreg.

306. *Forensic Science Techniques.* Boca Raton, FL: CRC Press, 2004–, irreg.

307. *International Forensic Science and Investigation Series.* Boca Raton, FL: CRC Press, 1997–, irreg.

308. *Practical Aspects of Criminal & Forensic Investigation.* Boca Raton, FL: CRC Press, 1992–, irreg.

309. *Progress in Forensic Genetics* (part of the **International Congress Series**). Amsterdam: Elsevier, 1998–, bi-annual.
    Proceedings of the International ISFG (International Society for Forensic Genetics) Congress (formerly the International ISFH Congress—International Society for Forensic Haemogenetics) held every two years. This series starts with the 17th Congress.

310.    **Protocols in Forensic Science.** Boca Raton, FL: CRC Press, 2000–, irreg.

In each volume, an expert in a specific forensic discipline provides enumeration and comprehensive discussion of hands-on protocols in that particular area or addresses a specific professional issue. Books in this series are written by the working professional for the working professional.

## Online Full Text Books

311.    **Interpol manual on disaster victim identification.** http://www.interpol.int/ Public/DisasterVictim/guide/default.asp (accessed May 13, 2005).

The revised edition of the 1984 manual based on the work of Interpol's Standing Committee on Disaster Victim Identification. It is circulated to all Interpol member countries and is designed to give practical advice on major issues of victim identification.

312.    **FORENSICnetBASE.** http://www.forensicnetbase.com/ (accessed January 23, 2005).

This subscription service from CRC Press, although not free, is an extremely important resource in forensic sciences because it provides online access to a growing list of full text books in forensics, criminal justice and law, and law enforcement.

313.    **Handbook of forensic services.** *(see Handbooks/Atlases section)*

314.    **Freedom of Information Act (FOIA) Electronic Reading Room.** http:// foia.fbi.gov/room.htm (accessed January 23, 2005).

The full text of selected FBI investigation files are available in this electronic reading room through the Freedom of Information Act (FOIA). Some portions are withheld under exemptions allowed by FOIA. The files are viewed using Adobe Acrobat Reader and are often split into several files because of their size.

315.    **National Institute of Justice.** http://nij.ncjrs.org/publications/pubs_db .asp (accessed January 23, 2005).

The National Institute of Justice maintains an extensive online collection of publications back to 1994 in PDF format, including such standards as *Death investigation: A guide for the scene investigator.*

## Career Information

The best career information is often obtained from practitioners in the field. There is no substitute for experience when describing career development. The following print and online resources can provide some basic guidance.

316.   Ryan, Alan S., ed. *A guide to careers in physical anthropology.* Westport, CT: Bergin & Garvey, 2002. 308 p. $89.95. ISBN 0897896939.

Chapter 18 discusses forensic science as a career for a physical anthropologist.

317.   U.S. Department of Labor, Bureau of Labor Statistics. *Occupational outlook handbook.* Washington, DC: GPO, 1949–. bi-e. $64. http://www.bls.gov/oco/home.htm (accessed December 10, 2004).

Published by the U.S. government, this is a classic for brief information on careers. Forensic science careers are covered in the science technicians, accountants and auditors, and psychologists categories.

318.   U.S. Department of Labor, Bureau of Labor Statistics. *Occupational outlook quarterly.* Washington, DC: GPO, 1958–. q. $15. http://www.bls.gov/opub/ooq/ooqhome.htm (accessed December 10, 2004).

Published by the U.S. government, this quarterly periodical supplements and updates information in the *Occupational outlook handbook*, providing current information on trends in the job market.

319.   Camenson, Blythe. *Opportunities in forensic science careers.* Chicago, IL: VGM Career Books, 2001. 149 p. $15.95 (cl.), $13.95 (pbk). ISBN 0658001019 (cl.), 0658001027 (pbk).

Part of the "Opportunities in" series, this publication defines and discusses the different fields in forensics, provides sample job listings and salaries, and discusses education and training. Specialty areas are discussed within the broad categories of forensic evidence, accident and fire investigation, forensic medicine, forensic anthropology, and forensic psychology and psychiatry. Four appendices list professional associations, further reading, forensic laboratories and institutes, and training programs.

# Selective Subject Collection Bibliography

### Introductory/General

320.   Nickell, Joe, and John F. Fischer. *Crime science: Methods of forensic detection.* Lexington, KY: University Press of Kentucky, 1999. 300 p. $25. ISBN 0813120918.

Aimed primarily at scientists and technicians; although there are plenty of technical terms used, they are generally translated into plain English for the non–technically minded. Each chapter is dedicated to a particular area of expertise and ends with details of a high-profile case related to the area discussed in the chapter and a recommended reading list.

321.   James, Stuart H., and Jon J. Nordby, eds. *Forensic science: An introduction to scientific and investigative techniques.* 2nd ed. Boca Raton, FL: CRC Press, 2005. 816 p. $79.95. ISBN 0849327474.

This textbook is specifically aimed at students enrolled in forensic science courses at the advanced high school and college undergraduate level. Contributors are highly respected forensic scientists and legal practitioners.

322.   Eckert, William G., ed. *Introduction to forensic sciences.* 2nd ed. Boca Raton, FL: CRC Press, 1997. 390 p. $99.95. ISBN 0849381010.

Written for students of all levels of education, each chapter is written by a different author (or authors) who has expertise in the particular field being discussed. Some of the chapters are more advanced than the "Introduction to" title implies, which might frustrate novices, but overall, this book has much to offer a student wanting to get an overview of the different specialties in the forensic sciences.

## Accounting

323.   Iannacci, Jerry, and Ron Morris. *Access device fraud and related financial crimes.* Boca Raton, FL: CRC Press, 2000. 176 p. $64.95. ISBN 0849381304.

A reference text for students, financial investigators, and law enforcement professionals on the wide spectrum of activity involving financial crimes.

324.   Manning, George A. *Financial investigation and forensic accounting.* 2nd ed. Boca Raton, FL: CRC Press, 2005. 616 p. $99.95. ISBN 0849322235.

This edition's updates include locating terrorist funds and computer fraud, and it relates new laws enacted since the first edition.

325.   Albrecht, W. Steven, and Chad Albrecht. *Fraud examination and prevention.* Mason, OH: Thomson South-Western, 2004. 416 p. $40.95. ISBN 053872689X.

A recognized expert in fraud detection and investigation, W. Steven Albrecht shares his considerable knowledge in this invaluable resource for fraud investigators.

326.   Madinger, John, and Sydney A. Zalopany. *Money laundering: A guide for criminal investigators.* Boca Raton, FL: CRC Press, 1999. 520 p. $94.95. ISBN 0849307104.

A compendium of the many types of money laundering and techniques involved in investigating financial crime.

327. Richards, James R. *Transnational criminal organizations, cybercrime, and money laundering: A handbook for law enforcement officers, auditors, and financial investigators.* Boca Raton, FL: CRC Press, 1999. 344 p. $84.95. ISBN 0849328063.

Examining the workings of organized crime that transcend national boundaries, this detailed text is written for law enforcement officers and financial crime investigators, but it will also be of interest to students and the lay public interested in learning more about this growing area of criminal activity.

**Anthropology/Osteology**

328. Haglund, William D., and Marcella H. Sorg, eds. *Advances in forensic taphonomy: Method, theory, and archaeological perspectives.* Boca Raton, FL: CRC Press, 2002. 507 p. $99.95. ISBN 0849311896.

An excellent update/supplement to the editors' *Forensic taphonomy: The postmortem fate of human remains*, presenting some new and updated techniques.

329. Galloway, Alison, ed. *Broken bones: Anthropological analysis of blunt force trauma.* Springfield, IL: Charles C Thomas, 1999. 371 p. $76.95. ISBN 0398069921.

An excellent overview of the principles and processes for interpreting blunt force trauma, this landmark reference will be useful to all anthropologists in analyzing fracture patterns throughout the skeleton.

330. Clement, John G., and David L. Ranson, eds. *Craniofacial identification in forensic medicine.* London: Arnold Publishers, 1998. 306 p. $169.50. ISBN 0340607599.

An outstanding technical guide written by experts from Australia, Canada, the United Kingdom, and the United States that in no way limits the usefulness of the information to any geographical area. Suitable for all levels.

331. Killam, Edward W. *The detection of human remains.* 2nd ed. Springfield, IL: Charles C Thomas, 2004. 268 p. $69.95 (cl.), $45.95 (pbk.). ISBN 0398074836 (cl.), 0398074844 (pbk.).

This manual for investigators involved in locating buried, concealed, or discarded bodies updates the author's first innovative book.

332.    Scheuer, Louise, and Sue Black. *Developmental juvenile osteology.* San Diego, CA: Academic Press, 2000. 587 p. $176.95. ISBN 0126240000.

The definitive reference on juvenile osteology for physical anthropologists, archaeologists, and forensic pathologists.

333.    İşcan, Mehmet Yaşar, and Richard P. Helmer, eds. *Forensic analysis of the skull: Craniofacial analysis, reconstruction, and identification.* New York, NY: Wiley-Liss, Inc., 1993. 258 p. $152. ISBN 0471560782.

Still a useful book for detailed information on forensic analysis of the skull.

334.    Fairgrieve, Scott I., ed. *Forensic osteological analysis: A book of case studies.* Springfield, IL: Charles C Thomas, 1999. 340 p. $80.95. ISBN 0398069638.

This collection of cases written by a large number of experts is most useful for forensic anthropology students but will also be of interest to practitioners. The cases are largely from Canada and the United States.

335.    Reichs, Kathleen J., ed. *Forensic osteology: Advances in the identification of human remains.* 2nd ed. Springfield, IL: Charles C. Thomas, 1998. 567 p. $108.95. ISBN 0398068046.

A new, considerably broadened edition of Reichs's very successful first edition detailing developments in forensic anthropology. Chapters are written by 34 different authors. Reichs is a popular forensic fiction author in addition to being a practicing forensic anthropologist.

336.    Haglund, William D., and Marcella H. Sorg, eds. *Forensic taphonomy: The postmortem fate of human remains.* Boca Raton, FL: CRC Press, 1997. 636 p. $129.95. ISBN 0849394341.

Provides a solid foundation in forensic taphonomy. The editors' follow-up book, *Advances in forensic taphonomy*, should be read as an extension on this one.

337.    Dixon, Andrew D., David A. N. Hoyte, and Olli Rönning, eds. *Fundamentals of craniofacial growth.* Boca Raton: CRC Press, 1997. 497 p. $179.95. ISBN 0849345758.

The basis of forensic facial recognition is to understand craniofacial growth. This detailed text provides an in-depth look at this fascinating area of study.

338.    White, Tim D. *Human osteology.* 2nd ed. San Diego, CA: Academic Press, 2000. 563 p. $89.95. ISBN 0127466126.

A revised edition of a classic text for students and professionals for accurately identifying human skeletal remains. Content has been updated and additional content added on the many advances in the field since the first edition.

339. Byers, Steven N. *Introduction to forensic anthropology: A textbook.* Boston, MA: Allyn & Bacon, 2002. 444 p. $86.20. ISBN 020532181X.

An excellent textbook for undergraduate students in forensic anthropology courses. It is also useful for professional crime scene investigators, forensic pathologists, and forensic science educators.

## Art, Facial Imaging, and Facial Reconstruction

340. Taylor, Karen T. *Forensic art and illustration.* Boca Raton, FL: CRC Press, 2001. 580 p. $99.95. ISBN 0849381185.

A comprehensive landmark text examining forensic art and its role in criminal investigation. Essential for all audiences.

341. Wilkinson, Caroline. *Forensic facial reconstruction.* Cambridge: Cambridge University Press, 2004. 290 p. $120. ISBN 0521820030.

A useful book that provides a new perspective on forensic facial reconstruction.

## Botany

342. Weising, Kurt, Hilde Nybom, Kirsten Wolff, and Gunter Kahl. *DNA fingerprinting in plants: Principles, methods, and applications.* 2nd ed. Boca Raton, FL: CRC Press, 2005. 472 p. $99.95. ISBN 0849314887.

This is a completely revised edition of a 1994 text. It focuses on PCR-based techniques, in addition to more sophisticated techniques.

343. Coyle, Heather Miller, ed. *Forensic botany: principles and applications to criminal casework.* Boca Raton, FL: CRC Press, 2005. 318 p. $119.95. ISBN 0849315298.

The first book to focus solely on the emerging field of forensic botany, this primer is recommended for all those with a basic knowledge of plant science and forensic sciences.

## Chemistry and Toxicology

344. Yinon, Jehuda, ed. *Advances in forensic applications of mass spectrometry.* Boca Raton, FL: CRC Press, 2004. 296 p. $129.95. ISBN 0849315220.

Yinon has updated the information from her first volume on *Forensic applications of mass spectrometry*.

345.    Klaassen, Curtis D., ed. ***Casarett and Doull's toxicology: The basic science of poisons***. 6th ed. New York, NY: McGraw-Hill Medical Publishing Division, 2001. 1236 p. $99. ISBN 0071347216.

The latest edition of this widely used text for graduate courses in toxicology. There is one chapter specifically focused on forensic toxicology, but all of the chapters will be of use to the forensic toxicologist.

346.    Petersen, R., and Amin A. Mohammad, eds. ***Clinical and forensic applications of capillary electrophoresis***. Totowa, NJ: Humana Press, 2001. 453 p. $135. ISBN 0896036456.

An excellent source of basic information on the main capillary electrophoresis (CE) techniques and their applications.

347.    Trestrail, John Harris, III. ***Criminal poisoning: Investigational guide for law enforcement, toxicologists, forensic scientists, and attorneys***. Totowa, NJ: Humana Press, Inc., 2000. 166 p. $59.50 (cl.), $34.50 (pbk.). ISBN 0896035921 (cl.), 1588291332 (pbk.).

A useful starting point for those launching a poisoning investigation or prosecution.

348.    Kintz, Pascal, ed. ***Drug testing in hair***. Boca Raton, FL: CRC Press, 1996. 293 p. $119.95. ISBN 0849381126.

A comprehensive review of the applications for hair analysis and the analytical methodology involved, written for those with potential involvement in the technique in forensics or clinical analysis. Content is evenly split between European and American contributors and covers analytical and interpretive issues.

349.    Yinon, Jehuda, ed. ***Forensic applications of mass spectrometry***. Boca Raton, FL: CRC Press, 1995. 296 p. $149.95. ISBN 0849382521.

Mass spectrometry is the primary analytical technique for investigating many types of evidence; thus this book is a valuable resource for the practicing forensic scientist and students. Content is updated in Yinon's *Advances in forensic applications of mass spectrometry* (see above).

350.    Drummer, Olaf H., and Morris Odell. ***The forensic pharmacology of drugs of abuse***. London: Arnold, 2001. 462 p. $98.50. ISBN 0340762578.

An invaluable reference in forensic pharmacology and forensic toxicology for students and experienced practitioners.

351.    Tebbett, Ian, ed. *Gas chromatography in forensic science.* London: Ellis Horwood Limited, 1992. 188 p. $139.95. ISBN 0133271986.

Written for forensic scientists and students addressing the problems specific to the examination of forensic samples.

352.    Newman, Reta, Michael Gilbert, and Kevin Lothridge. *GC-MS guide to ignitable liquids.* Boca Raton, FL: CRC Press, 1998. 750 p. $139.95. ISBN 0849331072.

Written by experienced forensic chemists, this compilation of ignitable liquid formulations and chromatograms will be a useful reference to fire and arson investigators.

353.    Karch, Steven B. *Karch's pathology of drug abuse.* 3rd ed. Boca Raton, FL: CRC Press, 2002. 568 p. $99.95. ISBN 0849303435.

This updated edition of this comprehensive and authoritative guide is a must for professionals.

354.    Levine, Barry, ed. *Principles of forensic toxicology.* 2nd ed. Washington, DC: American Association for Clinical Chemistry, 2003. 385 p. $67. ISBN 1890883875.

A new edition of a classic bestselling textbook for forensic toxicology students in one-semester courses.

## Computing

355.    Ratha, Nalini, and Ruud Bolle, eds. *Automatic fingerprint recognition systems.* New York, NY: Springer-Verlag New York, Inc., 2004. 475 p. $69.95. ISBN 0387955933.

A thorough survey of the field and recent advances of interest to anyone with an interest in automated fingerprint recognition systems.

356.    Mohay, George, Alison Anderson, Byron Collie, Olivier de Vel, and Rodney D. McKemmish. *Computer and intrusion forensics.* Norwood, MA: Artech House, Inc., 2003. 420 p. $85. ISBN 1-58053-369-8.

An excellent introduction to the study of computer forensics, especially for novices.

357.    Casey, Eoghan. *Digital evidence and computer crime: Forensic science, computers and the Internet.* 2nd ed. San Diego, CA: Elsevier Academic Press, 2004. 690 p. $69.95. ISBN 0121631044.

An update to Casey's successful first edition of this introductory text written so that technical details can be easily understood by the layperson with little or no computer-related experience. This in no way limits it from also being an essential book to knowledgeable experts in the field.

358.    Phillips, Amelia, Bill Nelson, Frank Enfinger, and Chris Steuart. *Guide to computer forensics and investigations.* Boston, MA: Thomson Course Technology, 2005. 650 p. $67.95. ISBN 0619217065.

An updated edition of one of the best books with a technical focus on cyberforensics, for both professionals and students who have a firm grasp on computer and network basics.

359.    Casey, Eoghan, ed. *Handbook of computer crime investigation: Forensic tools and technology.* San Diego, CA: Academic Press, 2002. 448 p. $44.95. ISBN 0121631036.

A detailed technical guide, useful for novices in understanding the forensic analysis of computer systems.

360.    Maltoni, Davide, Dario Maio, Anil K. Jain, and Salil Prabhakar. *Handbook of fingerprint recognition.* New York, NY: Springer-Verlag New York, Inc., 2003. 360 p. $59.95. ISBN 0387954317.

Useful to researchers, students, and practitioners who wish to understand or develop a fingerprint-based recognition system.

361.    Stephenson, Peter. *Investigating computer-related crime.* Boca Raton, FL: CRC Press, 2000. 304 p. $89.95. ISBN 0849322189.

Written for corporate information professionals and investigators, this well-written book is also useful as an introduction for students in this area.

**Crime Scene Investigation**

362.    Zonderman, Jon. *Beyond the crime lab: The new science of investigation.* Rev ed. New York, NY: John Wiley & Sons, 1999. 254 p. $29.95. ISBN 0471254665.

An intermediate-level book aimed at nontechnical readers such as police officers, attorneys, and the general public who need to know about advances in forensics.

363.  Wonder, Anita Y. *Blood dynamics.* San Diego, CA: Academic Press, 2001. 168 p. $79.95. ISBN 0127624570.

Wonder covers a variety of topics, including a novel theory on the "non-Newtonian, visoelastic" properties of blood. Some topics you would expect in a book like this are missing, but overall, this is a useful resource for a bloodstain pattern analyst.

364.  Bevel, Tom, and Ross M. Gardner. *Bloodstain pattern analysis: With an introduction to crime scene reconstruction.* 2nd ed. Boca Raton, FL: CRC Press, 2002. 393 p. $99.95. ISBN 0849309506.

This edition, blending practical crime scene knowledge and the application of scientific methodology to crime scene reconstruction, has become the basis for standardization of blood spatter analysis.

365.  MacDonell, Herbert Leon. *Bloodstain patterns.* Rev. ed. Corning, NY: Laboratory of Forensic Science, 1997. 182 p. $25.

MacDonell is widely acknowledged as the father of modern bloodstain pattern analysis.

366.  Byrd, Mike. *Crime scene evidence: A guide to the recovery and collection of physical evidence.* Temecula, CA: Staggs Publishing, 2001. 102 p. $29.95. ISBN 0966197054.

A quick, practical reference for the collection, handling, and packaging of crime scene evidence. The photographs are a little dark, but the text of the book is quite useful.

367.  Bodziak, William J. *Footwear impression evidence: Detection, recovery, and examination.* 2nd ed. Boca Raton, FL: CRC Press, 2000. 497 p. $99.95. ISBN 0849310458.

This book contains virtually everything a footwear impression examiner should know. Information in the first edition has been updated and three new chapters added, the most useful of which concerns the examination of barefoot evidence.

368.  Hilderbrand, Dwane S. *Footwear, the missed evidence: A field guide to the collection and preservation of footwear impression evidence.* Temecula, CA: Staggs Publishing, 1999. 118 p. $35.95. ISBN 0966197011.

A handbook designed to provide essential information the crime scene investigator will need to recognize, collect, and preserve footwear impression evidence.

369.   Pollanen, Michael S. *Forensic diatomology and drowning.* Amsterdam: Elsevier, 1998. 159 p. $162. ISBN 0444828443.

A useful book for libraries for quick reference, but there is really nothing new of value for practitioners that has not been covered in other publications.

370.   Christian, Donnell R. *Forensic investigation of clandestine laboratories.* Boca Raton, FL: CRC Press, 2004. 371 p. $79.95. ISBN 0849312272.

Written to provide investigators with general information they need to understand clandestine labs. The categorized reference list in Appendix R provides a wealth of information.

371.   Nause, Lawren. *Forensic tire impression identification.* Ottawa, ON: Canadian Police Research Centre, 2001. 290 p. CDN98. ISBN 0660186403.

A well-researched technical manual based on the author's 30 years of crime scene experience.

372.   O'Hara, Charles E., and Gregory L. O'Hara. *Fundamentals of criminal investigation.* 7th ed. Springfield, IL: Charles C Thomas, 2003. 907 p. $59.95. ISBN 0398073295.

The seventh edition of this classic continues to focus on the essential elements of a criminal investigation. It is not a technical volume for forensic scientists but more of an overview of the whole investigative process.

373.   Lee, Henry C., Timothy Palmbach, and Marilyn T. Miller. *Henry Lee's crime scene handbook.* San Diego, CA: Academic Press, 2001. 416 p. $79.95. ISBN 0124408303.

Useful for students interested in crime scene reconstruction and for experienced investigators wanting to read more on the scientific method applied to crime scene investigations. It is not as useful as a technical reference for experienced investigators, due to a scarcity of published references from sources other than Lee in the book and less than exhaustive coverage on some topics.

374.   James, Stuart H., and William G. Eckert. *Interpretation of bloodstain evidence at crime scenes.* 2nd ed. Boca Raton, FL: CRC Press, 1999. 324 p. $99.95. ISBN 0849381266.

Updated resource for law enforcement officers, medicolegal personnel, and attorneys. Fascinating case studies are presented in each chapter.

375.   Perlmutter, Dawn. *Investigating religious terrorism and ritualistic crimes.* Boca Raton, FL: CRC Press, 2004. 453 p. $69.95. ISBN 0849310342.

Written by one of the leading experts in the areas of religious violence and ritualistic crimes. This is a treasure-trove of information for researchers in this growing area.

376.    Hazelwood, Robert R., and Ann Wolbert Burgess, eds. *Practical aspects of rape investigation: A multidisciplinary approach.* 3rd ed. Boca Raton, FL: CRC Press, 2001. 517 p. $89.95. ISBN 0849300762.
Best suited for practicing investigators and new prosecutors. Unlike other books on this topic, this one discusses victimology as well as investigative methods.

377.    Gardner, Ross M. *Practical crime scene processing and investigation.* Boca Raton, FL: CRC Press, 2005. 391 p. $69.95. ISBN 0849320437.
Written as a refresher for all officers and investigative personnel involved in crime scene processing, it is also useful for students and those who need to understand the basics of crime scene processing.

378.    Bell, William R. *Practical criminal investigations in correctional facilities.* Boca Raton, FL: CRC Press, 2002. 303 p. $79.95. ISBN 0849311942.
Directed at detectives in prison towns and criminal investigators working within the prison systems. The focus is on an American audience, although several of the topics discussed are transferable to correctional facilities in other countries.

379.    Redsicker, David R., and John J. O'Connor. *Practical fire and arson investigation.* 2nd ed. Boca Raton, FL: CRC Press, 1997. 416 p. $89.95. ISBN 084938155X.
This edition has been significantly revised, updated, and expanded from the original bestseller.

380.    Carney, Thomas P. *Practical investigation of sex crimes: A strategic and operational approach.* Boca Raton, FL: CRC Press, 2004. 221 p. $69.95. ISBN 0849312825.
This is a systematic guide for investigating sex crimes written for law enforcement investigators.

381.    Horswell, John, ed. *The practice of crime scene investigation.* Boca Raton, FL: CRC Press, 2004. 418 p. $99.95. ISBN 0748406093.
Contributions are primarily from Australian experts, with each chapter being separately authored, but this does not limit its relevance to other geographic

areas. The chapters on light sources and photographic techniques are particularly useful for their thoroughness.

382.    James, Stuart H. ed. *Scientific and legal applications of bloodstain pattern interpretation.* Boca Raton, FL: CRC Press, 1998. 274 p. $79.95. ISBN 0849381088.

Written for attorneys and investigators, this publication is intended as a companion to *Interpretation of bloodstain evidence at crime scenes* by James and Eckert.

383.    Goldstein, Seth L. *The sexual exploitation of children: A practical guide to assessment, investigation, and intervention.* 2nd ed. Boca Raton, FL: CRC Press, 1999. 604 p. $94.95. ISBN 0849381541.

A comprehensive textbook for the practitioner that should be required reading for anyone who investigates or evaluates the sexual abuse of children.

384.    McDonald, Peter. *Tire imprint evidence.* New York, NY: Elsevier Science Publishing Co., Inc., 1989. 244 p. $129.95. ISBN 044401456X.

Reprinted in 1992 by CRC Press (ISBN 0849395151). Although an older imprint, this title is still one of the best around for this topic.

**Criminalistics and Trace Evidence**

385.    Lee, Henry C., and R. E. Gaensslen, eds. *Advances in fingerprint technology.* 2nd ed. Boca Raton, FL: CRC Press, 2001. 444 p. $89.95. ISBN 0849309239.

Each chapter in this thoroughly researched text is written by well-respected identification and forensic experts. The intent is to update readers on advances in this most important area of physical evidence, although the chapter on the history and development of fingerprinting and the chapter on latent print identification provide an excellent introduction to the area.

386.    Coppock, Craig A. *Contrast: An investigator's basic reference guide to fingerprint identification concepts.* Springfield, IL: Charles C Thomas, 2001. 131 p. $39.95 (cl.), $25.95 (pbk.). ISBN 0398071306 (cl.), 0398071314 (pbk.).

*Contrast* is written for the layman to understand the concepts and basics of fingerprint science, although it contains enough information to engage experienced crime science investigators as well.

387.    Murray, Raymod C. *Evidence from the Earth: Forensic geology and criminal investigation.* Mountain Press Publishing Company, 2004. 240 p. $20. ISBN 0878424989.

For general readers and practitioners, this is a completely revised and updated edition of Murray's classic earlier publication, *Forensic geology.*

388.    Menzel, E. Roland. ***Fingerprint detection with lasers.*** 2nd rev. exp. ed. New York, NY: Marcel Dekker, Inc., 1999. 272 p. $95. ISBN 0824719743.

Written for the latent print examiner, Menzel explains some complex concepts using simple ideas that make this book accessible to those without a background in quantum chemistry.

389.    Champod, Christophe, Chris J. Lennard, Pierre Margot, and Milutin Stoilovic. ***Fingerprints and other ridge skin impressions.*** Boca Raton, FL: CRC Press, 2004. 285 p. $89.95. ISBN 0415271754.

A relevant and informative practical manual on the topic of fingerprints and other ridge skin impressions. The appendices and references are particularly useful.

390.    Chisnall, Robert. ***The forensic analysis of knots and ligatures.*** Salem, OR: Lightning Powder Company, Inc., 2000. 157 p. $49.95. ISBN 0962230529.

Books specifically on the forensic analysis of knots and ligatures are very rare, so this is a welcome addition to the literature. Chisnall goes beyond previously published books in this area to provide specific guidelines for interpreting various knots and configurations of knots.

391.    Robertson, James, and Michael Grieve, eds. ***Forensic examination of fibres.*** 2nd ed. London: Taylor & Francis, 1999. 447 p. $149.95. ISBN 0748408169.

Completely revised, updated, and expanded edition of this thorough coverage of forensic fiber examination. Suitable for students and practitioners.

392.    Caddy, Brian, ed. ***Forensic examination of glass and paint: Analysis and interpretation.*** London: Taylor & Francis, 2001. 292 p. $119.95. ISBN 0748405798.

A useful read for the practicing forensic scientist but not really suitable for the novice. The book has a European leaning when it comes to popular methods and approaches, so some parts might not be as useful to an American audience as others.

393.    Robertson, James, ed. ***Forensic examination of hair.*** London: Taylor & Francis, 1999. 267 p. $119.95. ISBN 0748405674.

A useful reference for the practicing forensic scientist, although students with a biology background might also find it usable.

394.    Curran, James Michael, Tacha Natalie Hicks, and John S. Buckleton. ***Forensic interpretation of glass evidence.*** Boca Raton, FL: CRC Press, 2000. 178 p. $129.95. ISBN 084930069X.

An overview for forensic practitioners of the statistical tools and methodology of glass evidence interpretation in a Bayesian context.

395.    Budworth, Geoffrey. *Knots and crime.* London: Police Review Publishing Co. Ltd., 1985. 203 p. $10. ISBN 0851640176.

A seminal work on forensic knot analysis by a renowned authority and proponent of modern forensic knot analysis.

396.    Houck, Max M. *Mute witnesses: Trace evidence analysis.* San Diego, CA: Academic Press, 2001. 192 p. $74.95. ISBN 0123567602.

Chapters are case histories written by the forensic scientists who actually investigated them, illustrating the science of trace evidence analysis. This volume is especially useful to those new to the field, but it is just as appealing to experienced analysts.

397.    Inman, Keith, and Norah Rudin. *Principles and practice of criminalistics: The profession of forensic science.* Boca Raton, FL: CRC Press, 2001. 392 p. $89.95. ISBN 0849381274.

Unlike other criminalistics books that are written for the investigator, attorney, beginning student, or the lay public, this book is written specifically for the forensic science professional. It assumes a strong background and familiarity with the physical and forensic sciences. This is a thinker's book.

398.    Ashbaugh, David R. *Quantitative-qualitative friction ridge analysis: An introduction to basic and advanced ridgeology.* Boca Raton, FL: CRC Press, 1999. 234 p. $79.95. ISBN 0849370078.

A classic text for all latent print examiners. It goes into great detail, which may not be understandable to those without a background in the area.

399.    Houck, Max, M. *Trace evidence analysis: More cases in mute witnesses.* Burlington, MA: Elsevier Academic Press, 2004. 259 p. $69.95. ISBN 0123567610.

Another fascinating volume of cases on trace evidence analysis.

**DNA Analysis** *(see also Statistics)*

400.    Kobilinsky, Lawrence, Thomas F. Liotti, and Jamel Oeser-Sweat. *DNA: Forensic and legal applications.* Hoboken, NJ: John Wiley & Sons, Inc., 2005. 381 p. $89.95. ISBN 0471414786.

A comprehensive and invaluable guide to the science of DNA identification and presenting and explaining that science in a court of law. It is written primarily for lawyers, students of science and law, and forensic scientists who do not currently work in the field of DNA identification but who want to know more about the scientific and legal procedures involved.

401.    Budowle, Bruce, Jenifer A. L. Smith, Tamyra Moretti, and Joseph DiZinno. *DNA typing protocols: Molecular biology and forensic analysis.* Natick, MA: Eaton Publishing, 2000. 304 p. $54.95. ISBN 1881299236.

This is a lab manual detailing a comprehensive compendium of DNA typing techniques compiled by a team of molecular biologists from the FBI. This is an extremely useful publication for forensic students and experts alike.

402.    Lincoln, Patrick J., and Jim Thomson, eds. *Forensic DNA profiling protocols.* Totowa, NJ: Humana Press Inc., 1998. 309 p. $99.50. ISBN 0896034437.

A highly useful compilation of the major lab procedures in human identification aimed at the practicing scientist. It also contains information of value to forensic students.

403.    Butler, John M. *Forensic DNA typing: Biology, technology, and genetics behind STR markers.* 2nd ed. Burlington, MA: Elsevier Academic Press, 2005. 688 p. $79.95. ISBN 0121479528.

An excellent detailed guide for forensic scientists, providing a single source of information about STR typing.

404.    Rudin, Norah, and Keith Inman. *An introduction to forensic DNA analysis.* 2nd ed. Boca Raton, FL: CRC Press, 2002. 292 p. $79.95. ISBN 0849302331.

A concise guide to DNA analysis aimed at the layperson or those tangentially involved in forensics. Information on outdated methods, such as RFLP and DQá/ Polymarker, which was detailed in the first edition, is still included in the second edition. Readers should beware of this.

**Engineering**

405.    Carper, Kenneth L., ed. *Forensic engineering.* 2nd ed. Boca Raton, FL: CRC Press, 2001. 401 p. $99.95. ISBN 0849374847.

Each chapter is written by specialists in their respective fields, with the intention of providing an overview of several fields in forensic engineering.

406.    Brown, John Fiske, Kenneth S. Obenski, and Thomas R. Osborn. *Forensic engineering reconstruction of accidents.* 2nd ed. Springfield, IL: Charles C.

Thomas, 2002. 271 p. $56.95 (cl.), $38.95 (pbk.). ISBN 0398073406 (cl.), 0398073414 (pbk.).

This book is intended as an introduction to traffic accident reconstruction, with principles presented simply and understandably for the investigator, attorney, or other nontechnical reader.

407.    Ratay, Robert T., ed. *Forensic structural engineering handbook.* New York, NY: McGraw-Hill, 2000. 791 p. $99.95. ISBN 0070526672.

A comprehensive, practical reference book on the investigation of structural failures. It addresses technical, nontechnical, and legal matters related to an investigation. Its intended audience is structural engineers.

408.    Lewis, Gary L., ed. *Guidelines for forensic engineering practice.* Forensic Engineering Practice Committee, Technical Council on Forensic Engineering, American Society of Civil Engineers. Reston, VA: American Society of Civil Engineers, 2003. 140 p. $45. ISBN 078440688X.

Written by a committee of the American Society of Civil Engineers, these guidelines are for civil engineers who might be called upon to testify as an expert witness. Topics covered include qualifications, investigations, ethics, a brief overview of the court system applied to the construction industry, and the nontechnical management side of forensic engineering practices.

409.    Campbell, Peter, ed. *Learning from construction failures: Applied forensic engineering.* Caithness, U.K.: Whittles Publishing, 2001. 356 p. $90. ISBN 047039949X.

Written by numerous international experts, this text explores the various areas of forensic engineering, with an emphasis on the United States and the United Kingdom.

410.    Van Kirk, Donald J. *Vehicular accident investigation and reconstruction.* Boca Raton, FL: CRC Press, 2001. 512 p. $99.95. ISBN 0849320208.

A step-by-step guide to analyzing vehicular accidents, for the novice and professional.

## Entomology

411.    Catts, Elmer Paul, and Neal H. Haskell, eds. *Entomology and death: A procedural guide.* Clemson, SC: Joyce's Print Shop, Inc., 1990. 182 p. $25. ISBN 0962869600.

A useful guide for forensic investigators, especially those without an entomological background, but the information is in need of revision.

412.    Greenberg, Bernard, and John Charles Kunich. *Entomology and the law: Flies as forensic indicators.* Cambridge: Cambridge University Press, 2002. 306 p. $100. ISBN 0521809150.

Greenberg is considered the father of forensic entomology in America. Written for entomologists, law enforcement personnel, and lawyers preparing for trial, Part I focuses on carrion flies whereas Part II focuses on law and scientific evidence worldwide (although there is an American emphasis). An extensive reference list at the end of Part I is a boon of information for the researcher.

413.    Goff, Madison Lee. *A fly for the prosecution: How insect evidence helps solve crimes.* Cambridge, MA: Harvard University Press, 2000. 225 p. $25. ISBN 0674002202.

Primarily aimed a general audience, this publication provides a useful, if geographically limited, overview of forensic entomology, including case examples. Highly readable.

414.    Byrd, Jason H., and James L. Castner, eds. *Forensic entomology: The utility of arthropods in legal investigations.* Boca Raton, FL: CRC Press, 2001. 418 p. $139.95. ISBN 0849381207.

Each chapter is written by leading forensic entomologists bringing together the results of research past and current. A background in entomology by the reader makes the text more useful.

415.    Smith, Kenneth George Valentine. *A manual of forensic entomology.* Ithaca, NY: Cornell University Press, 1986. 205 p. ISBN 0801419271.

A wealth of information that is still quite useful, although some information needs to be updated.

**Environmental and Wildlife**

416.    Morrison, Robert D. *Environmental forensics: principles & applications.* Boca Raton, FL: CRC Press, 2000. 351 p. $99.95. ISBN 0849320585.

A good text for the environmental scientist or the well-informed attorney. It is not a quick reference book.

417.    Murphy, Brian L., and Robert D. Morrison, eds. *Introduction to environmental forensics.* San Diego, CA: Academic Press, 2002. 560 p. $84.95. ISBN 0125113552.

An excellent introductory text for all audiences that also manages to cover the topic of environmental forensics comprehensively.

418.    Sullivan, Patrick J., Franklin J. Agardy, and Richard K. Traub. *Practical environmental forensics: Process and case histories.* New York, NY: John Wiley & Sons, Inc., 2001. 606 p. $130. ISBN 0471353981.

Compiled by experts in the field, the primary goal of this text is to help engineering and scientific professionals understand the forensic process related to environmental problems. It is useful for anyone whose work involves environmental contamination.

## Ethics

419.    Barnett, Peter D. *Ethics in forensic science: Professional standards for the practice of criminalistics.* Boca Raton, FL: CRC Press, 2001. 231 p. $84.95. ISBN 0849308607.

Excellent as a source of discussion topics—especially the case studies—for training scientists new to the field.

## Explosives and Fire

420.    Yereance, Robert A. *Electrical fire analysis.* 2nd ed. Springfield, IL: Charles C Thomas, 1995. 343 p. $83.95 (cl.), $52.95 (pbk.). ISBN 039805987X (cl.), 0398059888 (pbk.).

Written by an electrical engineer with years of experience investigating fires of electrical origin, this detailed guide is a must-have for fire investigators.

421.    Karlsson, Björn, and James G. Quintiere. *Enclosure fire dynamics.* Boca Raton, FL: CRC Press, 2000. 315 p. $99.95. ISBN 0849313007.

This is a textbook for those with a basic knowledge of mathematics, physics, chemistry, and heat transfer, on the behavior of fire in an enclosed space by two experts in the field of fire protection engineering. It is also a useful resource for the practicing fire investigator.

422.    Yinon, Jehuda. *Forensic and environmental detection of explosives.* New York, NY: John Wiley & Sons, Inc., 1999. 302 p. $287. ISBN 0471983713.

Yinon is a world-renowned expert on the analysis of explosives. This reference book complements Yonon's previous book, *Modern methods and applications in analysis of explosives.* It is highly recommended for those working in this area.

423.   Icove, David J., and John David DeHaan. *Forensic fire scene recon-struction.* Upper Saddle River, NJ: Pearson Education, Inc., 2004. 397 p. $66.80. ISBN 0130942057.

This textbook for fire and law enforcement investigators, prosecutors, and forensic scientists is written by a principal member of the NFPA 921 Technical Committee on Fire Investigations (Icove) and the author of *Kirk's Fire Investigation* (DeHaan). It describes and illustrates a new systematic approach for reconstructing fire scenes.

424.   Beveridge, Alexander, ed. *Forensic investigation of explosions.* London: Taylor & Francis Ltd., 1998. 512 p. $179.95. ISBN 0748405658.

A multidisciplinary reference for professionals, students of the forensic sciences, and law enforcement and legal personnel who need a readable account of the topic. Each chapter is written by a different practitioner in the field.

425.   Technical Working Group for Bombing Scene Investigation. *A guide for explosion and bombing scene investigation.* Washington, DC: U.S. Dept. of Justice, Office of Justice Programs, National Institute of Justice, 2000. 52 p. Free. http://www.ncjrs.org/pdffiles1/nij/181869.pdf (accessed January 12, 2005).

An outline of investigative tasks that should be considered at every explosion scene. The guide was created by a working group of experts on explosions and bombing investigations.

426.   DeHaan, John David. *Kirk's fire investigation.* 5th ed. Upper Saddle River, NJ: Prentice Hall, 2002. 656 p. $74.33. ISBN 0130604585.

Written by a forensic scientist with extensive training and experience in fire investigation, the latest edition of this classic text has been updated and expanded in closer accordance with *NFPA 921: Guide for fire and explosion investigations.*

427.   Yinon, Jehuda, and Shmuel Zitrin. *Modern methods and applications in analysis of explosives.* Chichester, U.K.: John Wiley & Sons Ltd., 1993. 316 p. $150 (pbk.). ISBN 0471965626.

This publication is written as a reference book for forensic chemists and graduate students. It should be used in conjunction with the author's other book on the topic, *Forensic and environmental detection of explosives.*

428.   *NFPA 921: Guide for fire and explosion investigations.* Quincy, MA: National Fire Protection Association, 2004. 262 p. $48.

The benchmark for safe and systematic fire and explosion investigations. Material from this guide is often used in certification courses.

429.   Mader, Charles L. *Numerical modeling of explosives and propellants*. 2nd ed. Boca Raton, FL: CRC Press, 1998. 451 p. $149.95. ISBN 0849331498.

An update of the author's landmark *Numerical modeling of detonations*, the second edition incorporates the use of the computer for numerical modeling of explosives and propellants, including three-dimensional modeling techniques. A CD-ROM is included with the programs used for modeling. It is written for the practitioner, so a background in the field is needed to best understand the text.

### Firearms, Tool Marks, and Ballistics

430.   Wilber, Charles G. *Ballistic science for the law enforcement officer*. Springfield, IL: Charles C Thomas, 1977. 309 p. ISBN 0398035792.

This book presents the science of ballistics, explaining the basic laws and principles governing the functioning of firearms at a level for those without an extensive knowledge of physics and mathematics.

431.   Schwoeble, A. J., and David L. Exline. *Current methods in forensic gunshot residue analysis*. Boca Raton, FL: CRC Press, 2000. 169 p. $99.95. ISBN 0849300290.

Useful for the beginning gunshot residue examiner, especially the extensive bibliography. Tends to focus on SEM/EDS (scanning electron microscope/ energy dispersive spectroscopy) as an analytical method, with little mentioned on other methods.

432.   Warlow, Tom. *Firearms, the law, and forensic ballistics*. 2nd ed. Boca Raton, FL: CRC Press, 2004. 456 p. $79.95. ISBN 0415316014.

Of particular value to those training in the forensic examination of firearms, Warlow covers a vast volume of information in this updated edition. The chapter on presentation of evidence to the courts focuses on the British court system, but the rest of the book is applicable to all geographic areas.

433.   Committee on Scientific Assessment of Bullet Lead Elemental Compo- sition Comparison, Board on Chemical Sciences and Technology, Division of Earth and Life Studies, National Research Council of the National Academies. *Forensic analysis: Weighing bullet lead evidence*. Washington, DC: National Academies Press, 2004. 226 p. $47. ISBN 0309090792 (pbk.), 0309527562 (PDF). http://www.nap.edu/books/0309090792/html/ (accessed December 12, 2004).

An impartial assessment of the soundness of the scientific principles under- lying the Compositional Analysis of Bullet Lead (CABL).

434.    DiMaio, Vincent J. M. *Gunshot wounds: Practical aspects of firearms, ballistics, and forensic techniques.* 2nd ed. Boca Raton, FL: CRC Press, 1999. 417 p. $99.95. ISBN 0849381630.

The second edition of this comprehensive text on gunshot wounds, including the forensic aspects of ballistics, makes this a must-read for the forensic firearms community.

435.    Heard, Brian J. *Handbook of firearms and ballistics: Examining and interpreting forensic evidence.* Chichester, U.K.: John Wiley & Sons Ltd., 1997. 278 p. $135. ISBN 0471965634.

An instructional text on firearms and ballistics, written for the practicing criminal lawyer and forensic science student. There are some printing errors that were widely discussed at the time it was published by firearms experts, so use the information with care.

436.    Rinker, Robert A. *Understanding firearm ballistics: Basic to advanced ballistics simplified, illustrated, and explained.* 4th ed. Apache Junction, AZ: Mulberry House Publishing, 2000. 427 p. $24.95. ISBN 0964559846.

A large amount of information on the science of ballistics explained for the understanding of all levels of knowledge. The presentation is less than appealing, but the content is useful.

437.    Sellier, Karl G., and Beat P. Kneubuehl. *Wound ballistics and the scientific background.* Amsterdam: Elsevier, 1994. 501 p. $158. ISBN 0444815112.

A text on the penetration behavior of bullets, fragments, and jets in the human body, from a physical and biological point of view. Extensive scientific knowledge is required for understanding this text.

## Linguistics/Stylistics/Phonetics

438.    McMenamin, Gerald R. *Forensic linguistics: Advances in forensic stylistics.* Boca Raton, FL: CRC Press, 2002. 355 p. $79.95. ISBN 0849309662.

An introduction to the field of forensic stylistics, updating the author's 1993 book. McMenamin writes extensively on forensic linguistics.

439.    Olsson, John. *Forensic linguistics: An introduction to language, crime, and the law.* London: Continuum, 2004. 269 p. $140 (cl.), $32.95 (pbk.). ISBN 0826461085 (cl.), 0826461093 (pbk.).

Intended as a core text for forensic linguistics courses, this text is best suited to forensic science students, not students of traditional academic linguistics. Olsson, a practitioner and academic linguist, delves into the many subdisciplines, looking at techniques for use in forensic linguistics and how forensic linguistics can be used at the investigation level. Legal discussions are not limited to the U.S. legal system.

440.   Rose, Philip. *Forensic speaker identification.* London: Taylor & Francis, 2002. 364 p. $129.95. ISBN 0415271827.

This highly detailed text is a must-read for forensic speaker identification practitioners.

441.   Hollien, Harry. *Forensic voice identification.* San Diego, CA: Academic Press, 2002. 240 p. $89.95. ISBN 0123526213.

An overview of forensic voice analysis in the United States, particularly useful for its chapter on earwitness line-ups.

442.   Cotterill, Janet, ed. *Language in the legal process.* New York, NY: Palgrave Macmillan, 2002. 293 p. $75 (cl.), $24.95 (pbk.). ISBN 0333969022 (cl.), 140393388X (pbk.).

An overview of current and ongoing issues in forensic linguistics and language and the law, gathering together content from some of the key researchers in this field from around the world.

**Odontology**

443.   Dorion, Robert B. J. *Bitemark evidence.* Boca Raton, FL: Dekker/CRC Press, 2004. 680 p. $129.95. ISBN 082475414X.

The first textbook devoted to the topic of bitemark evidence, bringing together the most current techniques of bitemark analysis from a team of 21 experts in the field.

444.   Johansen, Raymond J., and C. Michael Bowers. *Digital analysis of bite mark evidence using Adobe Photoshop.* Santa Barbara, CA: Forensic Imaging Services, 2000. 112 p. $79. ISBN 0967786606.

A practical step-by-step description of digital methods for analyzing bitemark evidence.

445.   Bowers, C. Michael. *Forensic dental evidence: An investigator's handbook.* San Diego, CA: Elsevier Academic Press, 2004. 231 p. $59.95. ISBN 0121210421.

This overview of forensic dentistry is written for law enforcement and legal professionals.

446.  Stimson, Paul G., and Curtis A. Mertz, eds. *Forensic dentistry.* Boca Raton, FL: CRC Press, 1997. 301 p. $119.95. ISBN 0849381037.

This is an excellent review text on forensic dentistry.

447.  Bowers, C. Michael, and Gary L. Bell, eds. *Manual of forensic odontology.* 3rd ed. Saratoga Springs, NY: American Society of Forensic Odontology, 1997. 357 p. $79. ISBN 0965022358.

This is a reprint of the successful 1995 third edition. It is meant as an overview of the field of forensic dentistry.

## Pathology

448.  Henssge, Claus, Bernard Knight, Thomas Krompecher, Burkhard Madea, and Leonard Nokes. *The estimation of the time since death in the early post-mortem period.* 2nd ed. London: Arnold, 2002. 271 p. $98.50. ISBN 0340719605.

The primary audience for this worthy addition to death investigation literature is death investigators, but a strong background in calculus is recommended.

449.  DiMaio, Vincent J. M., and Dominick DiMaio. *Forensic pathology.* 2nd ed. Boca Raton, FL: CRC Press, 2001. 565 p. $99.95. ISBN 084930072X.

A compact overview of forensic pathology for students and non-pathologists.

450.  Brogdon, Byron Gilliam. *Forensic radiology.* Boca Raton, FL: CRC Press, 1998. 477 p. $129.95. ISBN 0849381053.

The first book to cover the entire spectrum of forensic radiology, this text is not just for radiologists, but for everyone in forensics.

451.  Dix, Jay, and Robert Calaluce. *Guide to forensic pathology.* Boca Raton, FL: CRC Press, 1999. 257 p. $39.95. ISBN 0849302676.

The authors intended this book primarily as a guide for death investigators, but it is more for the novice with an interest in forensic pathology.

## Photography and Imaging

452.  Siljander, Raymond P., and Darin D. Fredrickson. *Applied police and fire photography.* 2nd ed. Springfield, IL: Charles C Thomas, 1997. 375 p. $97.95. ISBN 0398066876.

A welcome update to an excellent book. It is useful for both the experienced and novice forensic photographer.

453.    Staggs, Steven. *Crime scene and evidence photographer's guide.* Temecula, CA: Staggs Publishing, 1997. 64 p. $24.95. ISBN 0966197003.

A field reference for forensic photographers, it is designed to be carried in a camera bag or evidence kit.

454.    Blitzer, Herbert L., and Jack Jacobia. *Forensic digital imaging and photography.* San Diego, CA: Academic Press, 2002. 270 p. $83.95. ISBN 0121064115.

A hands-on guide to how and when to use digital cameras in a forensic setting. A CD-ROM is included with practical examples. It is written for a broad audience, from lawyers to the forensic photographer, but it will be most useful to the novice.

455.    Russ, John C. *Forensic uses of digital imaging.* Boca Raton, FL: CRC Press, 2001. 200 p. $94.95. ISBN 0849309034.

Written by the author of the bestselling *Image processing handbook*, this step-by-step guide shows how to use digital imaging to its best advantage. This book is very accessible to the non-"techie."

456.    Miller, Larry S. *Police photography.* 4th ed. Cincinnati, OH: Anderson Publishing Co., 1998. 288 p. $43.95. ISBN 087084816X.

This is the latest edition of Sam J. Sansone's classic police photography manual. It is designed to teach the fundamentals of photography and their application to police/forensic work. An extensive glossary is also included.

457.    Redsicker, David R. *The practical methodology of forensic photography.* 2nd ed. Boca Raton, FL: CRC Press, 2001. 290 p. $89.95. ISBN 0849320046.

An intermediate level how-to guide for those in the early stages of their careers and still learning the fundamentals.

**Psychology and Psychiatry**

458.    Needs, Adrian, and Graham Towl, eds. *Applying psychology to forensic practice.* Oxford, U.K.: Blackwell Publishing Ltd., 2004. 310 p. $52.95. ISBN 1405105429.

A well-written range of contributions on the recent developments in forensic psychology, useful to all forensic psychologists and forensic psychology students.

459.    Ackerman, Marc J. *Essentials of forensic psychological assessment.* New York, NY: John Wiley & Sons, Inc., 1999. 294 p. $34.95. ISBN 0471331864.

A quick reference of forensic psychology assessment techniques, and interpretive and administrative guidelines for each.

460.    Wrightsman, Lawrence S. *Forensic psychology.* Belmont, CA: Wadsworth/Thomson Learning, 2001. 479 p. $84.95. ISBN 0534526799.

A practical introduction to forensic psychology written by a practitioner in the field. Suitable for students new to the field.

461.    Gudjonsson, Gisli H., and L.R.C. Haward. *Forensic psychology: A guide to practice.* London: Routledge, 1998. 241 p. $87.95 (cl.), $34.95 (pbk.). ISBN 0415132908 (cl.), 0415132916 (pbk.).

Primarily meant to inform a U.K. forensic psychology and psychiatry audience of U.S. and European perspectives.

462.    Adler, Joanna R., ed. *Forensic psychology: Concepts, debates and practice.* Portland, OR: Willan Publishing, 2004. 361 p. $65 (cl.), $32.50 (pbk.). ISBN 1843920107 (cl.), 1843920093 (pbk.).

An intermediate textbook for forensic psychology students.

463.    Rossmo, D. Kim. *Geographic profiling.* Boca Raton, FL: CRC Press, 2000. 347 p. $89.95. ISBN 0849381290.

An extensive and exhaustive introduction to this investigative methodology. The bibliography itself is worth the read.

464.    Godwin, Grover Maurice. *Hunting serial predators: A multivariate classification approach to profiling violent behavior.* Boca Raton, FL: CRC Press, 2000. 310 p. $99.95. ISBN 0849313988.

Not suitable for the lay reader, this meticulously researched book has a great deal to offer researchers in the field of criminology and police investigators.

465.    Bartol, Curt R., and Anne M. Bartol. *Introduction to forensic psychology.* Thousand Oaks, CA: Sage Publications, Inc., 2004. 513 p. $69.95. ISBN 0761926062.

Designed for graduate and undergraduate students studying forensic psychology, this scholarly book provides a broad overview of the field, with a special focus on the application of the principles, concepts, and knowledge of psychology to the civil and criminal justice systems.

466.    Walker, Lenore E. A., and David L. Shapiro. *Introduction to forensic psychology: Clinical and social psychological perspectives.* New York, NY: Kluwer Academic/Plenum Publishers, 2003. 440 p. $69.95. ISBN 0306479087.

A comprehensive, introductory text in forensic psychology for students and practitioners. Cases and legislation are based in the U.S. legal system.

467.    Arrigo, Bruce A. *Introduction to forensic psychology: Issues and controversies in crime and justice.* San Diego, CA: Academic Press, 2000. 384 p. $66.95. ISBN 0120643502.

A U.S.-focused reference book for forensic science students and practitioners who want a quick introduction to the debates involved in the area where psychology, crime, and the law intersect. It is useful as a starting point for discussion topics, but it is too brief to serve as a comprehensive work.

468.    Craig, Robert G. *Personality-guided forensic psychology.* Washington, DC: American Psychological Association, 2005. 374 p. $59.95. ISBN 1591471516.

A guide to demonstrating the utility and relevance of assessing personality variables in forensic psychology. Indispensable for forensic psychology students and psychologists who serve as expert witnesses.

469.    Rosner, Richard, ed. *Principles and practice of forensic psychiatry.* 2nd ed. London: Arnold, 2003. 906 p. $149.50. ISBN 0340806648.

A revised and updated edition of an award-winning textbook, this is a comprehensive study of the practice of forensic psychiatry in the United States, suitable to all levels of audience.

470.    Holmes, Ronald M., and Stephen T. Holmes. *Profiling violent crimes: An investigative tool.* 3rd ed. Thousand Oaks, CA: Sage Publications, 2002. 299 p. $89.95 (cl.), $36.95 (pbk.). ISBN 0761925937 (cl.), 0761925945 (pbk.).

A thorough revision of this bestseller. It is a vital resource for students in criminology and criminal justice, as well as for criminal justice professionals and researchers.

## Questioned Documents

471.    Brunelle, Richard L., and Kenneth R. Crawford. *Advances in the forensic analysis and dating of writing ink.* Springfield, IL: Charles C Thomas, 2003. 215 p. $59.95 (cl.), $39.95 (pbk.). ISBN 0398073465 (cl.), 0398073473 (pbk.).

This update to Brunelle's 1984 *Forensic examination of ink and paper* is written for document examiners (specifically forensic chemists). It is suggested that the researcher read the 1984 book before reading this one.

472. Hilton, Ordway. *Detecting and deciphering erased pencil writing.* Springfield, IL: Charles C Thomas, 1991. 125 p. $35.95. ISBN 0398063966.

In this day and age of the pen and printer, books on pencil writing detection are not that common. Ordway's book is still of value to the document examiner.

473. Brunelle, Richard L., and Robert W. Reed. *Forensic examination of ink and paper.* Springfield, IL: Charles C Thomas, 1984. 289 p. $91.95. ISBN 0398049351.

A description of methods at the time the book was written, including the historical development of writing inks and their chemical properties, manufacturing processes, writing instruments, printing inks, typewriting inks, and the paper manufacturing process.

474. Kelly, Jan Seaman. *Forensic examination of rubber stamps: A practical guide.* Springfield, IL: Charles C Thomas, 2002. 221 p. $61.95 (cl.), $40.95 (pbk.). ISBN 0398072787 (cl.), 0398072795 (pbk.).

There is a lack of contemporary literature on the topic of rubber stamps, so this publication is a welcome addition in this field.

475. Morris, Ron. *Forensic handwriting identification: Fundamental concepts and principles.* San Diego, CA: Academic Press, 2000. 238 p. $79.95. ISBN 0125076401.

A solid grounding in basic concepts and principles for those with little or no experience in this field. It has limited usefulness for the veteran investigator.

476. Slyter, Steven A. *Forensic signature examination.* Springfield, IL: Charles C Thomas, 1995. 117 p. $42.95 (cl.), 28.95 (pbk.). ISBN 0398065411 (cl.), 039806542X (pbk.).

Slyter presents working parameters and systems he has developed in his 25 years of experience as a handwriting expert.

477. Huber, Roy A., and Alfred M. Headrick. *Handwriting identification: Facts and fundamentals.* Boca Raton, FL: CRC Press, 1999. 435 p. $89.95. ISBN 084931285X.

Overall an excellent book for forensic handwriting examiners.

478. van Renesse, Rudolf L., ed. *Optical document security.* 3rd ed. Norwood, MA: Artech House, Inc., 2005. 386 p. $139. ISBN 1580532586.

Unlike the second edition, which was a compilation of related articles on the topic of optical document security, the third edition is a more comprehensive and cohesive treatment of the topic.

479.    Ellen, David. *The scientific examination of documents: Methods and techniques.* 2nd ed. London: Taylor & Francis, 1997. 180 p. $99.95. ISBN 0748405801.

A useful outline of the methods and techniques suitable for an audience outside the field of document examination.

480.    Hilton, Ordway. *Scientific examination of questioned documents.* Rev. ed. Boca Raton, FL: CRC Press, 1993. 424 p. $169.95. ISBN 0849395100.

Reprint of a 1982 revised edition. Hilton is one of the better-known experts in this field.

### Scientific Testimony/Expert Witnessing

481.    Babitsky, Steven, and James J. Mangraviti. *Cross-examination: The comprehensive guide for experts.* Falmouth, MA: SEAK, Inc., 2003. 432 p. $99.95. ISBN 1892904233.

Suitable for expert witnesses testifying in trials, this excellent resource provides invaluable explanations of the process of testimony and cross-examination.

482.    Matson, Jack V., Suha F. Daou, and Jeffrey G. Soper. *Effective expert witnessing: Practices for the 21st century.* 4th ed. Boca Raton, FL: CRC Press, 2004. 160 p. $94.95. ISBN 0849313015.

An update to the bestselling third edition, this text presents the fundamentals of the litigation process and recent legal rulings and their application in recent litigation. The book and the accompanying CD-ROM video are indispensable to all who have to testify as expert witnesses.

483.    Telpner, Zeph, and Michael Mostek. *Expert witnessing in forensic accounting: A handbook for lawyers and accountants.* Boca Raton, FL: CRC Press, 2003. 360 p. $84.95. ISBN 0849308984.

Specifically aimed at forensic accountants and lawyers, this guide to testifying as an expert relates the experiences of the authors (certified public accountant and a trial lawyer) in this arena—the mistakes and the triumphs—and uses these experiences to present guidelines for both groups.

484.    Kiely, Terrence F. *Forensic evidence: Science and the criminal law.* Boca Raton, FL: CRC Press, 2001. 368 p. $94.95. ISBN 0849318963.

A useful primer for attorneys and forensic scientists on the most recent state and federal court decisions that address the use of forensic science in the investigation and trial of criminal cases.

## Statistics

485.    Good, Phillip I. *Applying statistics in the courtroom: A new approach for attorneys and expert witnesses.* Boca Raton, FL: Chapman & Hall/CRC Press LLC, 2001. 276 p. $79.95. ISBN 1584882719.

Aimed squarely at statisticians and attorneys who are at a level where they know little about each other's professions. Not really of interest to forensic scientists.

486.    Buckleton, John, Christopher M. Triggs, and Simon J. Walsh, eds. *Forensic DNA evidence interpretation.* Boca Raton, FL: CRC Press, 2005. 548 p. $129.95. ISBN 0849330173.

This book is written to be compatible with Evett and Weir's landmark textbook *Interpreting DNA evidence.* It includes developments in the six years since their book was published and is written for less mathematically inclined practitioners. The focus of this book is the Bayesian method, mostly used in Europe.

487.    Evett, Ian W., and Bruce S. Weir. *Interpreting DNA evidence: Statistical genetics for forensic scientists.* Sunderland, MA: Sinauer Associates, Inc., 1998. 293 p. $44.95. ISBN 0878931554.

A landmark textbook on interpreting DNA evidence. The core reader for this well-written, comprehensive volume is a forensic scientist with a degree in one of the biological sciences, although the authors have made the mathematics as simple as possible. Mitochondrial DNA evidence is not included. The focus of this book is the Bayesian method, mostly used in Europe.

488.    Royall, Richard M. *Statistical evidence: A likelihood paradigm.* London: Chapman & Hall, 1997. 191 p. $79.95. ISBN 0412044110.

A noted expert in this field, Royall has written a book on an alternative theory that will appeal to anyone who deals with statistical evidence.

489.    Gastwirth, Joseph L., ed. *Statistical science in the courtroom.* New York, NY: Springer-Verlag New York, Inc., 2000. 443 p. $64.95. ISBN 0387989978.

A collection of articles written by statisticians and legal scholars on the use of statistical evidence in the courtroom. A background in statistics is helpful when reading this worthwhile addition to the literature.

490.    Aitken, Colin G. G., and Franco Taroni. *Statistics and the evaluation of evidence for forensic scientists.* 2nd ed. West Sussex, U.K.: John Wiley & Sons Ltd., 2004. 540 p. $120. ISBN 0470843675.

A fully revised and updated edition of Aitken's authoritative work in the field. It is a useful book for grasping the fundamentals of the use and interpretation of statistics in the courtroom, for forensic scientists.

# 5
# Online Sources

Forensic science sites on the Internet have multiplied exponentially with the advent of television shows such as *CSI: Crime Scene Investigation*. Sites are produced by government and professional organizations, by forensic specialists, as well as by forensic scientist aspirants. With all of these sites to choose from, this chapter is intended to identify some of the more useful resources on the Internet. It is adapted and updated from a Webliography written by the author and published in the Spring 2003 issue of *Issues in Science and Technology Librarianship*, http://www.istl.org/03-spring/internet.html (accessed January 23, 2005).

## Starting Points

Metasites include the most frequently used Web sites for forensic science research and information; however, these sites are by no means comprehensive. Below is a list of the most popular metasites for forensic science research resources. Resources on these sites will overlap, although each also has unique links.

491. **Google Web Directory in Forensic Sciences.** http://directory. google.com/Top/Science/Science_in_Society/Forensic_Science/ (accessed January 23, 2005).
   Resources in the Google Web Directory in Forensic Sciences are arranged in a similar manner to the Yahoo directory. Google is a true search engine in that it has a robot or a software program that searches and indexes the Web. The Google

Web Directory integrates Google's sophisticated search technology with Open Directory pages. Web Directory pages are enhanced with importance ranking. The Web pages in the Google directory have been selected by thousands of volunteer editors from the Netscape Open Directory Project, a large public directory managed by Netscape.

492.  **Kruglick's Forensic Resource and Criminal Law Search Site.** http://www.kruglaw.com/ (accessed January 23, 2005).

Created by Kim Kruglick, a criminal defense lawyer in Mill Valley, California, this site pulls together resources arranged by forensic subspecialty. To see the forensic science categories from the main page, click on "Links to Over 1,000 Forensic Sites." The "Beginner's Primer on the Investigation of Forensic Evidence" link on the main page leads to some useful primers in forensic sciences. Each of the subject pages provides a link to a bibliography in that area, although the bibliographies are sometimes out-of-date.

493.  **Kulesh's Forensic Page.** http://vip.poly.edu/kulesh/forensics/list.htm (accessed January 23, 2005).

With the increasing growth of computer crimes in the world, the forensic sciences have seen the establishment of a new breed of forensic scientist, the cybercrime specialist. Kulesh Shanmugasundaram, a graduate student in the computer science department at Polytechnic University in New York, has created a growing list of digital/cyber/computational forensic–related resources. Although it may not be flashy and it lacks annotations, it is extensive. Resources are arranged into these categories: Conferences, People, "R&D Groups/Projects/News Groups," "News Groups/Mailing Lists, Papers, Articles/FAQs/Talks," Forensic Books, Tools, Other Forensic Links, and Organizations and Conferences.

494.  **Reddy's Forensic Page.** http://www.forensicpage.com/ (accessed January 23, 2005).

Reddy P. Chamakura is a forensic scientist with the Police Laboratory, New York City Police Department. Links to sites include, but are not limited to, forensic science organizations, forensic science journals, colleges/universities with forensic programs, job opportunities, forensic science laboratories, law enforcement agencies, forensic homepages, forensic chemistry/narcotics, mass spectrometry, fingerprints, ballistics/firearms, microscopy, crime scene processing/investigation/photography, arson, DNA, toxicology, questioned documents, digital photography/imaging, image enhancing, Web publishing/Internet, and forensic mailing lists.

495. **Yahoo Directory of Forensic Science Resources.** http://www.yahoo.com/science/forensics/ (accessed January 23, 2005).

Resources in this Yahoo directory are arranged by broad subject categories: Bloodstain Pattern Analysis, College and University Departments and Programs, Companies, Computer Forensics, DNA Evidence, Forensic Anthropology, Forensic Art, Forensic Document Examination, Forensic Entomology, Forensic Fingerprinting, Forensic Nursing, Forensic Odontology, Forensic Psychiatry, Forensic Psychology, Forensic Toxicology, Government Laboratories, Organizations, Research, and Web Directories. Yahoo is a searchable directory built by humans. They have a team of real live humans (Yahoo! Surfers), who visit and evaluate suggested sites and decide where they best belong.

496. **Zeno's Forensic Site.** http://forensic.to/forensic.html (accessed January 23, 2005).

Zeno Geradts is a forensic scientist at the Netherlands Forensic Institute of the Ministry of Justice at the Digital Evidence section in the area of forensic (video) image processing and pattern recognition. This comprehensive page is one of the most complete sites in the field. Zeno has links to an extensive collection of sites arranged by subspecialty, including—but not limited to—DNA, hair and fiber, firearms, handwriting, forensic entomology, and forensic anthropology.

# Societies, Associations, and Other Organizations

Links and information on societies, associations, and other organizations related to forensics are listed in Chapter 6. Specialty-specific organizations are listed in each specialty's section in this chapter if they provide access to significant resources on their Web sites. More information is available on specialty-specific organizations in Chapter 6.

# Education and Employment

497. **American Academy of Forensic Sciences Job Opportunities List.** http://www.aafs.org/default.asp?section_id=employment&page_id=current_openings (accessed January 23, 2005).

This is the main online job list for forensic scientists. Positions, covering the whole gamut of the forensic sciences, remain posted until the application deadline or, if no deadline is listed, for 60 days.

498.    **American Academy of Forensic Sciences Colleges & Universities.** http://www.aafs.org/default.asp?section_id=resources&page_id=colleges_and_ universities (accessed May 15, 2005).

The American Academy of Forensic Sciences maintains a list of forensic sciences programs in the United States and abroad. Programs are arranged under the following categories: (1) programs accredited by the AAFS Forensic Science Education Programs Accreditation Commission (FEPAC), (2) undergraduate programs within the United States, (3) undergraduate programs outside the United States, (4) graduate programs within the United States, (5) graduate programs outside the United States, (6) doctoral programs, and (7) undergraduate and graduate degrees in dentistry.

499.    **Anil Aggrawal's Forensic Careers Page.** http://www.fortunecity.com/ campus/electrical/314/career.html (accessed January 23, 2005).

Created by Anil Aggrawal (a professor of forensic medicine at the Maulana Azad Medical College in New Delhi, India), this site lists job opportunities in forensic toxicology in India. The FAQs at the bottom of the page and links to practitioners working in particular specialties in forensics are also quite useful and are not limited to India.

500.    **Choosing a Career.** http://www.aafs.org/default.asp?section_id=resources &page_id=choosing_a_career (accessed May 11, 2005).

Created by the Forensic Sciences Foundation, Inc. (American Academy of Forensic Sciences), this online guide provides an overview of what forensic scientists do, how to become a forensic scientist, and the different disciplines in the forensic sciences. There is also a resource list at the end of career information sites.

501.    **National Association of Medical Examiners Jobs Web Page.** http:// www.thename.org/ (accessed October 12, 2005).

Although the association name implies medical examiner positions, there are several forensic pathologist positions included in this site. Click on the Jobs link.

502.    **Zeno's Forensic Site Employment Links.** http://forensic.to/links/pages/ General_information_resources/Jobs/ (accessed January 23, 2005).

A collection of Web site links maintained by Zeno Geradts, the creator of Zeno's Forensic Site (see above), to sites with employment opportunities.

# Anthropology

503.    **International Association for Craniofacial Identification (IACI).** http:// www.forensicartist.com/IACI/index.html (accessed January 23, 2005).

The IACI, formed in 1988, is an organization comprised mainly of medical and scientific professionals throughout the world who specialize in Forensic Odontology, Forensic Anthropology, 2- and 3-dimensional Skull Reconstruction Techniques, Computer-Based Skull Reconstruction, Facial Aging for Law Enforcement, and Facial Mapping, as well as Composite Sketching. The Craniofacial Identification Links (http://www.forensicartist.com/IACI/links.html) are particularly useful. Craniofacial Identification Links are arranged into two columns, with no annotations. Links range from traditional to computerized methods of craniofacial reconstruction.

504.    **Forensic Art.** http://www.forensicartist.com/index.html (accessed January 23, 2005).

The site covers the various facets of forensic art, giving a brief description of each. This site is maintained by Wesley Neville, a forensic artist and polygraphist with the Florence County Sheriff's Office in Florence, South Carolina, and a member of the International Association for Identification (IAI) forensic art subcommittee. The abundance of graphics makes the site slow to load, but a lot of images are to be expected on an "art" site. The red print on black background and tiny font size might make the site somewhat hard to read for some folks, but persevere, as there are some excellent resources here.

505.    **OsteoInteractive.** http://medstat.med.utah.edu/kw/osteo/index2.html (accessed January 23, 2005).

A great introduction to human osteology, forensic anthropology, paleopathology, and histology by experts in their fields. Topics include age, sex, stature, race, pathology, trauma, taphonomy, identifying characteristics, and graduate education in forensic anthropology.

# Botany

506.    **Forensic Botany.** http://myweb.dal.ca/jvandomm/forensicbotany/ (accessed May 18, 2005).

One of the few comprehensive sites on the subject, the Forensic Botany site was created in 2002 as a project in the Web Literacy for the Natural Sciences class at Dalhousie University, Halifax, Canada. It offers excellent information through literature citations with information and definitions of the subdisciplines within the field, clearly explains botanical uses within forensics, and provides case examples illustrating the described procedures and botanical evidence used. The Cited Literature and Links section is particularly useful.

507.  **Forensic Palynology: A New Way to Catch Crooks.** http://www.cri meandclues.com/pollen.htm (accessed January 23, 2005).

A comprehensive overview of the field of palynology, the study of palyno-morphs (pollen) trapped in materials associated with criminal or civil investi-gation, is written by Vaughn M. Bryant, Jr., Palynology Laboratory, Texas A&M University, and Dallas C. Mildenhall, Institute of Geological and Nuclear Sci-ences, New Zealand.

# Chemistry and Toxicology

508.  **Alan Barbour's Forensic Toxicology Page.** http://www.abarbour.net/ (accessed January 23, 2005).

Created by Alan Barbour, a consulting forensic toxicologist, this site provides links to forensic toxicology sites, government laboratories, and directories of forensic expert witnesses. Barbour also maintains the World Wide Web Virtual Library: Forensic Toxicology.

509.  **The International Association of Forensic Toxicologists (TIAFT).** http://www.tiaft.org/ (accessed January 23, 2005).

Founded in 1963, this association groups over 1,400 members from all regions of the world. The aims of this association are to promote cooperation and co-ordination of efforts among members and to encourage research in forensic toxicology. The members come from the police force, medical examiners and coroners' laboratories, horseracing and sports doping laboratories, hospitals, departments of legal medicine, pharmacology, pharmacy, and toxicology. Enter the Open Area for resources for nonmembers. The Observatory provides a list of Web sites arranged by categories (on the left menu bar). Also useful is the MS Library, collections of homemade reference electron impact mass spectra of derivatives produced by TIAFT members and made available freely on the In-ternet. The intent of the MS Library is to supplement commercial databases with new or uncommon substances or less frequent derivatives of drugs.

510.  **The Society of Forensic Toxicologists (SOFT).** http://www.soft-tox.org/ (accessed January 23, 2005).

SOFT, officially incorporated in 1983, is an organization composed of prac-ticing forensic toxicologists and those interested in the discipline for the purpose of promoting and developing forensic toxicology. The Toxilinks section is par-ticularly useful.

511.   **The World Wide Web Virtual Library: Forensic Toxicology.** http://home.lightspeed.net/~abarbour/vlibft.html (accessed January 23, 2005).

This site is maintained by Alan Barbour, a forensic toxicology consultant with more than twenty-five years' experience in forensic toxicology and clinical laboratory science. Links are arranged within broad categories: forensic toxicology sites, directories of forensic expert witnesses, general forensic science links, and education and career guidance in forensic sciences.

512.   **Molecular Expressions: Optical Microscopy Primer.** http://micro.magnet.fsu.edu/primer/index.html (accessed January 23, 2005).

Microscopy is a very important field in forensic sciences, as microscopes are used extensively in crime labs. For forensic science students, this site—created by Michael W. Davidson, Mortimer Abramowitz, Olympus America Inc., and the Florida State University—provides an excellent introduction to Optical Microscopy, Digital Imaging, and Photomicrography. Topics covered include the physics of light and color, an anatomy of the microscope, specialized microscopy techniques, digital imaging in optical microscopy, photomicrography, concepts and formulas in microscopy, fundamentals of stereomicroscopy, and interactive tutorials.

513.   **Guidelines for the Interpretation of Analytical Toxicology Results and Unit of Measurement Conversion Factors.** http://www.leeds.ac.uk/acb/annals/Webwise/Webwise97-1.html (accessed January 23, 2005).

This alphabetical table contains details of over 700 compounds. The table has been compiled within the limitations currently imposed by the restricted character set implemented on the World Wide Web. This limitation should be understood by all who make use of the table. This site was posted as a Web table addition to an article appearing in the *Annals of Clinical Biochemistry* in 1998 (Flanagan 1998).

514.   **ChemFinder.com.** http://chemfinder.cambridgesoft.com/ (accessed January 23, 2005).

Individual access to ChemFinder is complimentary on a limited basis. This free database includes chemical structures, physical properties, CAS Registry Numbers, and links to other Web sites with information about compounds.

515.   **Mass Spectrometry Databases.** http://www.ualberta.ca/~gjones/mslib.htm (accessed January 23, 2005).

Created by the Mass Spectrometry Database Committee of the American Academy of Forensic Sciences Toxicology Section, this site provides Zip files of a comprehensive drug mass spectral library and the latest version of the mini-library of full mass spectra of newer drugs, metabolites, and some breakdown products. This library is a subset of one that has been compiled over a period of many years by Dr. Graham Jones and colleagues in Edmonton, Alberta, Canada. Pure drug spectra, plus a few breakdown products and pure metabolite standards, have been edited into a single library. The libraries use the Hewlett Packard DOS ChemStation and UNIX ChemSystem MSD operating systems.

# Crime Scene Investigation

516.    **Crime-Scene-Investigation.net.** http://www.crime-scene-investigator.net /index.html (accessed January 23, 2005).

One-stop shopping for crime scene investigation links, articles, crime scene response and evidence collection guidelines, information on crime scene and evidence photography, training and employment, and a bookstore. Links are arranged at the top level by broad categories and by subcategories within the pages. The site is maintained by the Crime Scene Investigator Network, based in Temecula, CA.

517.    **Bloodstain Pattern Analysis Tutorial.** http://www.bloodspatter.com/ BPATutorial.htm (accessed January 23, 2005).

To provide an interpretation of the physical events that gave rise to the origin of a bloodstain, forensic scientists analyze the patterns (shapes, locations, and distribution) of the stain. This tutorial by Joseph Slemko, a forensic consultant in Alberta, Canada, provides an introduction to bloodstain pattern analysis.

518.    **Footwear & Tire Track Impression Evidence.** http://members.aol.com/ varfee/mastssite/index.html (accessed January 23, 2005).

Presented by C.A.S.T. (Chesapeake Area Shoeprint and Tire track), this site includes an interactive footwear examination tutorial for investigating shoe prints recovered from a crime scene. As well, there are extensive links on outsole evaluation, shoe and tire manufacturer contact information, tire Web sites, and instructions for evidence gathering. C.A.S.T. is a consortium of Footwear & Tire Track examiners, organized as a Multi-Agency Forensic Cooperation (MAFC) group.

# Criminalistics and Trace Evidence

519.    **Latent Print Examination: Fingerprints, Palmprints and Footprints.** http://onin.com/fp/ (accessed January 23, 2005).

An extensive Web site devoted to links on latent fingerprints, including articles and a comprehensive list of legal challenges to fingerprints. Ed German of the U.S. Army Criminal Investigation Command, U.S. Army Criminal Investigation Laboratory, maintains this site.

520.   **Marks Working Group.** http://www.intermin.fi/intermin/hankkeet/wgm/home.nsf/ (accessed January 23, 2005).

The Marks Working Group is one of the technical working groups of the European Network of Forensic Science Institutes (ENFSI) and represents examiners working with shoeprint, tool mark, and other types of visual mark comparisons in forensic laboratories. The Group publishes the *Information Bulletin for Shoeprint/Toolmark Examiners.* The Marks Working Group collects a library of articles (bibliographies) covering various subdisciplines of comparative visual examinations of interest to the mark examiners. In the Links section, this Web site provides a link to an interesting article on taking measurements of tiremarks (http://home2.pi.be/volckery/tiremarks_taking_measurements.htm).

521.   **SWGFAST: Scientific Working Group on Friction Ridge Analysis, Study and Technology.** http://www.swgfast.org/ (accessed January 23, 2005).

A scientific working group of the Federal Bureau of Investigation (FBI) to create consensus standards for fingerprint analysis and technology. Guidelines are provided in PDF format.

522.   **Ridges and Furrows.**   http://www.ridgesandfurrows.homestead.com/ (accessed January 23, 2005).

"This web site is the culmination of many hours spent researching topics related to forensic science and [the author's] particular areas of interest: embryogenesis of friction skin . . ., enhancement of latent prints using digital technology and latent print identification" (Beeton 2001). Categories include history, friction skin anatomy, friction skin growth, the integumentary system, latent print development, scientific research, fingerprint patterns, and identification. Mary Beeton, an A.F.I.S. fingerprint technician with the Durham Regional Police Service in Ontario, Canada, created this site.

523.   **Optical Mineralogy Basics.** http://www.eos.ubc.ca/courses/eosc221/optics/optics.html (accessed January 23, 2005).

An illustrated tutorial on optical mineralogy created for an introductory petrology lab at the University of British Columbia.

524.   **Minerals Under the Microscope.** http://www.gly.bris.ac.uk/www/teach/opmin/mins.html (accessed January 23, 2005).

A brief introduction to optical mineralogy created by Charlotte Gladstone at the University of Bristol Department of Earth Sciences.

525.    **Forensic Fiber Examination Guidelines.** http://www.fbi.gov/hq/lab/fsc/backissu/april1999/houcktoc.htm (accessed January 23, 2005).

Guidelines created by the Scientific Working Group on Materials Analysis (SWGMAT) at the FBI outlining fiber analysis methods for use by forensic fiber examiners. References and a bibliography are included in this article.

526.    **Hairs, Fibers, Crime, and Evidence.** http://www.fbi.gov/hq/lab/fsc/backissu/july2000/deedrick.htm (accessed January 23, 2005).

A detailed introduction and overview of hair and fiber evidence analysis written by Douglas W. Deedrick, Unit Chief of the FBI Trace Evidence Unit. It appeared in the July 2000 issue of *Forensic Science Communications.*

527.    **Microscopy of Hair Part 1: A Practical Guide and Manual for Human Hairs.** http://www.fbi.gov/hq/lab/fsc/backissu/jan2004/research/2004_01_research01b.htm (accessed January 23, 2005).

This article was published in the January 2004 issue of *Forensic Science Communications.* It was written by Douglas D. Deedrick, Supervisory Special Agent of the FBI Scientific Analysis Section, and Sandra L. Koch, Physical Scientist/Forensic Examiner of the FBI Trace Evidence Unit. This illustrated article provides an excellent look at human hair analysis.

528.    **Microscopy of Hair Part II: A Practical Guide and Manual for Animal Hairs.** http://www.fbi.gov/hq/lab/fsc/backissu/july2004/research/2004_03_research02.htm (accessed January 23, 2005).

This second article on the microscopy of hair, focusing on animal hairs, appeared in the July 2004 issue of *Forensic Science Communications.* It was written by Douglas D. Deedrick, Supervisory Special Agent of the FBI Scientific Analysis Section, and Sandra L. Koch, Physical Scientist/Forensic Examiner of the FBI Trace Evidence Unit.

# DNA Analysis

529.    **MITOMAP: A Human Mitochondrial Genome Database.** http://www.mitomap.org/ (accessed January 23, 2005).

A searchable database of human mitochondrial DNA. The Mitomap Quick Reference section includes an extensive bibliography (Mitochondrial

References) arranged alphabetically by author; the full text of the Mitochondrial Human Genome Report; Amino Acid Translation Tables; the Human Mitochondrial Sequence; a link to the Human Mitochondrial Protein Database; and Illustrations.

530.  **mtDNA Population Database.** http://www.fbi.gov/hq/lab/fsc/backissu/april2002/miller1.htm (accessed January 23, 2005).

Published in the April 2002 issue of *Forensic Science Communications*, the mtDNA Population Database "is used to assess the weight of mtDNA associations developed in forensic casework. It consists of anonymous population profiles contributed by collaborating laboratories" (Monson, Miller, Wilson, DiZinno, and Budowle, 2002). The database program (data, search software, and user's manual) can be downloaded from a link in the article. Periodic updates will be published in subsequent articles in *Forensic Science Communications*.

531.  **Mitochondrial DNA Analysis in the FBI Laboratory.** http://www.fbi.-gov/hq/lab/fsc/backissu/july1999/dnalist.htm (accessed January 23, 2005).

An informative article from *Forensic Science Communications*, the journal of the FBI Laboratory, which explains mitochondrial DNA and its use in the forensics laboratory to solve crimes.

532.  **STRBase.** http://www.cstl.nist.gov/biotech/strbase/ (accessed January 23, 2005).

Database of literature on short tandem repeat DNA, intended to benefit research and application of short tandem repeat DNA markers to human identity testing.

533.  **National Center for Biotechnology Information.** http://www.ncbi.nlm.nih.gov/ (accessed January 23, 2005).

Established in 1988 as a national resource for molecular biology information, NCBI creates public databases, conducts research in computational biology, develops software tools for analyzing genome data, and disseminates biomedical information.

534.  **Forensic Mathematics.** http://dna-view.com/ (accessed January 23, 2005).

Charles Brenner has been a consultant in forensic mathematics, which mostly pertains to DNA identification, since 1977. His well-organized site presents discussions on topics in forensic mathematics, software, data, a bibliography with links to the full text of articles, and links to other sites in forensic DNA analysis.

# Economics and Accounting

535.    **Forensic Economics and Forensic Accounting.** http://www.willyancey.com/forensic.htm (accessed January 23, 2005).

Maintained by Will Yancey (a CPA in Dallas, Texas, and a consultant on audit sampling and litigation support), this page provides one-stop shopping for resources in forensic economics and accounting. Topics covered include associations and educational programs, demographic data, financial data, journals, legal references, malpractice, money laundering and financial crimes, and software and publishers. The Forensic Economics Bibliography is particularly useful.

# Engineering

536.    **National Academy of Forensic Engineers (NAFE) Links.** http://www.nafe.org/NafeMenuLink.htm (accessed January 23, 2005).

NAFE was formed to fill the needs of those who serve as consultants to members of the legal profession and as expert witnesses. The NAFE Web site has an extensive list of links to automotive, safety, government, and organizations and institutions related to forensic engineering.

# Entomology

537.    **American Board of Forensic Entomology (ABFE).** http://www.research.missouri.edu/entomology/ (accessed January 23, 2005).

The ABFE constitutes the first step toward a professional organization with strict educational, ethical, and maintenance standards. The ABFE site provides a short but informative overview of the science and history of forensic entomology, as well as case studies in forensic entomology.

538.    **Forensic Entomology Pages, International.** http://folk.uio.no/mostarke/forens_ent/forensic_entomology.html (accessed January 23, 2005).

Created by Morten Starkeby, a graduate student in entomology at the University of Oslo, now an independent consultant in forensic entomology in Norway, this Web site provides a comprehensive overview of the many uses of insect and arthropod evidence as evidence. The organized site lists sections describing protocol and information regarding entomology in establishing time of death, movement of corpses, common insects found on bodies, and case histories.

539.   **Forensic Entomology: Insects in Legal Investigations.** http://www. forensicentomology.com/index.html (accessed January 23, 2005).

Created by Dr. J. H. Byrd of the Department of Criminal Justice at the Virginia Commonwealth University, this site includes definitions, death scene procedures, life cycles, information on entomological collection equipment, an entomological field notes death scene form in PDF, and further links.

# Ethics in the Forensic Sciences

540.   **Ethics in Science.** http://www.chem.vt.edu/chem-ed/ethics/ (accessed January 23, 2005).

A hypermedia page residing in the Department of Chemistry, Virginia Polytechnic Institute and State University, Blacksburg, VA, with links to full text articles, bibliographies, and selected essays on ethics in science. This page is no longer updated on a regular basis, but most of the links are not dependent on their currency.

541.   **American Academy of Forensic Sciences Code of Ethics and Conduct.** http://www.aafs.org/default.asp?section_id=aafs&page_id=aafs_bylaws#article2 (accessed May 13, 2005).

Article II of the American Academy of Forensic Sciences Bylaws. Violation of the provisions of the Code can result in censure, suspension, or expulsion from the Academy.

542.   **American Academy of Psychiatry and the Law Ethical Guidelines for the Practice of Forensic Psychiatry.** http://www.forensic-psych.com/articles/ artEthics.html (accessed January 23, 2005).

Ethical guidelines for forensic psychiatrists adopted May, 1987, and revised October, 1989.

543.   **American Society of Crime Lab Directors Code of Ethics.** http:// www.ascld.org/ethics.html (accessed January 23, 2005).

The major responsibility of the Ethics Committee is to handle all ethics complaints brought before the ASCLD Board of Directors and apply them to the Code of Ethics via the Enforcement Procedure of the Code of Ethics.

544.   **Academy of Behavioral Profiling Ethical Guidelines for Professional Conduct.** http://www.profiling.org/abp_conduct.html (accessed January 23, 2005).

Ethical guidelines for behavioral profilers, with sanctions for violators of those guidelines.

# Explosives

545. **International Association of Bomb Technicians and Investigators (IABTI).** http://www.iabti.org/ (accessed January 23, 2005).

Founded in 1973, the IABTI is a professional association formed for countering the use of explosives for criminal purposes. The site provides information on the organization and links to explosives manufacturers (http://www.iabti.org/manulinks.html). Links to explosives manufacturers are limited to advertisers in *The Detonator* and exhibitors at the International Association of Bomb Technicians and Investigators (IABTI) regional and international conferences. Links to bomb squad Web sites are accessible only to members.

546. **Analysis and Detection of Explosives: Published Papers, Reports and Presentations, 1988–1998.** http://www.ncfs.ucf.edu/twgfex/Analysis%20and%20Detection%20of%20Explosives.pdf (accessed January 23, 2005).

A reference bibliography compiled in 1999 by Charles R. Midkiff of the Technical Working Group for Fire and Explosives (TWGFEX) of the National Center for Forensic Science, a program of the National Institute of Justice.

# Firearms, Tool Marks, and Ballistics

547. **Association of Firearm and Tool Mark Examiners (AFTE).** http://www.afte.org/ (accessed January 23, 2005).

Formed in 1969 to address the requirements of firearms and tool mark examiners, the AFTE publishes the *AFTE Journal*. This site includes: Ammunition Manufacturers/Distributors, an alphabetical list of ammunition manufacturers and distributors; Firearm Manufacturers/Distributors, an alphabetical list of firearm manufacturers and distributors; and Ballistics Links, an alphabetically arranged metasite of ballistics links.

548. **firearmsID.com.** http://www.firearmsid.com/ (accessed January 23, 2005).

firearmsID.com is a nonprofit Web site maintained by Jeffrey Scott Doyle (firearm and tool mark examiner with the Kentucky State Police Jefferson Regional Forensic Lab), that exists solely as an educational and/or investigative aid.

This Web site provides an extensive introduction to firearms identification. It is arranged by broad categories: firearm identification, distance determinations, firearm function testing, expert witness testimony, new technologies (e.g., INIS, DrugFire), case profiles, the history of firearms ID, and career information.

549. **Firearms Tutorial.** http://medstat.med.utah.edu/WebPath/TUTORIAL/ GUNS/GUNINTRO.html (accessed January 23, 2005).

This illustrated tutorial is designed to give readers "a working knowledge of the types of firearms, the types of ammunition used, the nature of injuries that can be produced in the body, and the investigative techniques used by the forensic pathologist in assessing firearms injuries" (Klatt 2004). This tutorial is one of many created by the Internet Pathology Laboratory for Medical Education at Florida State University College of Medicine. This resource is designed for students and workers in the health care sciences studying pathology. *Warning:* Some of the images are quite graphic.

550. **How Do Bullets Fly?** http://www.nennstiel-ruprecht.de/bullfly/index.htm (accessed January 23, 2005).

This Web site attempts to explain the basics of bullet motion through the atmosphere. It avoids formulas as well as mathematics, but it does assume a familiarity with the way of physical thinking. Included are experimental observations of bullets fired from small arms, at both short and long ranges. Numerous illustrations are included and can be viewed via links. The intended audience is all levels (sportsmen, ballisticians, forensic scientists) and is intended to act as an introduction for those interested in the exterior ballistics of bullets fired from small arms. The author, Ruprecht Nennstiel of Wiesbaden, Germany, includes links to formulas related to bullet motion.

551. **The Making of a Rifled Barrel.** http://www.border-barrels.com/articles/ bmart.htm (accessed January 23, 2005).

Geoffrey Kolbe wrote this detailed article in 1995 for *Precision Shooting Annual.* Kolbe starts at the beginning, discussing the steel used in making a rifle barrel, and works his way through drilling the hole, reaming the hole, different rifling types (cut, button, and hammer), profiling, lapping, and barrel accuracy, and ends on an analysis of which rifling makes the best rifle barrel.

552. **Feasibility of a California Ballistics Identification System.** http:// caag.state.ca.us/newsalerts/2003/03-013_report.pdf (accessed January 23, 2005).

The California Department of Justice submitted the results to the legislature in January 2003 on the feasibility of a ballistic fingerprinting database in California.

The more technical information is contained in the appendices to the report. Some of the "exhibits" in the appendices are not provided full text in the report but can be found full text on the Web or by contacting the authors of each appendix.

# Linguistics

553.   **International Association of Forensic Linguists: Bibliography.** http://www.bham.ac.uk/IAFL/bib/biblio.html (accessed January 23, 2005).

This organization is comprised primarily of linguists whose work involves the law. This means linguistic evidence in court, such as authorship attribution, disputed confessions, interpreting and translating in court, the readability/comprehensibility of legal documents, and interviews with children in the legal system. The association's Web site includes a useful, searchable bibliography of notable references about forensic linguistics.

# Odontology

554.   **American Board of Forensic Odontology (ABFO).** http://www.abfo.org/ (accessed January 23, 2005).

The American Board of Forensic Odontology was organized in 1976 under the auspices of the National Institute of Justice, with the mission to establish, enhance, and revise as necessary, standards of qualifications for those who practice forensic odontology and to certify as qualified specialists those voluntary applicants who comply with the requirements of the Board. Detailed ABFO guidelines on human identification, bitemarks, development of a dental ID team, and missing person and unidentified body cases are available in the ID & Bitemark Guidelines (http://www.abfo.org/guide.htm) section.

555.   **Bureau of Legal Dentistry (BOLD).** http://www.boldlab.org/ (accessed January 23, 2005).

The Bureau of Legal Dentistry provides current bibliographies on "Human, Animal Bites," "DNA Methods," "Mass Fatalities," "Human Identification," "Domestic Violence," and "Dental Jurisprudence" in the Research area.

556.   **Forensic Dentistry Online.** http://www.forensicdentistryonline.org/ (accessed January 23, 2005).

A Web site by the International Organisation for Forensic Odontostomotology (IOFOS) devoted to forensic dentistry. The site includes information on identifications, bitemarks, and journals and books on this fascinating subject. The links on the right side of the page are particularly useful; many lead to full text articles. The IOFOS publishes the *Journal of Forensic Odonto-Stomatology*.

**557.   Issues in Human and Animal Bite Mark (Bitemark) Management.** http://www.forensic.to/webhome/bitemarks/ (accessed January 23, 2005).

Created by Mike Bowers, a forensic odontologist, this site provides a comprehensive overview, accessible through a hyperlinked table of contents, of bitemarks in forensic sciences.

# Photography

**558.   Crime Scene Photography.** http://www.rcmp-learning.org/docs/ecdd1004.htm (accessed January 23, 2005).

Created by the Royal Canadian Mounted Police, this informative guide walks through the steps and techniques in crime scene photography, using illustrations to explain some of the concepts. Topics include sharpness, light, exposure, use of the flash, ideas to consider, and a pre-shooting checklist.

**559.   Crime Scene and Evidence Photography.** http://www.crime-scene-investigator.net/csi-photo.html (accessed January 23, 2005).

This directory of Web sites on crime scene photography has some great links to articles and Web sites related to forensic photography and photography in general. It is hosted on the crime-scene-investigator.net Web site.

# Questioned Document Examination

**560.   American Society of Questioned Document Examiners.** http://www.asqde.org/ (accessed January 23, 2005).

The ASQDE was formally established in 1942. The society's goals are to foster education, establish standards, exchange experience, sponsor scientific research, provide instruction in the field of questioned document examination, and promote justice in matters that involve questions about documents. The site has a current database of court decisions relating to expert testimony about handwriting and document comparisons. ASQDE publishes the *Journal of the American Society of Questioned Document Examiners*.

**561.   American Board of Forensic Document Examiners.** http://www.abfde.org/index.htm (accessed January 23, 2005).

Established in 1977, this organization provides a program of certification in forensic document examination, with the dual purpose of serving the public interest and promoting the advancement of forensic science. Current employment opportunities are listed in the Jobs section, and the Links section has some interesting links to cases involving questioned documents and legal issues.

562.  **Questioned Documents Site of Emily J. Will.** http://www.qdewill.com/ (accessed January 23, 2005).

Created by Emily J. Will, a certified document examiner, this is a useful place to start for an overview of questioned document examination.

563.  **Identifont.** http://www.identifont.com/index.html (accessed January 23, 2005).

"Identifont uses a proprietary expert system to identify a typeface based on information about specific characteristics of the typeface" (Human–Computer Interface 2004). Identifont was designed and developed by Human–Computer Interface, a documentation and information design company specializing in high-tech products. Scan the text, upload the image, and this site will attempt to identify the font.

564.  **Virtual Typewriter Museum.** http://www.typewritermuseum.org/ (accessed January 23, 2005).

The Virtual Typewriter Museum was conceived, designed, and produced by mmworks, a Dutch-based Web design company, and is edited by Paul Robert. This virtual museum is based on private collections from around the world.

565.  **The Classic Typewriter Page.** http://staff.xu.edu/~polt/typewriters/index.html (accessed January 23, 2005).

Information on typewriters is becoming harder to find, so this site is a welcome addition to the Internet. Maintained by Richard Polt, a professor of philosophy at Xavier University in Cincinnati, Ohio, the Typewriter Facts section is useful to questioned document examiners, whereas the remainder of the links are more for typewriter enthusiasts.

566.  **Omniglot.** http://www.omniglot.com/ (accessed January 23, 2005).

This Web site provides a guide to over 200 different alphabets, syllabaries, and other writing systems, including a few you will find nowhere else. It also contains details of many of the languages written with those writing systems and links to a wide range of language-related resources, such as fonts, online dictionaries, and online language courses. The A–Z Index of all the writing systems and languages featured on this site is comprehensive and extensive, detailing the alphabets of each language. Simon Ager, a Web developer from England with a keen interest in languages, created the site.

567.   **CounterSpace.** http://www.counterspace.us/typography/ (accessed October 12, 2005).
A Web site dedicated to typography and its history. Although there is not much information on the authority of the site, the content is trustworthy and well designed. Particularly of use to someone new to questioned document examination is the Anatomy section.

568.   **fonts.com.** http://www.fonts.com/findfonts/ (accessed October 12, 2005).
This site allows for online viewing of samples of all fonts in the monotype catalogue. The Search By Sight feature enables you to identify a font from a sample by answering a series of simple questions. It is ideal if you want to match an existing typeface, or identify a typeface you have seen in a publication. You can also search by keyword, classification, or designer, in addition to browsing alphabetically by font family. Fonts.com is owned and operated by Agfa Monotype Corporation, a worldwide marketer of over 8,000 high-quality fonts.

569.   **Handwriting.** http://www.bham.ac.uk/english/bibliography/handwriting/HandwritingHome.html (accessed January 23, 2005).
Tom Davis is a handwriting expert and English professor at Birmingham University in England. This site contains two interesting articles on handwriting found in the United Kingdom, as well as a link to a fully analyzed and fully keyworded hypertext bibliography of over 1,500 references to books and articles in English on forensic handwriting analysis and related topics.

# Scientific/Expert Testimony and Legal

570.   ***Daubert* on the Web.** http://www.daubertontheweb.com/ (accessed January 23, 2005).
Maintained by Peter Nordberg, a Philadelphia lawyer, this comprehensive site on the *Daubert* decision includes links to the decision itself, Supreme Court decisions elaborating on *Daubert*, an overview of *Daubert*, guides to resolving *Daubert* challenges, federal appellate decisions related to *Daubert*, *Daubert* decisions by field of expertise, related links, a blog, and a user forum on *Daubert*.

571.    **Forensic-Evidence.com.** http://www.forensic-evidence.com/ (accessed January 23, 2005).

An information center in forensic science, law, and public policy for lawyers, forensic scientists, educators, and public officials, maintained by Andre A. Moenssens, a Douglas Stripp Missouri Professor of Law Emeritus.

# Terminology

572.    **Glossary of Terms of the Death Investigation.** http://www.vifsm.org/overview/glossary.html (accessed January 23, 2005).

A single-page glossary of forensics terms maintained by the Virginia Institute of Forensic Science and Medicine.

573.    **Forensic DNA Glossary.** http://www.forensicdna.com/emailforms/DNAGlossary.html (accessed October 11, 2005).

This work appears as Appendix A in *An Introduction to Forensic DNA Analysis, 2nd edition*, by Keith Inman and Norah Rudin (Inman and Rudin 2002). There is an intermediate page, where you will need to acknowledge the copyright agreement to proceed to the glossary.

574.    **Glossary of Typography.** http://www.counterspace.us/typography/ (accessed October 12, 2005).

Choose the glossary option from the menu bar at the top of the screen to access the extensive definitions of terms of interest to questioned document examiners. Created by CounterSpace.

575.    **SWGFAST Glossary.** http://www.swgfast.org/Glossary_Consolidated_ver_1.pdf (accessed January 23, 2005).

Created by SWGFAST, a scientific working group of the Federal Bureau of Investigation (FBI) to create consensus standards for fingerprint analysis and technology. This consolidated glossary (viewed using Adobe Acrobat Reader) covers friction ridge automation, anatomy, identification, fingerprint classification, and latent print processing.

576.    **Bloodstain Pattern Analysis Terminology.** http://www.iabpa.org/Terminology.pdf (accessed January 23, 2005).

Created by the Terminology Committee of the International Association of Bloodstain Pattern Analysts, this list consists of basic terms taught and used by the majority of bloodstain analysts in the field.

577.   **Genetics and DNA Glossaries.**
Glossaries created by Promega Corporation, a reagent and reagent systems supply company. Both glossaries are arranged alphabetically with a hyperlinked alphabetic index at the top.

- **Genetic Identity Glossary.** http://www.promega.com/techserv/apps/hmnid/ referenceinformation/glossary.htm (accessed January 23, 2005)
- **Acronyms Used in the Literature of Genome Research.** http://www.dpw .wau.nl/PV/aflp/acronyms.html (accessed January 23, 2005)

578.   **The On-Line Medical Dictionary (OMD).** http://cancerweb.ncl.ac.uk/ omd/index.html (accessed January 23, 2005).

OMD is a searchable dictionary created by Dr. Graham Dark and contains terms relating to biochemistry, cell biology, chemistry, medicine, molecular biology, physics, plant biology, radiobiology, science and technology. It includes acronyms, jargon, theory, conventions, standards, institutions, projects, eponyms, history, in fact anything to do with medicine or science. It aims to provide a one-stop source of information about all medical and scientific terms and includes many useful cross-references and pointers to related resources elsewhere on the Internet, as well as bibliographical reference to paper publications. It lacks many entries which one can find in paper dictionaries but contains more encyclopedia-like entries and entries on various subjects. It also contains many definitions in related areas. The dictionary started in early 1997 and has grown, to contain over 46,000 definitions. (American Medical Publishing 2003)

Entries are cross-referenced to each other and to related resources elsewhere on the Internet.

579.   **Forensic Botany Glossary.**   http://myweb.dal.ca/jvandomm/forensic botany/glossary.html (accessed October 12, 2005).
Created by the Forensic Botany site as a project in the Web Literacy for the Natural Sciences class at Dalhousie University, Halifax, Canada. All definitions are hyperlinked to their original source.

580.   **Useful Definitions for Forensic Economists.** http://www.umsl.edu/ divisions/artscience/economics/ForensicEconomics/definitions.html   (accessed January 23, 2005).
A glossary of forensic economics terms created and maintained by the University of Missouri–St. Louis Economics Department.

## Mailing Lists and Discussion Groups

581.   **Criminal Poisoning (cr_po).** http://groups.yahoo.com/group/cr_po/ (accessed January 23, 2005).

Criminal Poisoning is a discussion group hosted on Yahoo Groups. It was created by Anil Aggrawal, a professor of forensic medicine at the Maulana Azad Medical College, New Delhi, India. Membership is open, but messages require approval from the listowner.

582.   **Forens (Forensic Medicine and Sciences Interest Group).** http:// statgen.ncsu.edu/majordomo/forens.php (accessed January 23, 2005).

Forens is an unmoderated discussion list dealing with forensic aspects of anthropology, biology, chemistry, odontology, pathology, psychology, serology, toxicology, criminalistics, and expert witnessing and presentation of evidence in court. To subscribe to Forens, send an email to forens@statgen.ncsu.edu with the following message: "subscribe forens".

583.   **Forens-Arch.** http://www.soton.ac.uk/~jb3/forens-arch.html (accessed January 23, 2005).

The Forens-Arch mailing list was set up to gather people in archaeology and anthropology who have an interest in applying their skills to forensic science. To subscribe, send an email to majordomo@lists.soton.ac.uk with the following message: "subscribe forens-arch".

584.   **FORENSICS.** http://www.securityfocus.com/archive/104 (accessed October 12, 2005).

FORENSICS is a moderated mailing list for the detailed discussion of computer security forensics. FORENSICS is hosted by SecurityFocus, a vendor-neutral site for all members of the security community. A Spanish version of the listserv is available at http://www.securityfocus.com/archive/128.

585.   **forensic-science.** http://groups.yahoo.com/group/forensic-science/ (accessed January 23, 2005).

This Yahoo-based discussion group is for professional discussions related to the use of science in matters of law.

586.   **ICSIA-PublicForum.** http://groups.yahoo.com/group/ICSIA-PublicForum/ (accessed January 23, 2005).

The International Crime Scene Investigators Association hosts this public forum on Yahoo for people interested in crime scene investigations. It is not restricted to law enforcement officers.

587. **Investigative Image Processing.** http://spie.org/app/forums/ (accessed October 12, 2005).

The SPIE (International Society for Optical Engineering)-sponsored group focuses on forensic investigations of image and video material. Methods for investigation and presentation as forensic evidence are discussed.

588. **NAFE-L.** http://www.nafe.net/NAFE-L.aspx (accessed October 12, 2005).

The National Association of Forensic Economics (NAFE) sponsors a forum for its members to exchange ideas, information, and new developments in the field of forensic economics. Subscribers are also interested in expert and legal testimony by economists.

589. **PSYLAW-L.** http://www.geocities.com/Athens/7429/psychlaw.html (accessed January 23, 2005).

An open discussion list on the topic of forensic psychology.

# Miscellaneous Web Sites

590. **Forensic Science Timeline.** http://www.forensicdna.com/Timeline020702 .pdf (accessed January 23, 2005).

Norah Rudin, a forensic consultant and expert witness in forensic DNA, compiles this "work in progress." It can also be found as an appendix in the book *Principles and Practice of Forensic Science: The Profession of Forensic Science*, published by CRC Press in 2000 (Inman and Rudin 2000).

591. **Forensic Science Time Lines.** http://www.quincy.ca/TimeLine.cfm (accessed January 23, 2005).

Created by Shaunderson Communications Inc. (SCInc.), publishers of the *International Journal of Document Examination*, this collection of time lines by forensic science fields includes computer forensics, anthropology, chemistry, document examination, engineering, entomology, firearms and tool marks, impression evidence, medicine and pathology, odontology, profiling, serology and DNA, toxicology, trace evidence, and crime scene. Each time line includes a list of references.

# References

American Medical Publishing. 2003. *The on-line medical dictionary.* http://www.cancerweb.ncl.ac.uk/omd/about.html (accessed January 23, 2005).

Beeton, Mary. 2001. *Ridges and furrows.* http://www.ridgesandfurrows.homestead.com/ (accessed September 9, 2004).

Flanagan, Robert J. 1998. Guidelines for the interpretation of analytical toxicology results and unit of measurement conversion factors. *Annals of Clinial Biochemistry* 35: 261–7. http://www.leeds.ac.uk/acb/annals/Webwise/Webwise97-1.html (accessed January 23, 2005).

Holt, Cynthia. 2003. Forensic science resources on the Internet. *Issues in Science and Technology Librarianship* Spring 2003. http://www.istl.org/03-spring/internet.html (accessed January 23, 2005).

Human–Computer Interface. 2004. About Identifont. http://www.identifont.com/about.html (accessed January 23, 2005).

Inman, Keith, and Norah Rudin. 2002. *An Introduction to Forensic DNA Analysis, 2nd edition.* Boca Raton, Florida: CRC Press.

Inman, Keith, and Norah Rudin. 2000. *Principles & Practice of Criminalistics: The Profession of Forensic Science.* Boca Raton, Florida: CRC Press.

Klatt, Edward C. 2004. Firearms Tutorial. http://medstat.med.utah.edu/WebPath/TUTORIAL/GUNS/GUNINTRO.html (accessed January 23, 2005).

Monson, Keith L., Kevin W. P. Miller, Mark R. Wilson, Joseph A. DiZinno, and Bruce Budowle. 2002. The mtDNA Population Database: An Integrated Software and Database Resource for Forensic Comparison. *Forensic Science Communications* 4(2). http://www.fbi.gov/hq/lab/fsc/backissu/april2002/miller1.htm (accessed January 23, 2005).

# 6

# Other Non-Bibliographic Information Sources

## Genetic Population Databases

DNA analysis has become an integral part of forensic investigations, advancing the field in much the same way as fingerprints did when they were introduced as an identification tool in the 1890s. Until the 1980s, the most common method of genetic typing in forensics was the ABO blood group system combined with the examination of certain genetic markers. The combination of the frequency of a population with a certain blood type and the frequency of a population with certain genetic markers results in a percentage of the population who can be included as possible donors of a sample. Unfortunately, this often still leaves a large pool of possible donors. Forensic DNA typing is able to decrease this pool to a much smaller number.

The first forensic DNA profiling test involved the detection of multiple loci RFLP (restriction fragment length polymorphism) patterns. It was developed in 1984 by Sir Alec Jeffreys and published in a 1985 article in *Nature*. Although this technique has the highest degree of discrimination per locus, it requires a greater amount of higher quality DNA than other techniques and is difficult to automate.

At approximately the same time that Jeffreys was developing a forensics use for RFLP, Kary Mullis, a scientist at the Cetus Corporation, first conceptualized polymerase chain reaction (PCR), but he did not publish it in the mainstream literature until later. This technique amplifies DNA, allowing scientists to make many copies of a DNA molecule in a short time. This technique has significantly changed the field of molecular biology and is the basis for most DNA typing systems used by crime labs today. These systems include STR (short tandem repeats), Y-STRs (STRs found on the human Y chromosome), mitochondrial DNA (mtDNA) that is inherited from the mother, and gender identification through analysis of the amerogenin locus (also the gene for tooth pulp). The method used depends on the material being analyzed and its condition.

The exclusion of a person as the donor of a sample is absolute, and the inclusion of a person as the donor is expressed as a statistical probability. To calculate these probabilities, genetic population databases have been created and are constantly updated. Some of these databases are accessible only to members of the organization that created the database or to those who also contribute content to the database. Below are four that are freely accessible to all forensic scientists.

**592.  GEP-ISFG Nuclear DNA Database.** http://www.ertzaintza.net/cgi-bin/db2www.exe/adn.d2w/INPUT?IDIOMA=INGLES (accessed January 11, 2005).

This is a computerized database of allelic frequencies of DNA nuclear markers in populations from Spain, Portugal, and Latin America, analyzed by PCR. It was created as a result of a suggestion at the 16th International Conference of ISFH (now ISFG—International Society for Forensic Genetics) in 1995.

**593.  mtDNA Population Database.** http://www.fbi.gov/hq/lab/fsc/backissu/april2002/miller1.htm (accessed September 15, 2004).

This article from the FBI Forensic Science Research Unit discusses a new database of mtDNA control region nucleotide sequences. A link to download the database to your personal computer is included in the article.

**594.  The Short Tandem Repeat Internet DataBase (STRBase).** http://www.cstl.nist.gov/biotech/strbase/ (accessed July 28, 2004).

This Web site brings together the literature on the use of STRs for genetic mapping and identity testing. There are facts and sequences on each STR system, population data, commonly used multiplex STR systems, a review of various technologies for analysis of STR alleles, and PCR primers and conditions. In addition, there is a comprehensive listing of materials on STR for DNA typing.

**595.  YHRD—Y Chromosome Haplotype Reference Database.** http://www.yhrd.org/index.html (accessed February 7, 2005).

Established in 2000, this database was created to generate reliable Y-STR haplotype frequency estimates to be used in quantitative assessment of matches in forensics. Searching is available among geographically defined metapopulations and ethnically defined metapopulations.

# Dissertations

Dissertations can be a wealth of information for researchers. Since those writing dissertations must do a literature review as part of the dissertation process, these publications can be a great source of references on a topic. The identification of relevant dissertations is not difficult in the forensic sciences. Many are covered in several databases including *Dissertation Abstracts International* and *Chemical Abstracts* (see Chapter 2). The difficulty lies in obtaining these items, as some university libraries do not lend their dissertations. If interlibrary loan does not work, **UMI**—the producers of the *Dissertation Abstracts International* database (see Chapter 2)—sells copies of dissertations in multiple formats (paper, microfilm, or electronic) through its Dissertation Express service (http://www.umi.com/umi/dissertations/disexpress.shtml, accessed February 8, 2005). Price depends on the format you require and your user class (academic, nonacademic, or international). Another option is the Networked Digital Library of Theses and Dissertations.

596. **Networked Digital Library of Theses and Dissertations (NDLTD).** http://www.ndltd.org/ (accessed December 9, 2004).

NDLTD is an international organization with a mission to promote the adoption, creation, use, and dissemination and preservation of electronic versions of theses and dissertations. The project is spearheaded by Virginia Tech, but the organization includes over 200 members (universities and institutions) who also maintain collections. NTLTD has created a searchable Union Catalog of free, full text graduate theses and dissertations that have been submitted electronically by students via the Web. The electronic publications are in PDF and are broken into sections for smaller downloads.

# Societies, Associations, and Other Organizations

597. **Academy of Behavioral Profiling (ABP).** http://www.profiling.org/ (accessed December 1, 2004).

This association is dedicated to the application of evidence-based criminal profiling techniques within investigative and legal venues. Their goal is to foster the development of a class of practitioners capable of raising the discipline of evidence-based behavioral profiling to the status of a profession.

598. **American Academy of Forensic Psychology (AAFP).** http://www.abfp.com/academy.asp (accessed December 1, 2004).

The Academy is the education and training arm of the American Board of Forensic Psychology. It was organized for the purpose of contributing to the development and maintenance of forensic psychology as a specialized field of study, research, and practice. It is approved by the American Psychological Association.

599. **American Academy of Forensic Sciences (AAFS).** http://www.aafs.org/ (accessed Januray 23, 2005).

A professional society dedicated for over 50 years to the application of science to the law. The AAFS publishes the *Journal of Forensic Sciences*. The Resources section includes forensic science programs at universities and colleges worldwide, information on the forensic sciences as a career (an excellent overview of the various subspecialties in the forensic sciences), and links to forensic science organizations and publications.

600. **American Academy of Psychiatry and the Law (AAPL).** http://www.aapl.org/ (accessed December 1, 2004).

The AAPL promotes scientific and educational activities in forensic psychiatry. They sponsor continuing education programs, develop ethical guidelines, provide a forum for the presentation of the results of research, develop guidelines for education and training, and facilitate the exchange of ideas through the *Journal of the American Academy of Psychiatry and the Law*.

601. **American Association of Anthropological Genetics (AAAG).** http://www.ac.wwu.edu/~aaag/ (accessed May 13, 2005).

The AAAG was established in 1994 as an educational and scientific organization. Its purpose is to promote the study of anthropological genetics, facilitate communication between individuals in the field, and foster cooperation among anthropological geneticists. The AAAG publishes *Human Biology*.

602. **American Association of Physical Anthropologists (AAPA).** http://www.physanth.org/ (accessed December 2, 2004).

The AAPA is the world's leading professional organization for physical anthropologists. Forensic anthropologists use their knowledge of osteology and anatomy to make forensic determinations and identifications involving human remains. The AAPA publishes the *American Journal of Physical Anthropology*.

603. **American Board of Criminalistics (ABC).** http://www.criminalistics.com/ (accessed December 2, 2004).

The ABC is a federation of regional and national organizations that represent forensic scientists. This organization is involved in the certification of criminalists. It has developed rules of professional conduct, with disciplinary actions for behavior contrary to these rules.

604.   **American Board of Forensic Anthropology (ABFA).** http://www .csuchico.edu/anth/ABFA/ (accessed December 2, 2004).

The ABFA provides a certification in forensic anthropology. It establishes standards of ethics, conduct, and professional practice in forensic anthropology in addition to its mandate to establish and enhance standards that advance the science of forensic anthropology.

605.   **American Board of Forensic Document Examiners (ABFDE).** http:// www.abfde.org/ (accessed December 2, 2004).

The ABFDE is the only certifying board for forensic document examiners recognized by the American Academy of Forensic Sciences, the American Society of Questioned Document Examiners, and the Canadian Society of Forensic Scientists.

606.   **American Board of Forensic Entomology (ABFE).** http://www .research.missouri.edu/entomology/ (accessed July 28, 2004).

The ABFE constitutes the first step toward a professional organization with strict educational, ethical, and maintenance standards. The ABFE site provides a short but informative overview of the science and history of forensic entomology, as well as case studies in forensic entomology.

607.   **American Board of Forensic Odontology (ABFO).** http://www.abfo .org/ (accessed July 28, 2004).

The American Board of Forensic Odontology was organized in 1976 under the auspices of the National Institute of Justice, with the mission to establish, enhance, and revise as necessary, standards of qualifications for those who practice forensic odontology, and to certify as qualified specialists those voluntary applicants who comply with the requirements of the board. Detailed ABFO guidelines on human identification, bitemarks, development of a dental ID team and missing person and unidentified body cases are available in the ID & Bitemark Guidelines (http://www.abfo.org/guide.htm) section.

608.   **American Board of Forensic Psychology (ABFP).** http://www.abfp .com/board.asp (accessed December 1, 2004).

ABFP is responsible for the diplomating (credentialing) process in forensic psychology.

609.   **American Board of Forensic Toxicology (ABFT).** http://www.abft.org/ (accessed December 2, 2004).

The objective of the Board is to establish, enhance, and revise as necessary, standards of qualification for those who practice forensic toxicology, and to certify as qualified specialists those voluntary applicants who comply with the requirements of the Board. The Board also establishes, enhances, and maintains standards of qualification for those laboratories that practice postmortem forensic toxicology, and accredits as qualified laboratories those applicants who comply with the requirements of the Board.

610.   **American Board of Medicolegal Death Investigators, Inc. (ABMDI).** http://www.slu.edu/organizations/abmdi/ (accessed December 2, 2004).

ABMDI is a national, independent certification board established to promote the highest standards of practice for medicolegal death investigators. This is a voluntary certification program for individuals who have the proven knowledge and skills necessary to perform medicolegal death investigations as set forth in *Death investigation: A guide for the scene investigator*, published in 1999 by the National Institutes of Justice.

611.   **American Board of Forensic Document Examiners.** http://www.abfde .org/index.htm (accessed July 28, 2004).

Established in 1977, this organization provides a program of certification in forensic document examination with the dual purpose of serving the public interest and promoting the advancement of forensic science. Current employment opportunities are listed in the Jobs section, and the Links section has some interesting links to cases involving questioned documents and legal issues.

612.   **American College of Forensic Examiners International.** http://www .acfei.com/main.php (accessed December 2, 2004).

The College is an independent, scientific, and professional society with a multidisciplinary scope. The society's purpose is the continued advancement of forensic examination and consultation across the many professional fields of forensics. The society publishes the *Forensic Examiner* and provides workshops and continuing education courses.

613.   **The American Polygraph Association.** http://www.polygraph.org/ (accessed December 2, 2004).

The Association is dedicated to providing a valid and reliable means to verify the truth and establish the highest standards of moral, ethical, and professional conduct in the polygraph field. The Web site includes a code of ethics, standards of practice, a quick guide to the law relating to polygraphs, and an FAQ.

614.  **American Society for Investigative Pathology (ASIP).** http://www.asip. org/ (accessed December 10, 2004).

The ASIP is a society of biomedical scientists whose role it is to investigate mechanisms of disease. The Society publishes the *American Journal of Pathology*.

615.  **American Society of Crime Laboratory Directors.** http://www.ascld. org/ (accessed January 23, 2005).

The American Society of Crime Laboratory Directors (ASCLD) is a nonprofit professional society formed in 1974 and devoted to the improvement of crime laboratory operations through sound management practices. In the Forensic Links section links are arranged into three categories: forensic-related links, advocacy-related links, and safety-related links. The Forensic Students section has an overview of what is needed to become a forensic scientist, as well as information on the career itself (how much one makes, the type of work environment). For the practicing forensic scientist, the Employment section lists current job postings.

616.  **American Society of Forensic Odontology (ASFO).** http://www .forensicdentistryonline.org/new_asfo/newasfo.htm (accessed December 2, 2004).

The ASFO is the largest worldwide organization representing those interested in forensic dentistry. The site includes downloadable identification forms, links to related resources, a guide to forensic odontology books, research grant information, and information on courses and meetings.

617.  **American Society of Questioned Document Examiners (ASQDE).** http://www.asqde.org/ (accessed July 28, 2004).

The ASQDE was established in 1942. The purposes of the Society are to foster education, sponsor scientific research, establish standards, exchange experience, provide instruction in the field of questioned document examination, and promote justice in matters that involve questions about documents. The site has a current database of court decisions relating to expert testimony about handwriting and document comparisons. ASQDE publishes the *Journal of the American Society of Questioned Document Examiners*.

618.  **Armed Forces Institute of Pathology (AFIP).** http://www.afip.org/ (accessed January 23, 2005).

The Armed Forces Institute of Pathology (AFIP) is an agency of the Department of Defense specializing in pathology consultation, education, and research. The site provides instructions on submitting consultation requests in surgical pathology and autopsy through an online form. All AFIP departments are represented on the site.

The Office of the Armed Forces Medical Examiner presents autopsy diagrams (http://www.afip.org/Departments/oafme/diagrams.html) and information on the Department of Defense's DNA specimen repository and Armed Forces DNA Identification Laboratory. Its Forensic Toxicology Division provides guidelines for collection and shipment of toxicological analysis. The site also provides information on its medical education courses for physicians and professionals in other interrelated medical disciplines, some of which are available through the Internet.

**619. Association for Crime Scene Reconstruction (ACSR).** http:// www.acsr.org/ (accessed December 2, 2004).

The purpose of the ACSR is to encompass an understanding of the whole crime scene and the necessity of reconstructing that scene in order to better understand the elements of the crime and to recognize and preserve evidence. Members are law enforcement investigators, forensic experts, and teachers from all over the United States and a growing number of countries around the world.

**620. Association of Certified Fraud Examiners (ACFE).** http://www.cfenet .com/home.asp (accessed December 2, 2004).

The ACFE is a global, 31,000-member professional association whose members are dedicated to fighting fraud. One of their mandates is to provide anti-fraud training and education. The ACFE publishes *Fraud Magazine*. The Web site has a resource library that includes an index to fraud information and articles.

**621. Association of Firearm and Tool Mark Examiners (AFTE).** http:// www.afte.org/ (accessed July 28, 2004).

Formed in 1969 to address the requirements of firearms and tool mark examiners, the AFTE publishes the *AFTE Journal*. This site includes: Ammunition Manufacturers/Distributors (http://www.afte.org/aftelinks/aftelinks_ammunition. htm), an alphabetical list of ammunition manufacturers and distributors; Firearm Manufacturers/Distributors (http://www.afte.org/aftelinks/aftelinks_firearms.htm), an alphabetical list of firearm manufacturers and distributors; and Ballistics Links (http://www.afte.org/aftelinks/aftelinks_forensic.htm), an alphabetically arranged metasite of ballistics links.

622.  **Australian and New Zealand Forensic Science Society (ANZFSS).**
http://www.nifs.com.au/ANZFSS/ANZFSS.html (accessed December 2, 2004).

The Society's objectives are to enhance the quality of the forensic sciences,
providing both formal and informal lectures, discussions, and demonstrations
encompassing the various disciplines within the science. The Web site has a
Links section that is particularly useful to forensic scientists in Australia and New
Zealand.

623.  **Bureau of Legal Dentistry (BOLD).** http://www.boldlab.org/ (accessed
July 28, 2004).

The Bureau of Legal Dentistry provides current bibliographies on "Human,
Animal Bites," "DNA Methods," "Mass Fatalities," "Human Identification,"
"Domestic Violence," and "Dental Jurisprudence" in the Research area.

624.  **Canadian Society of Forensic Science (CSFS).** http://www.csfs.ca/index
htm .(accessed January 23, 2005).

The Canadian Society of Forensic Science is a nonprofit professional organization incorporated to maintain professional standards and to promote the study
and enhance the stature of forensic science. The CSFS publishes the *Canadian
Society of Forensic Science Journal*. The STR DNA Data link is particularly
interesting, as it leads to the Population Studies Data Centre, which provides raw
DNA data and frequency tables by ethnic groups from the Royal Canadian
Mounted Police and the Centre of Forensic Sciences in Toronto, Ontario, Canada.

625.  **Evidence Photographers International Council, Inc. (EPIC).** http://
www.epic-photo.org/ (accessed December 2, 2004).

EPIC is a worldwide organization of evidence photographers. It provides
workshops (including the School of Evidence Photography) and conferences on
forensic photography, and it has created standards for evidence photography.
Ceased publication.

626.  **Federal Bureau of Investigation (FBI).** http://www.fbi.gov/ (accessed
January 23, 2005).

The FBI Web site provides access to thousands of pages of frequently requested FBI documents (case files) through the **Freedom of Information Act
(FOIA) Electronic Reading Room** (http://foia.fbi.gov/room.htm—accessed
January 23, 2005). Documents are accessible through an alphabetical index and
crime type categories. Some portions are withheld under exemptions allowed by
FOIA. The files are viewed using the Adobe Acrobat Reader and are often split
into several files because of their size.

The FBI has been involved in many **famous cases** (http://www.fbi.gov/libref/ historic/famcases/famcases.htm—accessed January 23, 2005) since its founding in 1908. The Office of Public and Congressional Affairs (OPCA) has prepared monographs on some of the most frequently requested, closed investigations. The monographs, arranged alphabetically and by crime, should be considered to be overviews rather than exhaustive treatments.

The Web site is home to three publications of the FBI: *Forensic Science Communications* (the journal of the FBI Laboratory), the *FBI Law Enforcement Bulletin*, and the *Handbook of Forensic Services*.

627.  **The Fingerprint Society.** http://www.fpsociety.org.uk/ (accessed December 2, 2004).

This British society is a worldwide organization of fingerprint examination professionals. Its aim is to advance the study and application of fingerprints and to facilitate the cooperation among persons in the field of personal identification. The Society publishes *Fingerprint Whorld*.

628.  **The Forensic Science Society.** http://www.forensic-science-society .org.uk/ (accessed January 23, 2005).

Founded in 1959, this British multidisciplinary society is dedicated to the application of science to the cause of justice. The Forensic Science Society publishes the journal *Science & Justice*. The Web Links section allows you to search the Forensic Science Society's WebLinks Database by keyword to find links. In the Publications section is a keyword-searchable index to articles in the *Journal of the Forensic Science Society* and *Science & Justice*. The society also maintains a keyword index to book reviews published in its journal.

629.  **High Technology Crime Investigation Association (HTCIA).** http:// htcia.org/ (accessed December 2, 2004).

The purpose of the HTCIA is to encourage, promote, aid, and effect the voluntary interchange of data, information, experience, ideas, and knowledge about methods, processes, and techniques relating to investigations and security in advanced technologies among its membership. The association holds conferences and seminars for members. The Web site has a forensic toolkit that includes links to computer crime–related sites.

630.  **International Association for Craniofacial Identification (IACI).** http:// www.forensicartist.com/IACI/index.html (accessed July 28, 2004).

The IACI, formed in 1988, is an organization comprised mainly of medical and scientific professionals throughout the world who specialize in forensic odontology, forensic anthropology, 2- and 3-dimensional skull reconstruction techniques, computer-based skull reconstruction, facial aging for law enforcement, and facial mapping, as well as composite sketching. The Craniofacial Identification Links (http://www.forensicartist.com/IACI/links.html) are particularly useful. Craniofacial Identification Links are arranged into two columns with no annotations. Links range from traditional to computerized methods of craniofacial reconstruction.

**631. International Association for Forensic Phonetics and Acoustics (IAFPA).** http://www.iafpa.net/ (accessed December 3, 2004).

The IAFPA seeks to foster research and provide a forum for the interchange of ideas and information on practice, development, and research in forensic phonetics and acoustics. It also sets down and enforces standards of professional conduct and procedure for those involved in forensic phonetic and acoustic casework through its Code of Practice. The journal of the IAFPA is the *International Journal of Speech, Language and the Law: Forensic Linguistics*.

**632. International Association for Identification.**   http://www.theiai.org/ (accessed January 23, 2005).

The International Association for Identification was incorporated in 1919. The Association publishes the *Journal of Forensic Identification*. The Links section lists a hodge-podge of identification links. The Job Listings section contains current job ads.

**633. International Association of Accident Reconstruction Specialists (I.A.A.R.S.).** http://www.iaars.org/ (accessed December 7, 2004).

I.A.A.R.S. was established as a resource for members to use when the inevitable questions arose while trying to reconstruct a crash. The Association provides seminars and other development opportunities. Membership is peer reviewed to provide for greater acceptability of members as expert witnesses to judges.

**634. International Association of Arson Investigators (I.A.A.I.).** http://www.firearson.com/ (accessed January 30, 2005).

The goal of this association of fire investigation professionals is to foster support, and promote fire prevention and arson awareness through education and training. The Web site has a links section organized by industry topic. They conduct annual and regional seminars, administer the Certified Fire Investigator program, and publish the quarterly publication, the *Fire and Arson Investigator*.

635. **International Association of Bloodstain Pattern Analysts (IABPA).** http://www.iabpa.org/ (accessed December 2, 2004).

The IABPA is an organization of forensic experts specializing in the field of bloodstain pattern analysis. The IABPA publishes the *IABPA Newsletter*. The purpose of the IABPA is to promote education and encourage research in the field of bloodstain pattern analysis. The IABPA also encourages the study and research of, and promotes the standardization of, bloodstain pattern analysis training and terminology.

636. **International Association of Bomb Technicians and Investigators (IABTI).** http://www.iabti.org/ (accessed July 28, 2004).

Founded in 1973, the IABTI was formed for the purpose of countering the criminal use of explosives. It is an independent, non-profit professional association. The site provides information on the organization and links to explosives manufacturers (http://www.iabti.org/manulinks.html). Links to explosives manufacturers are limited to advertisers in *The Detonator* and exhibitors at International Association of Bomb Technicians and Investigators (IABTI) regional and international conferences. Links to bomb squad Web sites are accessible only to members.

637. **International Association of Computer Investigative Specialists (IACIS).** http://www.cops.org/ (accessed December 3, 2004).

IACIS is an international volunteer nonprofit corporation composed of law enforcement professionals dedicated to the education and certification of law enforcement professionals in the field of forensic computer science. The Web site includes the association's code of ethics and procedures for the forensic examination of computers and digital and electronic media.

638. **International Association of Forensic Linguists (IAFL).** http://www.iafl.org/ (accessed December 3, 2004).

This organization is comprised primarily of linguists whose work involves the law. This means linguistic evidence in court, such as authorship attribution, disputed confessions, interpreting and translating in court, the readability/comprehensibility of legal documents, and interviews with children in the legal system. The Association's Web site includes a useful, searchable bibliography of notable references about forensic linguistics.

639. **International Association of Forensic Nurses (IAFN).** http://www.forensicnurse.org/ (accessed December 3, 2004).

The IAFN is the only international professional organization of registered nurses formed exclusively to develop, promote, and disseminate information about the science of forensic nursing. This covers the application of nursing science to public or legal proceedings, and the application of the forensic aspects of health care to the scientific investigation and treatment of trauma and/or death of victims and perpetrators of abuse, violence, criminal activity, and traumatic accidents. The Association is also involved in the certification of forensic nurses through the Forensic Nursing Certification. The Web site has a Resources link that contains useful sources of information in this area, including a compilation of publications. The official journal of the IAFN is the *Journal of Forensic Nursing.*

640.   **The International Association of Forensic Toxicologists (TIAFT).** http://www.tiaft.org/ (accessed July 28, 2004).

Founded in 1963, this association groups over 1,400 members from all regions of the world. The aims of this association are to promote cooperation and co-ordination of efforts among members and to encourage research in forensic toxicology. The members come from the police force, medical examiners and coroners' laboratories, horseracing and sports doping laboratories, hospitals, and departments of legal medicine, pharmacology, pharmacy, and toxicology. Enter the Open Area for resources for nonmembers. The Observatory provides a list of Web sites arranged by categories (on the left menu bar). Also useful is the MS Library, collections of homemade reference electron impact mass spectra of derivatives produced by TIAFT members and made available freely on the Internet. The intention is to complete commercial databases with new upcoming or uncommon substances or less frequent derivatives of drugs.

641.   **International Association of Investigative Locksmiths, Inc. (IAIL).** http://www.iail.org/ (accessed December 3, 2004).

The IAIL is a group of locksmiths, security professionals, police officers, insurance investigators, and others with an interest in the benefits of investigative locksmithing to the community. Members provide technical advice to the insurance industry, community protection groups, and law enforcement.

642.   **International Crime Scene Investigators Association (ICSIA).** http://www.icsia.org/ (accessed October 12, 2005).

The ICSIA was created to assist law enforcement personnel who are involved in the processing of crime scenes. It is strictly Internet based. Its focus is to allow practitioners to directly discuss techniques and tips, or to share other pertinent information with crime scene personnel throughout the world.

643.   **International Homicide Investigators Association (IHIA).** http://www.ihia.org/ (accessed December 3, 2004).

The primary purpose of the IHIA is to assist and support law enforcement agencies and death investigation professionals by providing leadership, training, resources, and expertise that will enhance their ability to solve cases.

644.   **International Society for Forensic Genetics (ISFG).** http://www.isfg .org/ (accessed December 3, 2004).

Formerly the International Society for Forensic Haemogenetics (ISFH), the ISFG is an international organization responsible for the promotion of scientific knowledge in the field of genetic markers analyzed with forensic purposes. It hosts several working groups, with membership in these working groups based on the language of the member. One of the working groups is EDNAP, the European DNA Profiling Group, which consists of a group of forensic scientists from various European countries who came together to find a way of harmonizing DNA technology for crime investigation. The society's bi-annual congress proceedings are published by Elsevier in the series *Progress in Forensic Genetics*.

645.   **Microscopy Society of America (MSA).** http://www.microscopy.org/ (accessed October 12, 2005).

The purpose of the MSA is to promote and advance knowledge of the science and practice of all microscopical imaging, analysis, and diffraction techniques useful for elucidating the ultrastructure and function of materials in diverse areas of biological, materials, medical, and physical sciences. The MSA publishes the journal *Microscopy and Microanalysis*.

646.   **National Academy of Forensic Engineers (NAFE).** http://www.nafe .org/ (accessed December 7, 2004).

The Academy was formed to serve the needs of those who serve as consultants to members of the legal profession and as expert witnesses. NAFE's mission includes continuing education and the promotion of standards and ethics for its members.

647.   **National Association of Document Examiners (NADE).** http://www .documentexaminers.org/ (accessed December 7, 2004).

Members of NADE are private document examiners who work with cases relating to suspect signatures, anonymous letters, graffiti, reading obliterations, disputed handwriting, disputed legal documents, altered medical records, and sequence of writing issues.

648.   **National Association of Forensic Economics (NAFE).** http://www.nafe. net/default.aspx (accessed December 3, 2004).

Membership in NAFE includes economists, accountants, finance and business professionals, vocational counselors, lawyers, and actuaries. Forensic economists work in such areas as business valuation, commercial litigation, employment litigation, and personal injury and wrongful death torts. NAFE publishes the *Journal of Forensic Economics*.

649. **National Association of Medical Examiners (NAME).** http://www.the-name.org/ (accessed December 7, 2004).

NAME members include professional physician medical examiners, medical death investigators, and death investigation administrators who perform the official duties of the medicolegal investigation of deaths of public interest in the United States. NAME's purposes are to foster professional growth of death investigators and to disseminate professional and technical information to improve death investigation.

650. **National Association of Professional Accident Reconstruction Specialists (NAPARS).** http://www.napars.org/index2.htm (accessed December 7, 2004).

NAPARS is a nonprofit organization whose members have joined together to share the challenge of dealing with the complex problems of accident reconstruction and to upgrade, and ultimately professionalize, the accident reconstruction field.

651. **National Center for Biotechnology Information (NCBI).** http://www.ncbi.nlm.nih.gov/ (accessed July 28, 2004).

Established in 1988 as a national resource for molecular biology information, NCBI creates public databases, conducts research in computational biology, develops software tools for analyzing genome data, and disseminates biomedical information.

652. **National Institute of Justice (NIJ).** http://www.ojp.usdoj.gov/nij/ (accessed January 23, 2005).

NIJ serves as the research, development, and evaluation agency of the U.S. Department of Justice. The institute provides objective, independent, evidence-based knowledge and tools to serve those in the fields of crime and justice, particularly at the state and local levels. The NIJ publishes many of its reports full text online. Follow the Publications link on the left-hand menu bar to access these publications. NIJ also produces the National Criminal Justice Reference Service (NCJRS) Abstracts Database, an index to more than 180,000 criminal justice publications.

653.    **The Society of Forensic Toxicologists (SOFT).** http://www.soft-tox.org/ (accessed July 28, 2004).

SOFT, officially incorporated in 1983, is an organization composed of practicing forensic toxicologists and those interested in the discipline for the purpose of promoting and developing forensic toxicology. The Toxilinks section is particularly useful.

# 7
# Research Essentials

To maximize success, researchers in the forensic sciences must be aware of more than subject-specific tools such as indexes, journals, and books. They must also be familiar with tools such as bibliographic management products, copyright guidelines and laws, and reference citation styles.

## Bibliographic Management Tools

With the increasing quantities of information that is electronically available through bibliographic databases, it is essential for researchers to have a method of saving and organizing this information. Increasingly, software applications known as bibliographic management tools are filling this roll. These tools allow users to download sets of citations, save them, search them, and retrieve them for inclusion in papers and bibliographies.

For a long time there were really only three true bibliographic management packages, but recent years have seen several new competitors entering the market. The original products were **EndNote**®, **ProCite**®, and **Reference Manager**®. Thomson ResearchSoft, a division of Thomson Scientific, currently owns all three. With the prevalence of the Internet, Web-based products—such as **WriteNote**®, from Thomson ResearchSoft, and **RefWorks**, from RefWorks (distributed by CSA)—have recently entered the market.

**Features**

All of the bibliographic database tools mentioned previously share many common features such as:

- the ability to import citations from online, CD-ROM, the World Wide Web, and other sources into files that can be stored for later use (called libraries or bibliographies);
- search capabilities with field-limiting and connection (Boolean) operators;
- templates for citations in many bibliographic record formats (e.g., journal article, book, conference proceeding, technical report), with several defined fields specific to that record format (e.g., author, article title, publisher, conference location);
- the ability to interact directly with word processing programs;
- the ability to generate bibliographies from within word processing programs in a multitude of citation styles, such as APA, MLA, Chicago, or even specific journal styles; and
- the ability to link citations to Web sites, such as full text articles, from within a bibliographic file.

**Determining the Best Package for Your Needs**

With such similar products, how do you determine the best one for you? The factors to consider when choosing the best package for your needs are:

*Functionality with Local Databases and Catalogues:* Consider how easy it is to transfer citation lists from databases used at your institution and any library catalogues you may plan to search. Does the product handle the different material types (e.g., journal articles, conference proceedings, books, book chapters) from the databases that you will use in your searches, such as *FORS: Forensic Abstracts, Web of Science, NCJRS, Medline, Biological Abstracts*, among others? Your local librarian can provide information on the compatibility of these tools with local databases and systems. Also useful is the ability to directly connect to and search Z39.50-compatible databases. WriteNote does not support this option.

*Support and Training:* With an increasing number of features in these packages, local support and training—whether it is the library, writing center, or information technology department—is extremely important. All of the packages currently available on the market provide freely available filters (small programs that tell the tool how to parse the different pieces of information in each citation in a downloaded citation list into the appropriate fields in the bibliographic file/library) for most major databases. However, filters for all databases may not be available or may not work consistently for citation files. Editing existing filter files or creating new ones is not always simple, so local support to help with this is important. Thomson ResearchSoft and RefWorks both provide technical support for users in addition to user listservs.

*Portability:* If you intend to work in more than one location, the portability of your bibliographic files is important. EndNote, ProCite, and Reference Manager personal editions both require software to be loaded locally on your computer, so you will need to be on that particular computer (which could be a laptop for portability) to work with your bibliographic files. All three can also be installed on a network server, although ProCite and EndNote do not have true network capabilities. WriteNote and RefWorks are both Web-based, so files can be accessed from any computer with an Internet connection on most operating systems. If you have multiple users who might have to access the software and bibliographic files, then it is important to choose a product that offers real network operability.

*Price:* Some of these products are software that can be purchased for a one-time fee, whereas others are subscription-based services. Although these products should be considered an investment (in that they will be of use for several years), price can be a factor for many researchers, particularly students, and one-time vs. ongoing costs can also influence which product you use. Many products can be purchased at an academic discount price.

*Operating System:* EndNote and ProCite are available for Windows and Macintosh. Reference Manager is available only for Windows. Web-based products such as RefWorks and WriteNote are Web based, so they work on multiple platforms, such as Windows, Mac, and Linux.

*Language:* The majority of bibliographic management tools were developed for an English-speaking world. If your work is not based in the English language, choosing a product that supports your specific language is vital. EndNote, WriteNote, and RefWorks are all Unicode compliant, enabling you to work in languages other than English.

Reviews and comparisons of the different products are available at the following Web sites.

654. **Bibliography Formatting Software: An Evaluation Template** by Francesco Dell'Orso. http://www.burioni.it/forum/ors-bfs/index.html (accessed February 13, 2005).

This site by Francesco Dell'Orso of the Univerità degli studi di Perugia (Italy) that provides a detailed review of the various bibliographic database management software products is updated as new versions and products become available. Since the review is of software, Web-based products (WriteNote and RefWorks) are currently not included.

655. **Thomson ResearchSoft.** http://thomsonisiresearchsoft.com/compare/ (accessed February 13, 2005).

Thomson ResearchSoft provides a feature comparison in chart format of its four products, EndNote, Reference Manager, ProCite, and WriteNote.

656. **RefWorks Review from the** *Journal of the Medical Library Association.* http://www.pubmedcentral.gov/articlerender.fcgi?artid=314118 (accessed February 13, 2005).

**Product Information**

657. **EndNote 9** (Windows 2000 and XP, Palm OS 4.x or higher, Macintosh OS X). $299.95 (list), $199.95 (academic). http://www.endnote.com/ (accessed September 18, 2005).

658. **ProCite 5** (Windows and Macintosh). $299.95 (list), $179.95 (academic, nonstudent), $99.95 (student). http://www.procite.com/ (accessed February 13, 2005).

659. **Reference Manager 11** (Windows). Thomson ResearchSoft: Phone 800-722-1227; Fax 760-438-5573. $299.95 (list), $179.95 (academic, nonstudent), $99.95 (student). http://www.refman.com/ (accessed February 13, 2005).

EndNote was created by Niles Software. In 1999, the Institute for Scientific Information (ISI) acquired Niles Software and combined it with an ISI subsidiary, Research Information Systems (RIS), to create a new company called ResearchSoft. RIS was the producer of Reference Manager and ProCite, so the merger brought the three most popular bibliographic management tools into one development environment. Since the three products were united under one company, they have become increasingly similar—yet each has also developed a niche. EndNote is the most popular and easy-to-use package; ProCite provides flexibility to group references and create subject bibliographies using advanced searching techniques; and Reference Manager offers true network capabilities, such as simultaneous read/write access to databases.

660.   **WriteNote** (Windows, Macintosh, Linux). Thomson ResearchSoft. Phone: 800-722-1227; Fax: 760-438-5573. Pricing negotiated based on size of the institution. http://www.writenote.com/ (accessed February 13, 2005).

WriteNote is a Web-based product similar to EndNote but without some of EndNote's features, such as the ability to directly connect to, and search, Z39.50-compliant databases. Access is available to individuals or institutions on an annual subscription basis.

661.   **RefWorks** (Windows, Macintosh, Linux, Unix). RefWorks (distributed by CSA). Phone: 775-327-4105; Email: info@refworks.com. $100/yr. (individuals), (institutions call for quote). http://www.refworks.com/ (accessed February 13, 2005).

RefWorks is a Web-based bibliography and database manager. Access is available to individuals or institutions on an annual subscription basis.

# Copyright

Intellectual property legislation is complicated, and this book could not even pretend to explain all of the details surrounding the topic. This section will attempt to provide researchers with some basic guidelines, and links to further reading, on copyright laws in the United States.

On October 12, 1998, the Digital Millennium Copyright Act (DCMA) was passed by Congress, becoming effective in October 2000. Its intent was to update U.S. copyright law to address issues raised by the new digital era. The DCMA also conforms U.S. copyright law with treaties signed by the United States and the World Intellectual Property Organization (WIPO). It has been fully incorporated into the Copyright Act (U.S. Code Title 17—see link in resource section). The DCMA and the WIPO treaties strongly favor copyright holders, skewing the traditional balance between affording access to information and protecting information.

On November 2, 2002, President Bush signed the "Technology, Education and Copyright Harmonization" Act (TEACH). TEACH defines the terms on which accredited, nonprofit educational institutions in the United States may use copyrighted materials for distance education purposes. The TEACH Act was not intended to address concerns related to e-reserves.

## Copyright 101

For the researcher, there are four factors that must be considered when determining whether the use of a particular work constitutes "fair use" and copyright permission does not need to be obtained from the copyright holder. These criteria are listed in the U.S. Code, Title 17, Chapter 1, Section 107 (see link in resource section).

*The character of the use:* Is the use for a nonprofit educational purpose or a commercial purpose?

*The nature of the work:* Is the work a fact or published, or is it imaginative or unpublished?

*How much of the work will be used:* What portion of the work will be used in relation to the work as a whole?

*The effect of the use on the market for, or value of, the work:* If this kind of use were widespread, would this affect the market for the original work?

Weighting of these factors for a particular use is subjective. Two people reviewing a use with the same criteria can come to vastly different conclusions about the fairness of the use. The University of Texas has developed some rules of thumb in evaluating fair use: http://www.utsystem.edu/OGC/Intellectual Property/copypol2.htm#test (accessed February 13, 2005).

Some general rules of thumb regarding copyright are:

It is allowable to copy a single article for educational purposes and/or personal use in a nonprofit organization.

It is not allowable to copy materials that were created for educational use, such as textbooks and workbooks, if this would provide a substitute for purchasing the item.

It is not allowable to systematically copy materials to create a personal collection of articles if this would be a substitute for subscribing to one or more journals.

## United States Copyright Law Resources

662.  **U.S. Code Title 17. Copyrights.** http://www.law.cornell.edu/uscode/html/uscode17/usc_sup_01_17.html (accessed February 13, 2005).

663.  **U.S. Code Title 17, Chapter 1, Section 107. Limitations on Exclusive Rights: Fair Use.** http://www.law.cornell.edu/uscode/html/uscode17/usc_sec_17_00000107——000-.html (accessed February 13, 2005).

664.    **U.S. Code Title 17, Chapter 1, Section 108. Limitations on Exclusive Rights: Reproduction by Libraries and Archives.** http://www.law.cornell.edu/uscode/html/uscode17/usc_sec_17_00000108—-000-.html (accessed February 13, 2005).

665.    **University of Texas Crash Course in Copyright.** http://www.utsystem.edu/OGC/IntellectualProperty/cprtindx.htm (accessed February 13, 2005).

The University of Texas System has created a quick tutorial on copyright basics for faculty and other researchers.

666.    **Copyright Clearance Center.** http://www.copyright.com/ (accessed February 13, 2005).

The Copyright Clearance Center acts as an intermediary between copyright holders and content users. It manages requests for academic permissions and online course content, facilitating the exchange of rights, permissions, and royalties.

# Citation Styles

Hand-in-hand with copyright is proper citing in an author's work of another's intellectual property. Whether writing a research paper for a course or submitting a paper for publication, authors must be consistent in formatting references in their publication (reference lists and citations within the text). There are a multitude of styles that can be used. The most common are the American Psychological Association (APA) format, the Modern Language Association (MLA) format, the Chicago Manual of Style format, the Turabian style, and the American Medical Association (AMA) Manual of Style format. APA has become increasingly common in the social sciences, including psychology, criminology, nursing, economics and business, and social work; MLA is more common in literature, art, and the humanities; Turabian is intended to be used by college students in all subjects; Chicago is used with all subjects in the nonacademic books, magazines, newspapers, and other nonscholarly publications; and AMA is used in medicine, health, and the biological sciences. Each style often includes similar pieces of information, but the actual form and layout of this information can vary tremendously.

Due to the vast array of subdisciplines in the forensic sciences, there is no one standard style used by all. The legal medicine journals tend to use variations on the AMA style. The psychology journals tend to use APA. The style used depends very much on the publisher's requirements when submitting for publication, or a professor's preference for students writing a paper for a course. Guidelines for various forensics journals can often be found at the publisher's Web site or in a print issue of the journal. The publisher usually dictates guidelines for books.

The common styles listed above are based on print publications.

667.  *Publication manual of the American Psychological Association. 5th ed.* Washington, DC: American Psychological Association, 2001. 439 p. $39.95 (cl.), $26.95 (pbk.). ISBN 1557987904 (cl.), 1557987912 (pbk.). http://www.apastyle .org/pubmanual.html (accessed February 13, 2005).

668.    Gibaldi, Joseph. *MLA handbook for writers of research papers. 6th ed.* New York, NY: Modern Language Association, 2003. 378 p. $17.50. ISBN 0873529863. http://www.mla.org/publications/handbook (accessed February 13, 2005).

669.    University of Chicago Press Staff. *The Chicago manual of style. 15th ed.* Chicago, IL: University of Chicago Press, 2003. 984 p. $55 (cl. or CD), $95 (cl. + CD). ISBN 0226104036 (cl.), 0226104044 (CD), 0226104052 (cl. + CD). http://www.press.uchicago.edu/Misc/Chicago/cmosfaq/cmosfaq.html   (accessed February 13, 2005).

670.    Turabian, Kate L. *A manual for writers of term papers, theses, and dissertations.* 6th ed. Chicago, IL: University of Chicago Press, 1996. 318 p. $14. ISBN 0226816273.  http://www.press.uchicago.edu/cgi-bin/hfs.cgi/00/12917.ctl (accessed February 13, 2005).

671.    Iverson, Cheryl, Annette Flanagin, Phil B. Fontanarosa, and Richard M. Glass. *American Medical Association manual of style: A guide for authors and editors. 9th ed.* Philadelphia, PA: Lippincott Williams & Wilkins, 1997. 672 p. $42.95.  ISBN 0683402064.  http://www.lww.com/product/?0-683-40206-4 (accessed February 13, 2005).

There are several sites with excellent examples of how to cite different types of sources (e.g., books, journal articles, conference proceedings) in multiple styles. A few of the best sites follow.

672.    **Citation Style for Research Papers.**  http://www.liunet.edu/cwis/cwp/ library/workshop/citation.htm (accessed February 13, 2005).

Created by staff at the B. Davis Schwartz Memorial Library at C.W. Post Campus of Long Island University, this provides color-coded examples for the APA, MLA, Turabian, Chicago, and AMA styles. Examples are of the citations as they should appear in a paper's reference list. It does not describe how to cite a reference in the text of the paper.

673. **OWL (Online Writing Lab).** http://owl.english.purdue.edu/handouts/ research/index.html (accessed February 13, 2005).

Created by Purdue University Online Writing Lab, this site brings together information and sites on research and documenting sources. There are four specific links from this site that are most useful.

674. **Using American Psychological Association (APA) Format.** http://owl .english.purdue.edu/handouts/research/r_apa.html (accessed February 13, 2005).

An excellent guide to formatting references in a reference list and in the text of the paper. There is also an extensive list of links to additional sources for samples and guides.

675. **Using Modern Language Association (MLA) Format.** http://owl .english.purdue.edu/handouts/research/r_mla.html (accessed February 13, 2005).

An excellent guide to formatting references in a works cited list and in the text of the paper. There is also an extensive list of links to additional sources for samples and guides.

676. **Resources for Documenting Sources.** http://owl.english.purdue.edu/ handouts/research/r_docsources.html (accessed February 13, 2005).

A list of disciplines, the style used most often in that discipline, a link to the official Web site for that style, and a link to an explanatory Web site for that style are available at this site.

677. **Resources for Documenting Electronic Sources.** http://owl.english. purdue.edu/handouts/research/r_docelectric.html (accessed February 13, 2005).

Electronic sources of information have always had their own unique issues related to citation styles. With the Internet and other digital sources now being heavily used in research, various disciplines are still determining the best way to document these sources. OWL has compiled links to resources for MLA, APA, and several discipline-specific styles to help in formatting citations to electronic works in the correct manner.

# NAME / TITLE / ELECTRONIC RESOURCE INDEX

*Note:* Reference is to entry number or page number; page numbers are italicized.

# SUBJECT INDEX

*Note:* Reference is to entry number or page number; page numbers are italicized.

# ABOUT THE AUTHOR

CYNTHIA HOLT has been the librarian for the sciences and engineering programs at George Washington University in Washington, D.C., for six years. A
large part of this has been supporting the forensic sciences department. Her career
as a science and engineering librarian has spanned 12 years in various positions.
She is the past chair of the Physics-Astronomy-Mathematics Division of the
Special Libraries Association and is a past SLA Chapter Member of the Year
Award winner for the D.C. chapter of SLA.